LOAN

KU-422-563

Apple Pro Training Series
Motion

Damian Allen

PLEASE CHECK DISC ON ISSUE AND DISCHARGE

WITHDRAWN
WITHDRAWN

WS 2227182 1

3 07

Apple
Certified

Apple Pro Training Series: Motion
Damian Allen
Copyright © 2005 by Damian Allen

Published by Peachpit Press. For information on Peachpit Press books, contact:

Peachpit Press
1249 Eighth Street
Berkeley, CA 94710
(510) 524-2178
Fax: (510) 524-2221
http://www.peachpit.com
To report errors, please send a note to errata@peachpit.com.
Peachpit Press is a division of Pearson Education.

Editor: Anita Dennis
Managing Editor: Kristin Kalning
Production Coordinator: Laurie Stewart, Happenstance Type-O-Rama
Technical Editors: Abba Shapiro, Anne Renehan
Technical Reviewers: Bahram Foroughi, Bill Foster, Jeff Guenette, Vidas Neverauskas, Sean Safreed
Copy Editors: Elissa Rabellino, Karen Seriguchi
Compositor: Happenstance Type-O-Rama
Indexer: Jack Lewis
Cover Design: Frances Baca
Cover Illustration: George Mattingly

Notice of Rights
All rights reserved. No part of this book may be reproduced or transmitted in any form by any means, electronic, mechanical, photocopying, recording, or otherwise, without the prior written permission of the publisher. For information on getting permission for reprints and excerpts, contact permissions@peachpit.com. Music and media content are by Damian Allen, with the exception of:
The Butterfly animation, designed by Dave Tracey.
DVD Motion Menu, designed by Chris Parkinson.
Police footage (part of the Call 911 collection) licensed from Thinkstock, a division of Jupitermedia Corporation.
All rights reserved.

Notice of Liability
The information in this book is distributed on an "As Is" basis, without warranty. While every precaution has been taken in the preparation of the book, neither the authors nor Peachpit Press shall have any liability to any person or entity with respect to any loss or damage caused or alleged to be caused directly or indirectly by the instructions contained in this book or by the computer software and hardware products described in it.

Trademarks
Throughout this book trademarked names are used. Rather than put a trademark symbol in every occurrence of a trademarked name, we state we are using the names only in an editorial fashion and to the benefit of the trademark owner with no intention of infringement of the trademark.

ISBN 0-321-27826-7
Printed and bound in the United States of America

778.
59
ALL

Acknowledgments

A huge thanks goes to my beautiful wife, Marne, for her unbelievable support and for wrestling with my infant daughter while I hid away in my office writing this book.

Thanks, too, to my daughter Makenzie, for making this world colorful. I'd forgotten how to laugh until you showed up.

To God, for creating pixels. I don't think I could have handled a real job.

To Patty Montesion, a force of nature disguised as a mild-mannered girl from Boston. Kings and emperors have fallen to less. Thank you for being unfathomably generous with your resources and your encouragement. If they could bottle what makes you tick, we'd be that much closer to world peace. And we'd all be called Baby Cakes.

Dion Scoppettuolo, Guido Hucking, and Greg Niles—thanks for trusting a man from a land of criminals with your amazing work of art.

Thanks to the incredible people at Peachpit: Special thanks to Anita Dennis for bearing with the jarring production schedule, and for not editing out my punch lines. Thanks to Serena Herr for your grace in clandestine times and your straight shooting; it's rare to find people so instantly trustworthy. Thanks to the rest of the production team for firing on all cylinders towards the end.

To Dave Tracey, one of the most amazing animators in the world, and to Chris Parkinson, a man who designs motion graphics the way the rest of us breathe: Thank you that you're both hidden in the sleepy suburbs of Sydney unknown to the rest of the world. Otherwise I wouldn't be able to exploit you and your collective creative genius.

Thanks to Haiti Harrison for gracing the greenscreen, to the boys from Reflecmedia for providing it, to Diana Weynand and Shirley Craig for housing it, and to Boston Camera for capturing it.

I think I'm supposed to thank my sixth-grade English teacher as well, but I have no recollection of who it was. Oh, and thanks, Mum.

Contents at a Glance

Table of Contents

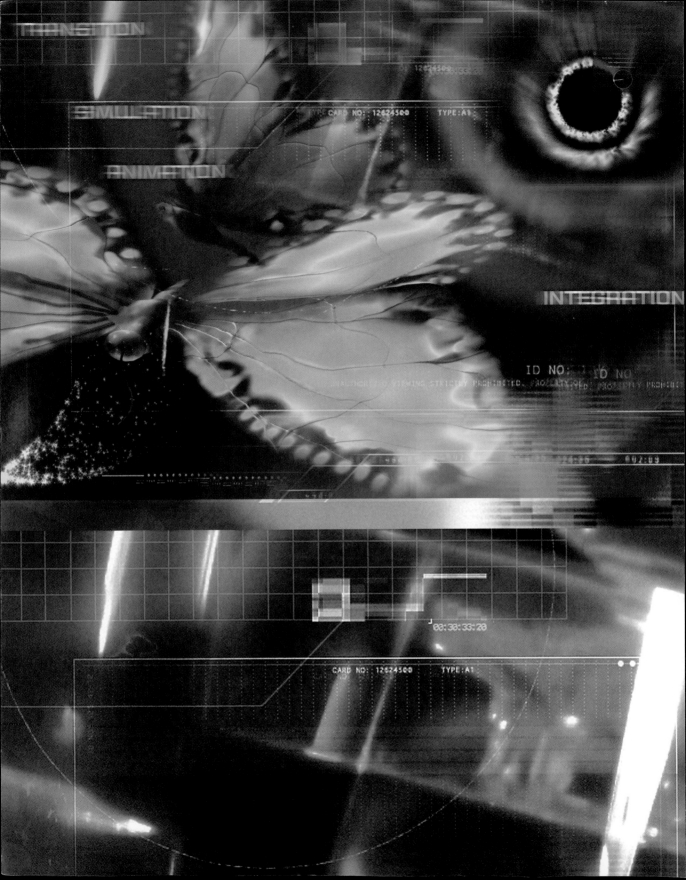

Getting Started

Welcome to the official Apple Pro training course for Motion, Apple Computer's revolutionary real-time-design motion graphics application. This book provides a comprehensive guide to designing with Motion, including the use of particle dynamics, behaviors, filters and effects, audio, bluescreen keys, text, and keyframing.

Whether you've been creating motion graphics for years or are encountering the art form for the first time, every chapter is worth reading. That's because Motion's way of designing is profoundly different from anything you've used before. Motion's real-time design engine and behavior system are easy to learn and yet open the door to expansive creative experimentation.

If you're already familiar with Adobe's After Effects software, you may wish to read through Appendix A, "Motion for After Effects Users."

The Methodology

This book takes a hands-on approach to learning the software. It's divided into projects, which gradually introduce the interface elements and ways of working with them, building progressively until you can comfortably grasp the entire application and standard workflow.

Motion comes with an exhaustive number of keyboard shortcuts and ways to access menus. We'll concentrate on learning the ones that are most important and most efficient; Motion's user guide (available from the Help menu) includes a comprehensive list if you need something specific.

Course Structure

This book contains several very detailed motion graphics projects, which cover all the different aspects of Motion. They're typical of the kinds of assignments motion graphics designers see in the real world. The lesson design projects break down as follows:

▶   Lessons 1–3: Fundamental concepts

▶   Lesson 4: Creating projects using templates

▶   Lessons 5–10: Creating a TV station promo ID

▶   Lessons 11–13: Creating a network-style title sequence

▶   Lesson 14: Creating a lower-third overlay and a DVD motion menu

Some Quick Terms

Before we move ahead, we need to touch on a few key terms used throughout the book.

▶   Composite—You'll see the word *composite* appearing often in the book. Usually it's referring to your final work—the image you see on the screen. You could also think of this as a *composition* (or *comp* for short). It's occasionally used as a verb: You *composite* several objects together to create the final product.

▶ Objects—This is the term Motion uses to describe the individual elements of a composite. *Objects* can include QuickTime movies, image sequences, still images, and text. The objects are layered together to create the composite.

For a fuller understanding of motion graphics–related terms, see the Glossary at the end of the book.

Copying the Motion Lesson Files

Apple Pro Training Series: Motion comes with a DVD containing all the files you need to complete each lesson. Each lesson has its own folder with project files, media, and a sample clip of the final version.

Installing the Lesson Files

1 Insert the *Apple Pro Training Series: Motion* DVD into your computer's DVD drive.

2 Double-click the DVD icon on the Desktop titled "APTS_Motion."

3 Drag the folder **APTS_Motion** onto your Macintosh HD icon.

It is important that you put this folder on the top level of your hard drive as described; this will ensure that the project files correctly link with the media they use.

System Requirements

Motion has a high set of minimum system requirements. Applications such as Final Cut Pro are designed to *scale* their performance from less powerful laptops all the way through to fully equipped G5 systems. While this is also true of Motion, the real-time performance that makes it so revolutionary requires certain hardware to be present in order to operate.

The minimum system requirements for Motion are an 867 MHz G4 with 512 MB of RAM running Mac OS X v10.3.5 or later, as well as one of the following AGP graphics cards (or better):

▶   ATI Radeon 9800 XT (R360)

▶   ATI Radeon 9800 Pro (R350)

▶   ATI Radeon 9700 Pro (R300)

▶   ATI Radeon 9600 XT (RV360)

▶   ATI Radeon 9600 Pro (RV350)

▶   ATI Mobility Radeon 9700 (RV M11)

▶   ATI Mobility Radeon 9600 (RV M100)

▶   nVidia GeForce 6800 Ultra DDL (NV40)

▶   nVidia GeForce Go5200 (NV34M)

▶   nVidia GeForce FX 5200 Ultra (NV34)

In addition, Motion requires a 1024x768-pixel display, 10 GB of hard disk space, QuickTime 6.5.1 or higher, a 4x AGP slot, and a DVD drive.

How Motion Uses Your Hardware

All systems are not created equal, and the more power you have in your hardware, the more you'll be able to do interactively (that is, without rendering) in Motion. Here's a brief explanation of how Motion leverages your hardware; if you're thinking of upgrading your system to run Motion, it might help you decide what will give you the best results.

The following sections are a little technical, so if you start to lose track, don't panic. Just remember: Faster equals better, and more RAM also equals better.

System Memory

Motion uses system RAM to cache all the different objects that make up your composite throughout your preview range. I know, we're getting a little ahead here since you're not yet familiar with the product, so let's look at an example.

Let's say you're combining three QuickTime movies in Motion to create a final, single image—your composite. For the example, let's imagine you have a moving fractal background clip (Element 1), a rotating web (Element 2), and some random boxes (Element 3).

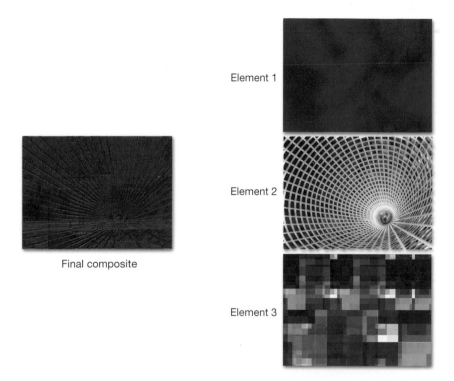

Element 1

Element 2

Element 3

Final composite

Each frame of NTSC video contains 720 pixels horizontally and 486 pixels vertically (480 for DV). When you add up the memory required to store every one of those pixels in the computer's memory, it works out to about 1.3 MB (including an alpha channel) per frame.

So if you wanted Motion to generate a real-time preview of your three-layer composite that lasted for 120 frames (about 4 seconds), you'd need 1.3x120 MB worth of RAM to cache each element. For all three elements to be cached, you'd need 1.3x120x3 = 468 MB.

So to be able to make real-time adjustments to the three clips in our hypothetical composite, you'd need at least 468 MB of available RAM—that's after the operating system, Motion, and other background applications had their fill of the memory. For this scenario to work well, you'd want at least 1 GB of system RAM. (The story for PAL would be essentially the same, since although the images are 720x576, there are only 25 of them each second.)

Have I lost you in geek speak? That's OK. All you really need to know is that if you have more system RAM, you can play back more objects in real time and watch a longer preview of your composite than you could with minimal RAM. Motion can use up to 4 GB of a G5's system RAM. Hang in there, though, as this is only part of the story.

Video Card Memory (VRAM)

In addition to your system RAM, your Macintosh has memory on the graphics card itself. This memory is known as *VRAM* (for *video RAM*) and is used by the graphics card while it's performing calculations to draw an image to your computer monitor. Your graphics card also has its own processor, called a *GPU* (for *graphics processing unit*), which calculates how things should get drawn.

When it comes time to draw a frame of your composite to screen, the different elements required for that frame are sent to the VRAM of your graphics card, along with a set of instructions telling the processor on the card where and how it's supposed to draw each image. The processor might be told to scale down an image, blur another, and color-correct another before combining them all into a single image. This is where the real-time part of Motion takes place.

Since the graphics card's processor can only render what's been put into its VRAM, the number of layers that can be processed in real time is going to be limited by how much VRAM you have. Once a single frame is drawn, the VRAM is free to load up the objects for the next frame. So the amount of VRAM determines how many layers and effects can be combined at *one frame* of the sequence, not the whole sequence. In other words, your system RAM ultimately decides how long your preview range can be, but the VRAM decides how many elements can be composited together at once.

Finally, even when you reach your VRAM limits, Motion has a clever RAM caching feature to allow you to render a real-time preview and still manipulate individual objects in real time via a soloing feature.

CPU Speed

You've always been told a faster CPU is better. That's also true for Motion, but not in the way you might think. Since all the heavy lifting is being done by the processor in your graphics card, the CPU doesn't really have much to do with the actual construction of the composite.

Where the main system's CPU comes into play most is in calculating Motion's behaviors, particle trajectories, motion paths, and curves before sending them to the graphics card. So if you're using a lot of complex behaviors in your project or working with particle systems, you'll definitely benefit from a faster processor.

You'll also see an improvement going from a G4- to a G5-based system due to the higher bandwidth on the latter, and a dual-processor system will perform better than a single-processor system. The G5 architecture allows more data to travel at faster speeds between the CPU, the system RAM, and ultimately the graphics card.

Summarizing Hardware Requirements

The good news from the preceding technobabble is that if your system meets the minimum system requirement (an 867 MHz G4 Macintosh), improving Motion's performance doesn't necessarily mean having to buy a faster computer; upgrading your graphics card may be all that's required.

Here's the story in a nutshell:

▶ System RAM determines how many frames of animation you can preview in real time (and, to some degree, how many objects in a composite can be viewed in real time before you have to perform a RAM preview render). Motion can address up to 4 GB of a G5's system RAM.

▶ VRAM (video RAM on the graphics card) determines how many objects in a composite can be rendered in real time before a RAM preview render is required. If you want more objects on the screen with more filters and effects, you'll need more VRAM.

▶ CPU speed determines how many complex behaviors and simulations can be applied to the composite objects in real time. It has less impact on the number of layers that can be drawn to screen; the amount of VRAM is more important in determining this.

About the Apple Pro Training Series

Apple Pro Training Series: Motion is both a self-paced learning tool and the official training curriculum of the Apple Pro Training and Certification Program, developed by experts in the field and certified by Apple Computer. The series offers complete training in all Apple Pro products. The lessons are designed to let you learn at your own pace. Although each lesson provides step-by-step instructions for creating specific projects, there's room for exploration and experimentation. You can progress through the book from beginning to end, or dive right into the lessons that interest you most. Each lesson concludes with a review section summarizing what you've learned.

Resources

Apple Pro Training Series: Motion is not intended as a comprehensive reference manual, nor does it replace the documentation that comes with the application. For comprehensive information about program features, refer to these sources:

▶ The user guide. Accessed through the Motion Help menu, the user guide contains a complete description of all Motion's features. You'll want to pay attention to the Late-Breaking News button on the first page of the online help; it provides a direct link to updated Motion information at Apple's Web site.

▶ Motion's Web site: www.apple.com/motion.

Apple Pro Certification Program

The Apple Pro Training and Certification Program is designed to keep you at the forefront of Apple's digital media technology while giving you a competitive edge in today's ever-changing job market. Whether you're an editor, graphic designer, sound designer, special effects artist, or teacher, these training tools are meant to help you expand your skills.

Upon completing the course material in these books, you can become a certified Apple Pro for most Apple Pro applications by taking the certification exam at an Apple Authorized Training Center. Certification is offered in Final Cut Pro, DVD Studio Pro, Shake, and Logic. Successful certification as an Apple Pro gives you official recognition of your knowledge of Apple's professional applications, allowing you to market yourself to employers and clients as a skilled, pro-level user of Apple products.

To find an Authorized Training Center near you, go to www.apple.com/software/pro/training.

For those who prefer to learn in an instructor-led setting, Apple offers training courses at Apple Authorized Training Centers worldwide. These courses, which use the Apple Pro Training Series books as their curriculum, are taught by Apple Certified Trainers and balance concepts and lectures with hands-on labs and exercises. Apple Authorized Training Centers have been carefully selected and have met Apple's highest standards in all areas, including facilities, instructors, course delivery, and infrastructure. The goal of the program is to offer Apple customers, from beginners to the most seasoned professionals, the highest-quality training experience.

1

Lesson Files	APTS_Motion > Lessons > Lesson01
Time	This lesson takes approximately 60 minutes to complete.
Goals	Become familiar with the basic elements of the interface
	Add movies to a project
	Work with the play range
	Add and modify filters and behaviors
	Create a particle effect

Lesson **1**

A Tour of Motion

The easiest way to understand why Motion is so revolutionary is to play with it. Rather than plow through pages and pages of information on windows, menus, and widgets, this chapter will take you straight into the thick of Motion's magic.

We'll learn the elements of the interface along the way, but just as important, we'll begin to get a handle on the workflow of Motion—real-time previewing, behaviors, particles, and the like. By the end of the lesson you'll have a clear sense of what Motion really is and just the first inkling of what you might be able to achieve with it creatively.

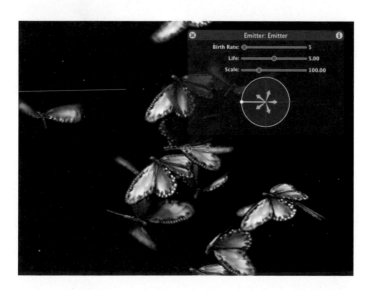

A Revolution in Motion: The Backstory

It's hard to overstate the sea change Motion brings to the postproduction world. For years there's been a great divide between the digital haves and have-nots. In the hopes of landing high-profile commercial work, artists have mortgaged houses and frayed marriages to purchase multimillion-dollar online suites.

For the editing world, the last ten years have seen a radical change in fortune. Systems like Apple's Final Cut Pro now make it possible to build a complete high-definition editing station for under $25,000.

That hasn't been the case in the realm of motion graphics, where the million-dollar machines still rule the big time. The issue isn't a dearth of powerful software. Applications such as Adobe After Effects can compete head-to-head in the quality of their output. The issue comes down to workflow.

Imagine the following scenario: Advertising agency McSwank & Spendit wants some fancy title and logo work done for a prestigious European manufacturer. This is a TV commercial designed to launch a foray into the American SUV market. The ad agency wants lots of motion—lots of frenetic, edgy graphics—and it's narrowed down the work to two post houses: PixelPuffVoodoo and JuxtaFish.

The owners of PixelPuffVoodoo decided to be smart and kind to their significant others, so when they opened their facilities they invested in several modest desktop boxes instead of mortgaging their houses for one of those million-dollar machines that go obsolete in the night. They've hired some talented up-and-coming digital artists, and when they win the McSwank & Spendit contract, they feel their ship has finally rendered.

When the creative director from McSwank & Spendit arrives at their office, he's a little disturbed to find out there's no cool-looking gray-carpeted suite to hang in, and he mumbles something about there being no cocktails.

One of the owners proudly takes him over to the workstation where the final composite of the commercial has been assembled and has the artist crank the speakers and play the clip.

"Hmmm, I like where it's going, but let's make the sky a little darker and add some blur to the parrot."

The PixelPuffVoodoo founder smiles and suggests they go get a cappuccino while the artist re-renders the clip with the changes. When the McSwank & Spendit creative director discovers this will take a half hour or so, he mumbles something else and storms out of the building, never to return.

Instead, he calls up JuxtaFish, agrees to pay the extra $20,000 the company was asking for the job, and heads over. The design work isn't as creative, but as soon as he enters, they drop a piña colada into his hand and lead him to a suite with wall-to-wall carpeting and a lava lamp. As he lies back and watches a preview, he casually asks the artist at the workstation to blur the parrot, and then smiles as he sees the bird instantly smear into the background. The director can do this because although the owners of JuxtaFish are in debt up to their eyeballs, they at least have a million-dollar motion graphics suite with real-time capabilities.

Enter Motion. Motion revolutionizes motion graphics the way Final Cut Pro revolutionized nonlinear editing. It provides real-time, interactive changes to animated graphic elements in a fashion comparable to and sometimes exceeding the capabilities of these million-dollar behemoths. And it does that all on a standard Macintosh workstation.

Paradigm shift is an overused term, particularly in the computer industry. But in this case it really does apply. Working in Motion is such a completely different way of creating motion graphics that it stands separate and distinct from all other existing mainstream software-based compositing applications.

Adding Motion to Your Dock

To make it easier to quickly launch Motion from the Desktop, we'll drag it into the Dock.

1   Click anywhere on the Desktop to make sure the Finder is active.

2   Press Cmd-Shift-A to open the Applications folder.

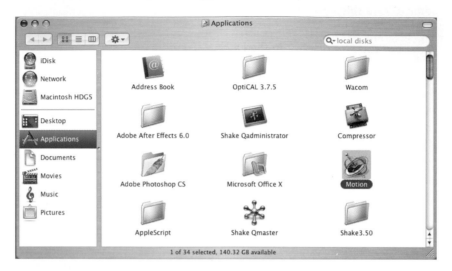

3   Locate the icon for Motion and drag it into the center of your Dock, then release the mouse. Other icons in the Dock should move out of the way to make room for it.

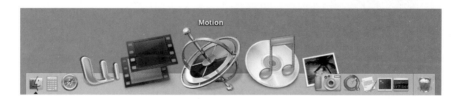

NOTE ▶ You may want to hide the Dock by opening the Apple menu in the top-left corner of the screen and choosing Dock > Turn Hiding On, or by pressing Cmd-Option-D. This will give you more screen real estate while working in Motion.

Launching Motion

Now let's launch Motion.

1   Click the Motion icon in the Dock.

When you first launch Motion, you'll be greeted with the Welcome screen. This enables you to choose from a list of options, including tutorials and templates. Since we'll be working with custom projects for our lessons, we can ignore this screen.

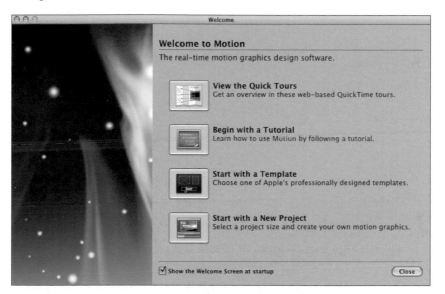

2   Uncheck the box labeled "Show the Welcome Screen at startup."

3   Click the Close button.

▶ **Configuring Startup Preferences**

If you later want the Welcome screen to appear when you launch
Motion, simply open the Preferences window by choosing Motion >
Preferences. In the General pane you'll find a pop-up menu called At
Startup. Set this to Show Welcome Screen.

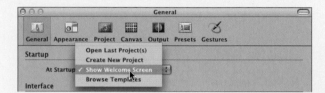

Alternatively, set this to Open Last Project(s) so that every time you
launch Motion, the last project you were working on will open, ready
for you to continue working.

4 From the main menu at the top of the screen choose File > New, or press
Cmd-N.

5 When the Select Project Preset dialog appears, choose NTSC Broadcast SD
from the Preset pop-up menu and click OK.

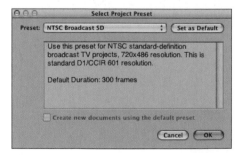

Normally you would choose an entry that matches the final output of
your composite. In this case, we're just here to experiment, so we'll use
standard-definition NTSC settings, even for those of you working in PAL
(since we're not exporting this session to tape).

Getting to Know the Interface

Before we start experimenting, let's take a bird's-eye view of the interface elements.

1   Press the F5 and then F6 function keys at the top of your Mac's keyboard. This will expose two sections of the interface that are hidden by default. If for some reason you notice part of the interface hiding itself when you press one of these keys, press the key again (the keys act as toggles to open and close these sections of the interface).

   NOTE ► If you're using a PowerBook or a keyboard with pre-defined shortcuts, consult your manual for equivalent function keys.

There are four main sections of the Motion interface: the Canvas, the Utility window, the Project pane, and the Timing pane. There's also a fifth element we'll meet in a little while, called the Dashboard.

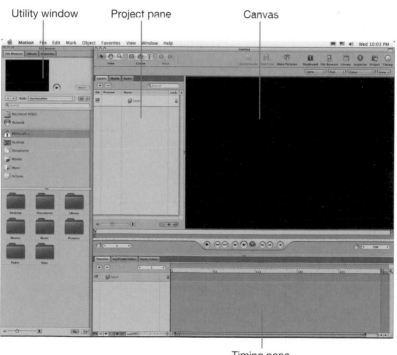

Timing pane

▶ The Canvas is well named: It's where you'll "paint" your composite. This is the part of the screen for previewing your work and making changes to the location of elements on the screen, their rotation, and so on. Think of it as the stage and the elements of your composite the actors and props, yours to move around as you see fit.

> **TIP** ▶ If at any time you want to hide all the other windows and just concentrate on the Canvas, press F8. It will center the Canvas and frame it in a neutral gray. To return to the normal view, press F8 again.

▶ The Utility window is a busy place. It's where you import footage, browse for filters and effects, and make changes to the *parameters* of your scene and its layers (parameters are all the properties you can change about an object, such as its scale, position onscreen, and opacity).

▶ The Project pane is all about organizing your elements, making sure they layer on top of each other in the right order. It also helps you single out specific parts of your composite to make changes.

▶ The Timing pane is where you decide what happens when. It's also where you can be more precise about how things speed up, slow down, or stop, via the Keyframe Editor. More on that later.

Some Windowing Hot Keys

I know, we're supposed to be diving into playtime, but we just need to make a quick stop to cover some hot keys. Anyone who's spent time in a professional software application like Motion knows that hot keys (keyboard combinations that help you perform common tasks quickly) are essential to working efficiently. Motion has a lot of hot keys; we'll be learning the ones that matter most.

Because of the density of windows and views in Motion, it's important to learn the keys that will quickly open or close the section of the interface you need. Check the following figure for details.

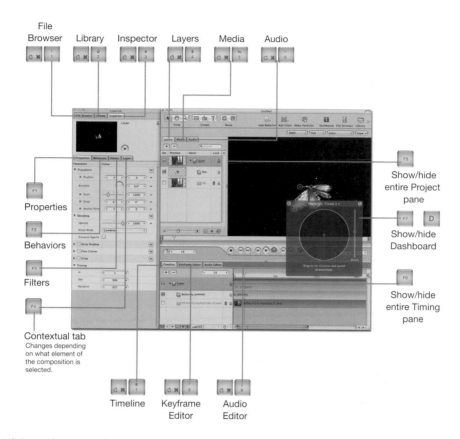

Of these, here are the most important to learn:

Cmd-1—opens and closes the File Browser

F1—opens the Properties tab of the Inspector

F2—opens the Behaviors tab of the Inspector

F3—opens the Filters tab of the Inspector

F4—opens the object tab of the Inspector (the name of this tab changes depending on the type of object selected)

F5—opens and closes the Project pane (which will usually be set to its Layers tab)

F6—opens and closes the Timing pane

F7—reveals and hides the Dashboard (more on this window later)

Don't panic—we'll be reminding you of these throughout the book, but they really are worth learning by heart. If you forget the hot keys to open and close windows, you can access them via the Window menu or use the buttons at the top of the Canvas.

> **TIP** ▶ Take advantage of these commands to close sections of the interface you're not currently working with. Not only will this unclutter the screen, but you also may find a slight performance increase, since Motion will have fewer things to redraw.

Bring On the Talent

OK, enough boring details. Let's start experimenting.

1   Press Cmd-1 to open the File Browser.

NOTE ► If your File Browser tab is already active, you obviously will not need to perform this step. If you do, you will close the File Browser and with it the entire Utility window. If that happens, press Cmd-1 to reopen your File Browser.

2 Click your hard drive icon in the top pane of the File Browser.

NOTE ► Motion supports all QuickTime-compatible formats, image sequences, multi-layered Adobe Photoshop files, and PDF vector graphics.

3 Double-click the APTS_Motion folder in the bottom pane of the File Browser.

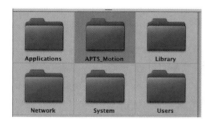

4 Double-click successively the following folders in the pane: Lessons > Lesson01.

You should find a single clip called **Butterfly.mov**.

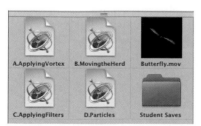

TIP To preview a clip without importing it into your composite, you can do one of two things: Either click its icon in the File Browser and then view the thumbnail preview at the top of the browser, or double-click its icon, which will launch a floating QuickTime window at the full size of the clip.

5 Click and hold the butterfly icon in the lower Browser pane—*not* the thumbnail icon at the very top of the Browser—and then drag it to the center of the Canvas, *but don't release the mouse.*

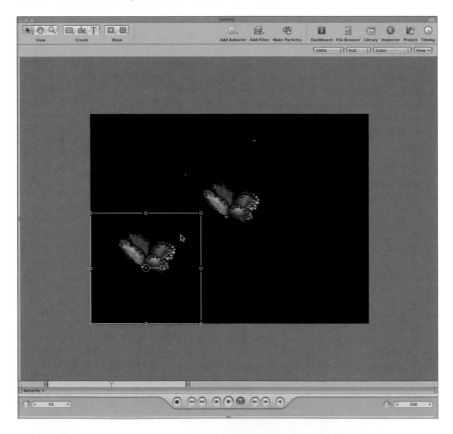

As you drag over the center of the Canvas, you'll notice yellow lines appearing onscreen. The image will snap to these lines. These are called *Dynamic Guides,* and they help you make sure your composite's elements are precisely centered. They can also be used to align several objects alongside each other.

TIP ▶ You can also import footage by clicking the Import button to the right of the thumbnail viewer at the top of the File Browser.

6   Release the mouse button when horizontal and vertical yellow lines form a cross at the center of the screen. This ensures that the clip is perfectly centered.

TIP ▶ If you ever have trouble executing a step and end up with something that looks markedly different from what you see in this book's illustrations, press Cmd-Z to undo the last step (or steps, by pressing Cmd-Z multiple times). This should return your project to the state it was in before things went awry.

7   To play back the clip, press the spacebar or click the Play button at the center of the control bank directly below the Canvas window.

Play button

You should now be watching the butterfly flap its wings as it floats in place.

NOTE ▶ If you find at times that pressing the spacebar fails to pause or resume playback, it may be that one of the other windows has lost "focus." To regain access to your Canvas hot keys, click back in the Canvas to give it focus, and then your hot keys should operate as expected again.

Setting the Play Range

OK, so we haven't done anything revolutionary just yet; we could have done the same by opening the movie in the QuickTime Player. Before we get more adventurous, though, we need to set up what's called the *play range* in preparation for real-time previewing.

1 Press the spacebar to halt playback. The spacebar toggles between play and stop.

2 Press F5 and then F6 to hide the Project and Timing panes. We're not using them right now, so there's no need to have them cluttering the screen. You may also notice a small, semi-transparent window called the Dashboard. Press F7 to hide it for now.

If you look at the very bottom of the Canvas, just above the Play button, you'll see a blue bar with the name Butterfly.

NOTE ▶ If you don't see the blue bar, you've probably deselected the butterfly object. Click the butterfly in the Canvas view to reselect the clip.

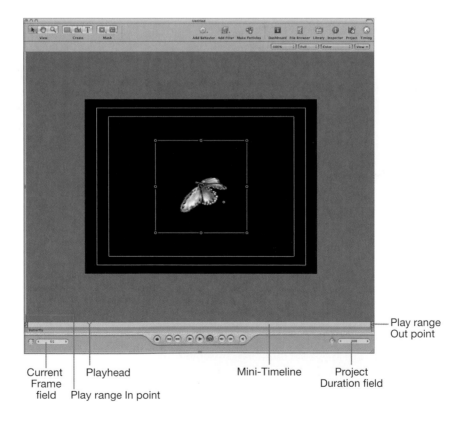

This bar is part of what's called the *mini-Timeline*. It shows you where a selected object starts and finishes. When projects get complicated with lots of objects and effects, it's much easier to make changes to the In and Out points of an object here than in the main Timeline.

Just above the bar is another little strip with three main features: the play range In point, the play range Out point, and the playhead. You may have noticed the playhead moving from left to right while you were playing the butterfly animation earlier.

Your final composite could last anywhere from a couple of seconds to a couple of minutes or even longer. Motion does its magic by loading all the objects into the system RAM, a process known as *caching*. At some point you're going to run out of RAM.

TIP If you want more RAM for your real-time Motion previews without having to run to the local Apple Store, make sure you have no other applications running in the background. Having Photoshop launched with an iLoad of images open is going to siphon off a lot of precious system RAM. Also, use high-resolution monitor settings and multiple monitors sparingly. The more pixels making up your Desktop, the more work the graphics processor needs to do, leaving it less power for Motion magic.

To make sure that Motion can comfortably play your entire sequence, we're going to adjust the play range. That way, Motion will need to cache only a portion of our project instead of the whole thing.

3   Drag the play range In point marker to the right. As you do so, a yellow tooltip appears, indicating the frame where your In point marker is positioned. When the tooltip reads 20, release the mouse. You've now set the new In point for the play range.

NOTE ▶ Even though we've set the play range In point to 20, the project itself still starts at frame 1. All this means is that while previewing our composite we'll only be able to preview frames 20 and beyond. The final render of our project will still include frames 1 through 19, as well as any frames beyond the play range Out point.

4   Click and hold the mouse in the Current Frame field just below the left side of the mini-Timeline. Drag the pointer left and right to change the frame value. Notice how the playhead moves as you adjust the value.

You're using a *hot scrub* numeric entry box. All of Motion's parameter boxes can be modified this way. You can also enter a specific number by clicking once inside the box, typing the number, and pressing Return.

5   When the current frame reads 120, release the mouse.

We're now going to set the play range Out point, but instead of dragging the marker, we'll use another hot key.

6   Press Cmd-Option-O. Instantly the play range Out point marker jumps to where the playhead is positioned—in our case, 120 (since we just set it there).

The play range is now set from frame 20 to frame 120. This means that when we press the spacebar to begin playback, Motion will play only the 101 frames contained within the play range region.

NOTE ▶ On systems with less RAM (under 512 MB) you may need to set your play range lower to fully cache the Timeline. Conversely, if you have 2 GB or greater RAM in your system, feel free to extend your play range Out point to 200 or more for this exercise. You should still be able to maintain real-time playback.

The play range Out point is a good hot key to learn—it saves you from having to constantly drag the markers around and gives you a way to select specific frames. To set the play range In point this way, use Cmd-Option-I.

Zooming the Canvas

At times you'll want to scrutinize fine details of your composite; other times you'll want to make the Canvas small enough to see what's going on even with several menus and windows open. Zooming the Canvas allows you to do both. Let's take a look at the different ways you can zoom the Motion Canvas.

1   At the top right of the Canvas, change the pop-up menu labeled 100% to 50%.

This is the Zoom Level menu, and it offers the preset zoom levels of 12%, 25%, 50%, 100%, 200%, 400%, 800%, and 1600%.

2   Press Cmd-+ and Cmd-– using the plus and minus keys on the main keyboard (*don't* use the numeric keypad plus or minus keys), and watch the zoom level in the top-right corner of the Canvas.

Cmd-+ and Cmd-– zoom the Canvas in and out by the specific preset intervals listed in the Zoom Level menu. This provides an easy way to quickly jump to a zoom level that suits your particular task.

3   Press Cmd-spacebar, and then click and drag the mouse left and right.

This allows you to do what's called *free-form zooming*. You can quickly zoom to any arbitrary size you choose. Note that you can do this even while the Timeline is playing back.

As you experiment, notice that Motion zooms into the part of the image that was under your pointer when you began the zoom. So if your pointer was over the butterfly's head, that's where you'll zoom to.

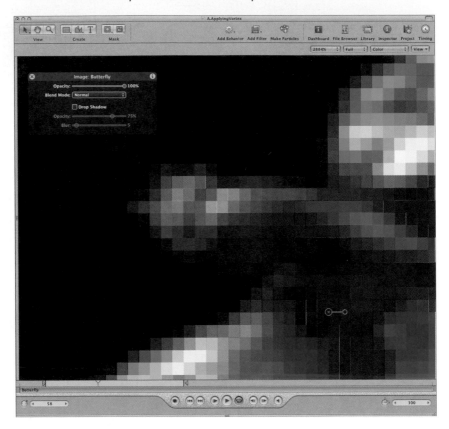

4   Press the spacebar and click and drag anywhere in the Canvas.

Holding down the spacebar allows you to pan the image around the Canvas. This is great when you're zoomed all the way in and need to see part of the image that's offscreen.

5   Press Option-Z.

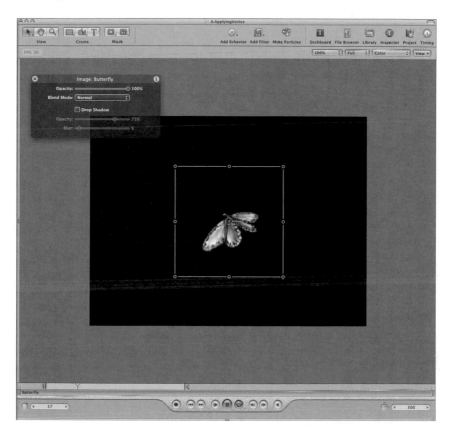

Option-Z jumps you back to 100%.

6   Press Shift-Z.

7   Press F5 a few times to open and close the Project pane.

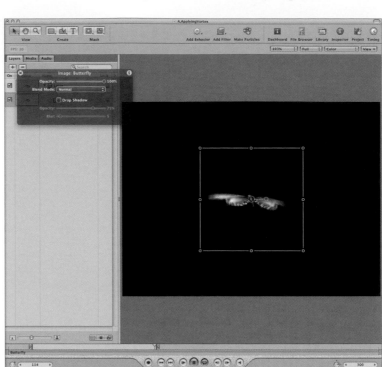

By pressing Shift-Z, you activated the Fit in Window zoom mode. In this mode, Motion zooms the image in the Canvas so that the entire composite is visible at all times.

8   Press Option-Z to return the Canvas to its default scale of 100%.

For additional zoom shortcuts, see Lesson 8.

Adding Objects

Now let's add some more objects to our scene.

1   Press the spacebar to resume playback. This time Motion loops from frame 20 through 120.

One butterfly is kind of boring the 20th time around. Let's add another one.

NOTE ▶ Unless you're instructed in this book to stop playback and move to a particular frame, make sure the preview is looping while you add clips to the Canvas. If you add clips to the Canvas while previewing in real time, they are automatically added to the Timeline at frame 1. If you add clips to the Canvas while playback is paused, they are added to the Timeline starting on the frame where the playhead is positioned. For example, if the playhead is paused at frame 39, a clip added to the Canvas will start at frame 39 in the master Timeline. If you accidentally add an object at a frame other than frame 1, press Home to jump to frame 1, and then press Shift-[to move the object so that it begins at that frame.

2   You should still see the **Butterfly.mov** clip in the lower pane of the File Browser. (If you can no longer see the File Browser, press Cmd-1 to retrieve it.) Drag the clip onto the lower-left corner of the Canvas and release the mouse.

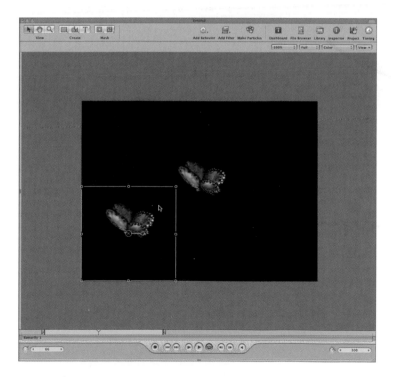

We now have two butterflies flapping away on the screen. Problem is, they're identical. We want them to look like two different butterflies.

3   In the Canvas, drag one of the corner circles of the new butterfly's bounding box in toward the center of the butterfly. As you do so, the butterfly will scale smaller.

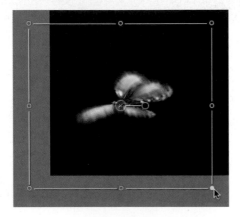

Notice how the butterfly is scaling in and out of the corner opposite the one you're dragging.

4   Press Option-Shift as you drag. Pressing the Option key as you drag scales from the center of the butterfly. Pressing the Shift key scales uniformly in both horizontal and vertical directions, preserving the butterfly's aspect ratio.

5   Make the butterfly about two-thirds the size of the original. Drag the center of the butterfly to reposition the butterfly if necessary.

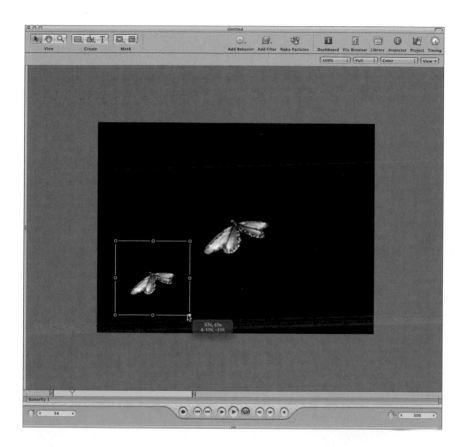

Both butterflies should still be playing back in real time, even as you were adjusting the scale of one of them. But we're just getting started.

The second butterfly is flapping its wings in perfect time with the first. If these were really two different butterflies, their wings would beat out of sync.

6   Drag the blue bar in the mini-Timeline to the left, but *do not* release the mouse. The blue bar should be labeled Butterfly 1, but you won't be able to see the label after you've dragged it to the left. It will be hidden before frame 1 in the Timeline.

As you drag, you'll see another tooltip appear, this one telling you what the new In and Out points on the project Timeline will be for the selected object (in our case, Butterfly 1). It also shows how far you've moved the clip from where it started—that's the number after the triangle, and it's called the *delta*.

7   Release the mouse when the delta value (that's the far-right number displayed in the yellow tooltip) reads –45.

We've now offset the timing of the second butterfly so that it's playing 45 frames ahead of the original butterfly. This helps the illusion that these are two distinct butterflies.

Let's create another butterfly, but this time we'll simply duplicate one of the butterflies already in the Canvas.

8   Pressing the Option key, drag the butterfly that you've just scaled (the one in the lower left) to the top left of the Canvas.

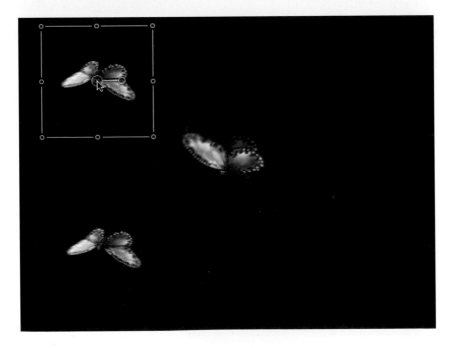

To recap: We added two of the butterflies by dragging from the File Browser, but we added this third butterfly by Option-dragging one of the two butterflies already in the Canvas. Dragging a butterfly in from the File Browser and duplicating one by holding down the Option key may seem to achieve the same result, but in Motion they are profoundly different things. It's important to understand the distinction between the two methods.

9 Press F5 to open the Project pane.

10 Click the Media tab to reveal its contents.

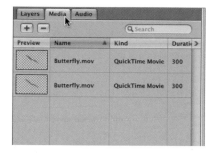

The Media tab lists all the actual media files that are *referred to* by objects in your project. Notice that there are two listings for **Butterfly.mov**, the QuickTime clip we dragged in from the File Browser. Hang on, aren't there *three* butterflies in the project right now?

Each time you drag an object in from the File Browser, that clip is cached into your system RAM and ready for Motion's real-time compositing. In this case we dragged the butterfly into the Canvas twice, so Motion considers these two clips to be cached in the system RAM. But because we Option-dragged the third butterfly, it's considered an *instance* of the second butterfly clip. That is, there are now two butterflies onscreen referring to the same clip that's been cached to RAM.

Even though it's the same clip on the hard drive, whenever you drag a clip from the File Browser into the Canvas, it's considered a new clip to be cached into RAM. So if you were to continue dragging additional butterflies into the Canvas, you'd be using more and more of your precious RAM. But if you simply Option-drag to make copies, all the copies refer to the same movie clip cached into RAM when the first clip was dragged into the Canvas. This significantly reduces the amount of RAM that Motion needs to preview the clip.

So why would you *ever* want to drag the same object into the Canvas twice, when it's more efficient to "clone" it by Option-dragging? Well, occasionally you might want the different butterflies to play back at different frame rates or behave differently once you reach the last frame of their movie sequence. Such properties can only be set for individual media clips in the Media tab, not the objects linked to them. The short answer, though, is that you almost *always* want to Option-drag to make another copy of an object.

11 Click the Layers tab (or press Cmd-4).

12 Press F5 to hide the Project pane.

13 Drag the mini-Timeline for the new butterfly until the delta value in the tooltip reads –35.

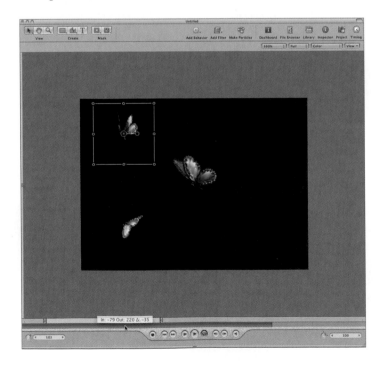

14 Repeat step 8 for a final, fourth butterfly to be positioned in the lower-right corner of the Canvas. Use a delta value of –45.

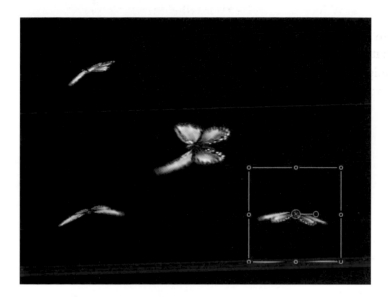

15 Click on the original center butterfly to select it.

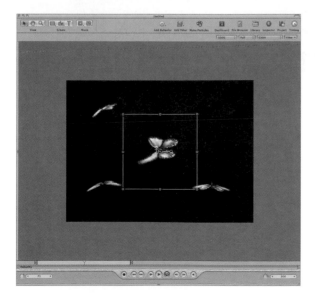

Notice that the mini-Timeline displays the position in time of whichever object on the Canvas is selected. Now that the original butterfly is selected, the blue bar is once again labeled Butterfly.

Applying Behaviors

Already Motion's shown us some pretty decent things. We've been able to play back four separate clips in real time and resize them on the fly. Not revolutionary yet, but nice nonetheless. Let's introduce another fundamental part of Motion: *behaviors.*

Behaviors are a form of artificial intelligence. Traditionally in motion graphics work, movements and actions onscreen are specified by *keyframes,* which tell the computer how an object should look at certain moments in time. It's very much like traditional cartoon animation: A senior artist blocks out key poses at certain moments in an animation, and then a second artist (who works much harder but doesn't get paid as well) is given the task of *tweening,* or drawing the in-between frames that connect the two poses of the character to make a final animation.

In conventional computer keyframe animation, the digital designer blocks out the keyframes in the animation, and the computer does the tweening. Using behaviors in Motion, however, is even better. You provide Motion with some basic information, and it figures out the rest. Say, for example, you were animating a cartoon character being flattened by a rock. You would just tell Motion what you wanted to happen, and the character would be flattened; you wouldn't even have to draw the keyframes. Motion does it for you.

Motion also supports sophisticated keyframe animation techniques. In fact, it's possible to "bake" behaviors into keyframes for further tweaking. The good news, though, is that behaviors can do things simply not possible with keyframes and with a lot less work.

Applying a Vortex Behavior

Let's apply a behavior called Vortex.

> **TIP** If you've fallen behind, feel free to open the project **A.ApplyingVortex** to catch up.

1   Make sure the center butterfly is still selected (the mini-Timeline should be labeled Butterfly).

2   With the Timeline still playing back, click the Add Behavior button at the top of the Canvas.

3   Choose Simulations > Vortex.

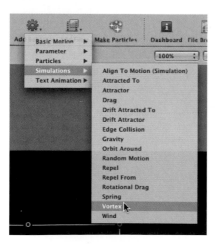

As soon as you choose Vortex, the other three butterflies will begin to fly around the center butterfly. That's because we've applied a behavior, one called Vortex, that influences other objects in the scene, causing them to rotate around the selected object.

You may or may not have noticed a translucent window appear during the course of earlier steps. If you can't see it, do the following:

4   Press F7 to show the Dashboard.

NOTE ▶ If the Dashboard disappears, just press F7 again to reveal it once more.

The Dashboard is a cool little window that gives you quick access to the most common features of objects and their filters and effects. If the title of the Dashboard doesn't say Butterfly: Vortex, you may have deselected it. That's OK. The Dashboard gives you an easy way to switch between the components of an object.

5   Make sure the center butterfly is still selected. If not, click it to select it.

6 Click the small triangle to the right of the Dashboard title, Butterfly:
Vortex.

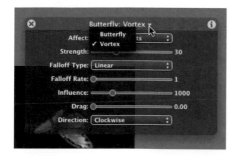

You'll see a menu of the object and all the filters and behaviors applied to
it. In this case we only have one behavior, Vortex.

7 Choose Vortex.

8 In the Dashboard, drag the Strength slider to 0. The butterflies are no
longer affected by the Vortex.

9 Set the Strength slider back up to 20, and then set the Drag to around 0.3.

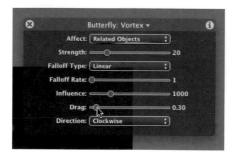

Now the butterflies are drawn toward the center butterfly over time. Notice how Motion instantly adjusts the preview to accommodate the new parameters.

TIP ▷ Sometimes you can't get the exact value you want by dragging the sliders in the Dashboard. If this happens, press Option and click just to the right or left of the slider knob. This should change the slider value by one unit, allowing you to home in on your desired value. Sometimes this doesn't work, in which case you'll need to visit the Inspector, but more on that later.

Moving the Herd

The whole thing looks a little static right now; let's add some momentum to this flock of butterflies.

TIP ▷ If you've fallen behind, feel free to open the project **B.MovingtheHerd** to catch up.

1   Make sure the center butterfly is still selected.

2   Click the Add Behavior button and choose Basic Motion > Throw.

Your Dashboard now shows controls for the Throw behavior. This behavior's job, believe it or not, is to throw things around the screen.

3   Drag the pointer from the center of the circle in the Dashboard to the upper-left corner.

The butterfly is now "thrown" up and to the left of the screen. Notice that the other butterflies are having a hard time keeping up with our lead butterfly. Instead of neatly rotating around it, they're lagging behind somewhat. That's because although they're influenced by the Vortex behavior we applied to the leader, its pull on them isn't quite strong enough to make them follow obediently without question.

It's actually a pretty cool effect, but let's say our storyboard calls for the butterflies to stay in close formation.

4   Press the D key a few times and watch the Dashboard.

Pressing D is a nice way to cycle through the Dashboard controls for all the filters and behaviors attached to a selected object. Pressing Shift-D cycles in the opposite direction. This saves you from selecting the controls via the pop-up menu.

5   Press D again until you return to the controls for the Vortex.

6 Set the Strength all the way to 100.

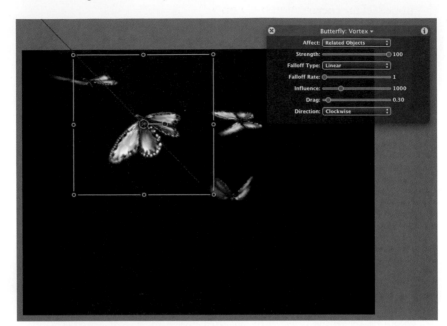

The butterflies now keep up with the leader.

Applying Filters

Let's start to stylize our winged friends, first by adding a splash of color using a color-correction filter.

> **TIP** If you've fallen behind, feel free to open the project
> **C.ApplyingFilters** to catch up.

1 Click one of the orbiting butterflies to select it. If you find it hard to "catch" one, press the spacebar to temporarily pause playback. Once you've selected one, press the spacebar again to resume playing.

2 Click the Add Filter button at the top of the main Canvas window and choose Color Correction > Colorize.

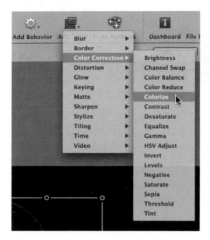

You should instantly see the butterfly's color change. Pretty cool, huh? Let's start tweaking the color.

3 In the Dashboard, click the color swatch (the colored rectangle) to the right of Remap White To. Remember, if you can't see the Dashboard, press D to reveal it.

NOTE ▶ Be sure to click the swatch only once. If you click twice, you'll open the Mac OS X Colors window with the first click and then deactivate the Remap White To swatch with the second click. If that happens, just click on the Remap White To swatch again to reactivate it so that it's ready for editing by the Mac OS X Colors window.

4   Drag your pointer around the color wheel in the Mac OS X Colors window that pops up, and watch as the butterfly you selected changes color, again in real time. Pick a color you like and close the Colors window.

Let's go a little out on the edge now.

5   Select one of the other butterflies.

6   Click the Add Filter button and choose Glow > Dazzle.

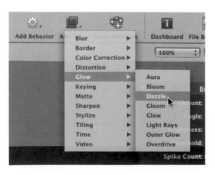

NOTE ▶ At this point you may experience a slowdown in playback. Dazzle is one of the most render-intensive effects in Motion, so that's to be expected.

7   In the Dashboard, set the Amount to 25 and the Threshold to 95.

That's better—a little more sunny afternoon, a little less Vegas.

Soloing Objects and RAM Previews

As mentioned, you may have noticed a slowdown after applying the Dazzle filter. Dazzle is an extremely render-intensive filter, and as such it may slow your playback rate below the intended 30 frames per second. You can see just how fast Motion is currently playing your sequence by looking at the FPS (frames per second) reading at the top left of the Canvas.

Whether or not Dazzle put the brakes on your system, at some point you'll be working with enough objects and filters that Motion will be unable to preview in real time. In these situations you have two options: soloing or rendering a RAM preview. Let's take a look at each in turn.

Let's suppose you'd like to adjust the color of the butterfly to which we applied the Colorize filter, and for some reason you have to do it in real time. This wouldn't be a problem if it weren't for that annoying Dazzle filter. Not to worry—we'll solve the problem by soloing.

1   Select the butterfly to which you applied the Colorize filter.

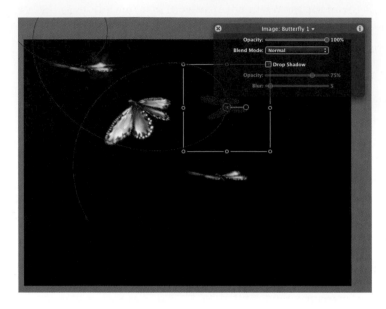

2   Press Ctrl-S to *solo* the object.

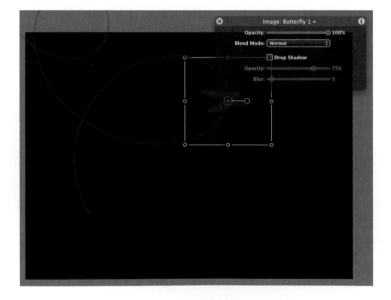

All other objects disappear from the screen. You should now have regained real-time performance. You can do this with any object in your project, which is great for tweaking parameters for specific objects in real time when projects become extremely complex.

3 Press Ctrl-S again to unsolo the object.

Another way to gain real-time performance is to use a RAM preview. However, RAM previews restore real-time playback at the expense of interactivity. When you generate a RAM preview, Motion effectively renders out a final version of your composite and then stores it in RAM for you to easily play back in real time. As soon as you change one of the properties in your project, however, the preview becomes unrendered and the real-time performance is lost until another RAM preview is initiated.

TIP ▶ Because Motion leverages the graphics card's GPU, RAM previews in Motion are usually several times faster than RAM previews in other motion graphics applications.

4 Choose Mark > RAM Preview > Play Range, or press Cmd-R.

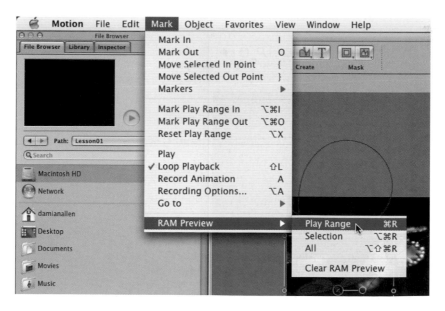

Motion begins to render a RAM preview. Notice how the play range in the mini-Timeline turns green as frames are cached into RAM. It's actually possible to stop the RAM preview while it's rendering and restart it later. As long as you haven't modified your project, the section of the Timeline already cached (the part that's turned green) will be remembered and the RAM preview render will pick up where it left off.

5   When the RAM preview is complete, resume playback (by pressing the spacebar or clicking the Play button at the bottom of the Canvas).

Your playback (as indicated in the top left of the Canvas) should now be 30 fps. Try changing one of the sliders in the Dashboard. The RAM preview immediately becomes uncached (as indicated by the removal of green in the mini-Timeline).

TIP If memory's tight, clear RAM previews when you're done with them. This should give you back precious RAM for other things. Choose Mark > RAM Preview > Clear RAM Preview.

Deactivating Behaviors and Filters

No doubt you've already started to throw on other filters and behaviors in a frenzy of experimentation. Go ahead, give them all a whirl. Just one thing before we leave you to it: Once you've thrown 20 behaviors on an object, here's how to turn some of them off.

1   Press F5 to open the Project pane.

2   In the Layers tab, uncheck the box for the Throw behavior to deactivate it.

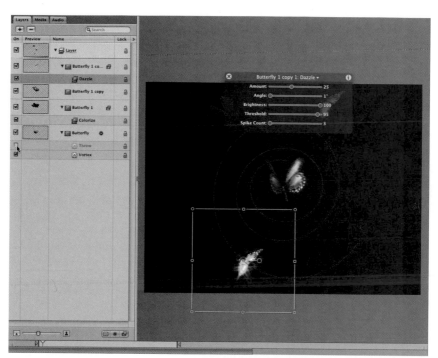

The center butterfly is no longer "thrown" offscreen. All of the filters and behaviors can be deactivated by clicking their respective check boxes here in the Layers tab.

3   Click the Throw behavior in the Layers tab to select it.

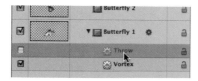

4   Press Delete. The Throw behavior is now completely removed from the layer.

5   Press Cmd-Z (for Undo).

Your command to delete the Throw is undone and the Throw returns to the Layers tab.

Using Particle Simulations

Motion comes with a great collection of predesigned particle simulations, but it's easy to create your own. If you've tried to use other particle systems and failed, fear not. Motion's real-time feedback and simple controls make the design process extremely intuitive. We'll take a look at designing particle systems later in the book. What you may not immediately realize is that anything in Motion can become a particle simulation. Take our humble butterfly, for example…

Generating a Particle System

Any object in the Motion layers tab can become a particle system with a simple click.

1   Press Cmd-Option-W to close any currently open projects. If you've created a masterpiece that you'd like to revisit later, save it when prompted. Otherwise, click Don't Save to continue.

2   Choose File > Open or press Cmd-O to open a project.

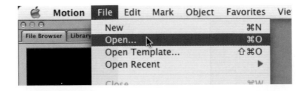

3 Navigate to APTS_Motion > Lessons > Lesson01 and open the project **D.Particles.**

Here we are again, with one simple butterfly flapping at the center of the screen. What if we want a whole lot of butterflies but don't want to have to drag them all onto the screen individually and change their Timeline offsets as we did in the opening exercise? We'd use particles, of course.

4 Make sure playback is halted. If not, press the spacebar to stop playback and move the playhead to frame 1 (by pressing the Home key).

5 Click the butterfly in the Canvas to select it, and then click the Make Particles button at the top of the Canvas.

Now, before you go playing this back, know that the default Birth Rate of 30 is way too high for what we're doing here. Because we have a relatively large animated sequence, Motion has a lot of work to do calculating all of the particles in real time.

6 In the Dashboard (press F7 to bring it up if it's hidden), drag the Birth Rate slider to around 5.

7 *Now* press the spacebar to begin playback.

TIP ▶ If you're having problems getting real-time playback on your system, try reducing the Birth Rate even further for a more modest number of butterflies. Alternatively, you could try reducing the play range by moving the play range Out point marker to the left. Another solution would be to run out to the local Apple Store and buy more RAM and a better graphics card, or even one of those shiny new G5s.

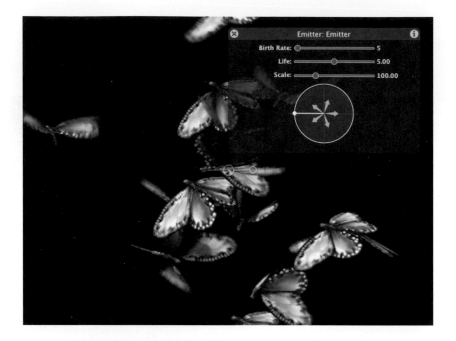

The butterflies explode outward. Notice how each one starts at a different frame of the butterfly's motion, creating the illusion that these are all different butterflies.

8   Drag the main radial line—the line with no arrows that's connected to the outside of the circle by a small round dot—and watch the result. It will divide into two separate lines.

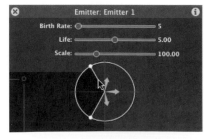

Moving the radial lines in this fashion allows you to decide how broad a spread of directions the butterflies will move in once they're "born."

9   Click and drag the gray arrows in the circle, watching the result.

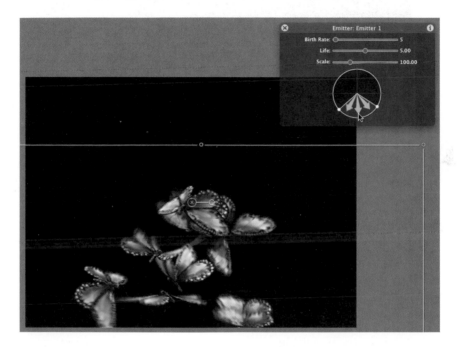

Dragging the arrows toward the outside of the circle increases the butter-flies' speed, while rotating the arrows around the circle changes their direction.

10   Set the arrowheads so that they're about halfway between the center and the outside of the circle, thus setting the speed of the butterflies to a medium level.

11 Drag one of the radial lines to close up the circle again, causing the butterflies to shoot out in all directions.

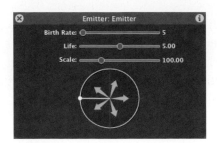

TIP ▶ To snap the circle shut again, press Shift as you drag.

It's a little disconcerting how the butterflies just pop out of nowhere. Let's
apply another behavior to change that.

Applying a Particle Behavior

Motion ships with just one particle behavior; no doubt we'll see more in the
future. It's an incredibly useful behavior, though: It's called Scale Over Life.

NOTE ▶ There are two parts to a particle system in Motion, the emitter
and the particle(s) that belong to it. In the case of Scale Over Life, the
behavior must be applied to the particle, *not* to the emitter.

1 Press F5 to reveal the Project pane.

2 Click the Layers tab if it's not currently active.

Notice there are four rows in the Layers tab. The row labeled Layer contains the particle object (we'll take a better look at the role of layers later). Next we have the emitter, Emitter, which spits out the butterflies. Third, we have a particle called Butterfly. It's what Emitter spits out. Finally, you'll notice a grayed-out row called Butterfly. This is the original reference footage used by the Butterfly particle. It's turned off because it's being used only as a reference for the particle system; it's not being drawn to the Canvas itself. If it were, we'd be seeing the original butterfly that was on the screen before we clicked Make Particles *as well as* the butterflies being fired out of the emitter.

Don't worry if this all sounds confusing—we'll spend a lot of time going through particle systems in Lessons 5 and 6. The important thing right now is that we apply the Scale Over Life behavior to the Butterfly particle, *not* to the emitter.

3   Click the layer titled Butterfly to select it.

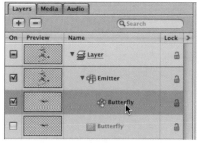

4   Click the Add Behavior button and choose Particles > Scale Over Life.

5   Press F5 to close the Project pane. If you've stopped playback, press the spacebar to resume.

6   In the Dashboard, choose Birth and Death Values from the Increment pop-up menu.

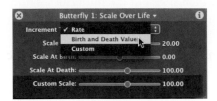

7   Set Scale At Birth to around 20 and Scale At Death to around 300.

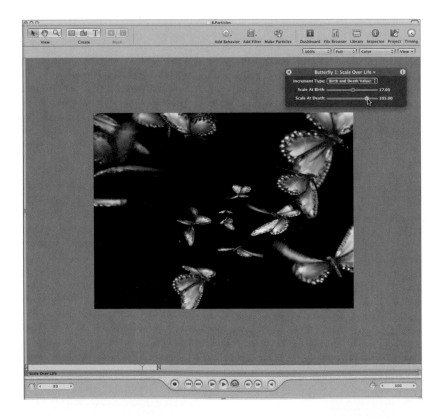

The butterflies now start their lives at a fairly humble size and grow bigger and bigger with age.

What You've Learned

▶ The main interface comprises the Utility window, the Canvas, the Project pane, and the Timing pane.

▶ Several useful hot keys reveal and hide these interface elements.

▶ The play range can be adjusted to create a real-time preview of a specific section of the Timeline.

▶ Behaviors create complex animations without the need for keyframing.

▶ Filters and behaviors can be added to selected objects via controls at the top of the Canvas.

▶ The Dashboard provides easy access to the most common parameters of objects, filters, and effects.

▶ Any object in the Canvas can be turned into a particle system.

Keyboard Shortcuts

File Commands

Cmd-O	opens a project

Windowing Keys

Cmd-1	opens and closes the File Browser
Cmd-2	opens and closes the Library
Cmd-4	opens and closes the Layers tab
F1	opens the Properties tab of the Inspector
F2	opens the Behaviors tab of the Inspector
F3	opens the Filters tab of the Inspector
F4	opens the object tab of the Inspector (this tab changes its name depending on the selected object)
F5	opens and closes the Project pane (which usually opens to its Layers tab)

Keyboard Shortcuts

Windowing Keys, continued

F6	opens and closes the Timing pane
F7	reveals and hides the Dashboard (see below)

Navigation

Cmd-+ **(main keyboard)**	zooms in by a discrete amount
Cmd-- **(main keyboard)**	zooms out by a discrete amount
Shift-Z	zooms Canvas to 100%
Option-Z	sets Canvas to Fit in Window zoom mode
Cmd-spacebar-drag	zooms
Spacebar-drag	pans the Canvas

Play Range Commands

Spacebar	begins and halts playback
Cmd-Option-I	sets the play range In point to the current time
Cmd-Option-O	sets the play range Out point to the current time
Home	sends the playback to frame 1
Shift-[	moves the beginning of the selected object to the current playhead position

Dashboard

D	reveals the Dashboard if hidden, then cycles through the filters and behaviors attached to the current object
Shift-D	cycles through the filters and behaviors attached to the current object in the opposite direction to the D hot key

Keyboard Shortcuts

Miscellaneous

Cmd-R	renders a RAM preview
Ctrl-S	solos a selected object
Cmd-Z	undoes the last action
Cmd-Option-D	reveals and hides the Dock in the Finder
Cmd-Shift-A	reveals the Applications folder in the Finder

2

Lesson Files   APTS_Motion > Lessons > Lesson02

Time   This lesson takes approximately 45 minutes to complete.

Goals   Become familiar with the Library

Apply and manipulate generators

Work with particle presets

Create a motion graphics background

Lesson 2
Using Generators

Motion projects frequently contain video footage and still images from a variety of sources. Very often, however, the design of a sequence requires you to generate unique abstract elements out of thin air. Fortunately, Motion comes with a generous set of tools for creating such elements. These tools are called *generators*, and along with particles they provide a great additional resource for building up your composite.

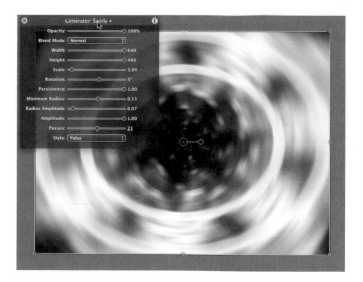

Applying Generators from the Library

In Lesson 1 we added filters and behaviors to an object using the pop-up menus in the Canvas. That's the quickest way to access them, but there's another place you can find them: the Library. You'll find generators and a host of other goodies in the Library.

1   Press Cmd-O and then navigate to and open the project APTS_Motion > Lessons > Lesson02 > **A.ExploringGenerators**.

2   Press Cmd-2 to select the Library tab.

Like the File Browser, the Library has two panes. The top pane lists the various categories of elements, such as fonts, particle emitters, gradients, and, of course, generators. The Library is a nice place to browse when you're looking for inspiration on a new project. Notice that behaviors and filters are accessible here as well as from the buttons at the top of the Canvas.

3   Select Behaviors in the top-left pane.

4   Make sure the List View button—just below the Apply button and above the upper-right pane—is selected.

Toggling between the List View and Icon View buttons allows you to view items in the Library in a list or as large icons. List view is preferable for most of what you do in the Library. An identical pair of buttons exists in the File Browser.

5   Select the All folder in the top-right pane, and then select Attractor from the Name list in the lower pane.

While filters and behaviors are easier to access via the buttons in the Canvas, the preview window in the Library helps when you're first learning what each behavior and filter does.

NOTE ▸ Notice the 3rd Party Filters icon. Motion supports Adobe After Effects–compatible filters in addition to those that come standard. Be aware that third-party filters are *not* accelerated for use with Motion, so they may not support Motion's real-time preview capabilities. To install third-party filters, you need to tell Motion where to look for them, via the General tab of Preferences (Motion > Preferences).

▶ Using Alternate Window Layouts

Do you have one of those wide Apple Cinema displays that make your studio look as though it teleported here from the year 2020? If you do (or even if you don't), you may want to take advantage of one of Motion's alternate window layouts. You can find these in the Window menu.

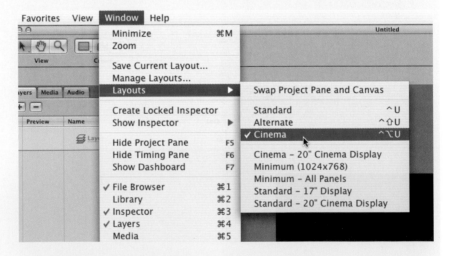

Bear in mind that this book assumes you're using the Standard layout, so you may want to stick with that at least while doing the exercises in this book.

6 Now select the Generators icon in the top-left pane of the Library and the All folder in the top-right pane.

7 Drag the Swirly preset icon from the lower pane of the Library (you may need to scroll to find it) into the center of the Canvas and release it when it snaps to the yellow Dynamic Guides.

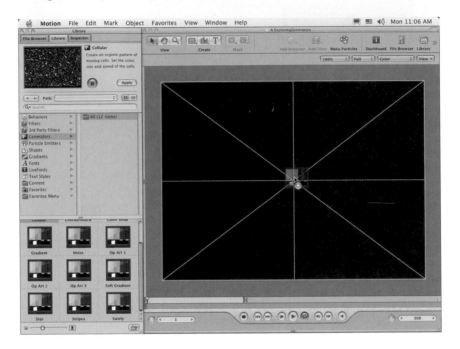

8 Click the Play button below the Canvas to begin playback.

At first glance Swirly seems a little unimpressive; it looks like a jaggy version of an iTunes visualization. But it can produce some very pleasing results, especially when combined with one or two other effects.

9 Click the Add Filter button and choose Blur > Radial Blur.

We've taken care of the jaggies (aliasing); now let's try modifying some of Swirly's parameters to create some interesting effects.

10 If you can't see the Dashboard, press F7 to bring it up. Press D to cycle from the Dashboard for Radial Blur to the Dashboard for Swirly.

> **NOTE** ▶ Remember that pressing D and Shift-D cycles through the Dashboards for the selected object. In this case, we only have the generator object itself—the Swirly—and the Radial Blur filter we applied to it, so these are the only two Dashboards you'll see when you press D and Shift-D.

11 Using the Swirly Dashboard, start dragging sliders around to see the various effects you can create.

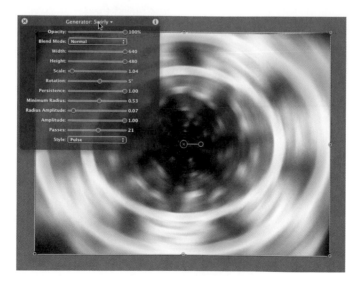

You may want to try selecting Spiderweb Spin or Spiky from the Style pop-up menu (at the bottom of the Dashboard) for completely different effects.

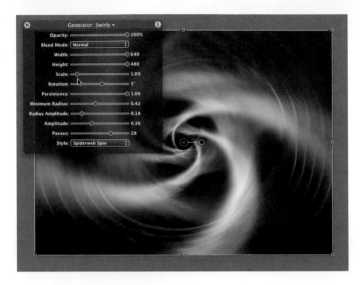

By applying other blur, glow, and stylize filters on top of the generator, you can create an almost infinite variety of elements to blend into your composite. Compositing these elements via the blend modes adds yet another creative dimension for exploration.

NOTE ▶ At some point in your compositing, you'll have applied so many objects, filters, behaviors, and particles that your system won't be able to play back in real time. Sometimes it's just a matter of caching files from disk into system RAM, so let the entire Timeline play through completely after adding a new object so that Motion can cache the composite correctly. At other times, you may simply reach your hardware's limit for real-time performance. As mentioned in Lesson 1, pressing Cmd-R to render a RAM preview can help.

There are several other generators available in Motion; some of them require keyframing while others, such as Swirly, automatically generate motion effects. However, before we go any further with generators, let's take a quick look at some "pseudo generators" hiding among the particle presets.

Exploring Abstract Particles

When most people think of particles, they think of explosions, fairy dust, and weather effects like rain and snow. But particles can be a useful way of creating generic elements for motion graphics. In this exercise we'll take a look at a few particle presets whose output is much more "generator-like" than you would expect from particles. We will, however, take a brief detour on the way to these more abstract particles. For some reason, people like to watch things explode and catch fire, so let's look at the more traditional particle offerings first (and get it out of your system).

1   Choose File > Revert. This returns us to the original state of our project (**A.ExploringGenerators**) without having to close and reopen it.

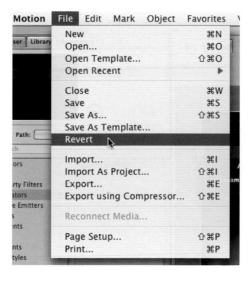

2   Still in the Library tab (press Cmd-2 if you're not there), click the Particle Emitters icon in the upper-left pane.

3 Click the Pyro folder in the upper-right pane.

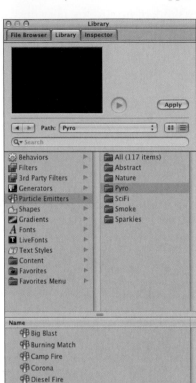

4 Resume playback by clicking the Play button at the base of the Canvas.

NOTE ▶ When you've been clicking in the Library as we have, pressing a key on the keyboard causes Motion to jump to a certain letter in the Library Name list. For example, if you're looking for the Oil Fire preset in a long list of presets, you can press O to jump there. What this means is that pressing the spacebar will *not* resume playback of the Timeline. The key press is being used to navigate the lists in the Library. In order to use hot keys again, you'll need to first click back into the Canvas. This is called giving the Canvas window *focus*.

5   Drag the preset Corona from the lower Library pane and release it when it snaps to the Dynamic Guides at the center of the Canvas.

Feel free to scale the Corona outward by Option-Shift-dragging a corner of its bounding box (pressing Option while dragging scales from the center; pressing Shift while dragging preserves the object's aspect ratio).

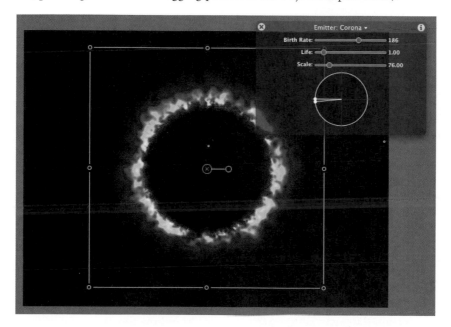

Without a lot of work, you now have something that looks eerily like the evil eye from *Lord of the Rings*.

6   Select the Layers tab (by pressing F5), select the item called Layer, and delete it by pressing Delete.

The item called Layer is the container for all the elements in your composite. By deleting it, you quickly delete everything else.

There are plenty of other combustible presets in the Library—feel free to try some out. When you're finished, delete the Layer item again to clear out your project.

7   Close the Layers tab (by pressing F5).

8   In the Library, click the Sparkles folder in the upper-right pane.

9   In the lower pane, select Magic Wand.

10 Drag your pointer around the preview window at the top of the Library pane.

As you drag, you get instant feedback about how the preset will look animated. (This is the sort of the thing you instantly feel like showing to your favorite 3-year-old.)

Let's move on to those more "generator-like" particles we were talking about earlier.

11 Click the Abstract folder in the upper-right pane of the Library.

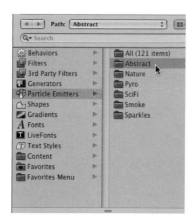

12 Resume playback if you've stopped it, clicking the Canvas to bring it to focus as necessary.

13 Drag Circle City from the lower Library pane into the center of the Canvas, releasing it when it snaps to the Dynamic Guides.

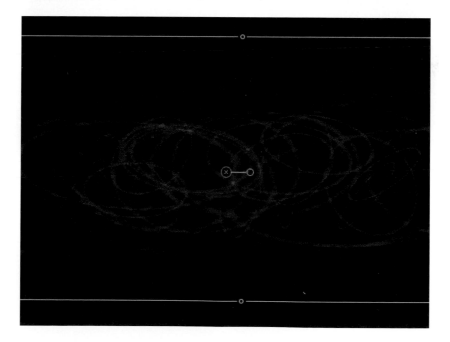

We've created a nice swirly mess. By itself it's not that spectacular, but used as an element of a multi-layered composite it could provide a sense of geometric chaos, complex rhythm on the verge of collapse. Or for those of you who are a little more pragmatic and less prone to aesthetic philosophy, let's just say it makes lots of pretty circles.

Nice, you say, but not the color you were looking for. Don't worry—we can fix that.

14 Click the Gradients preset icon in the upper-left pane of the Library.

15 From the lower pane, drag Icy Blue onto the Circle City particles in the Canvas.

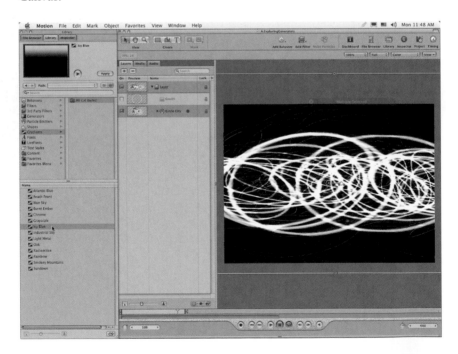

Instantly the particle system takes on the color scheme of the selected gradient. This could just as well have been a custom gradient you created yourself, as we'll see a little later in this lesson.

Let's take a look at a couple of other generator-like particles before going back to the "official" generator presets.

16 Choose File > Revert. This again returns us to the default project.

17 Resume playback by pressing the spacebar or clicking the Play button at the bottom of the Canvas.

18 In the Library, select Particle Emitters > Abstract, and then drag the Golden Cam preset emitter into the center of the Canvas.

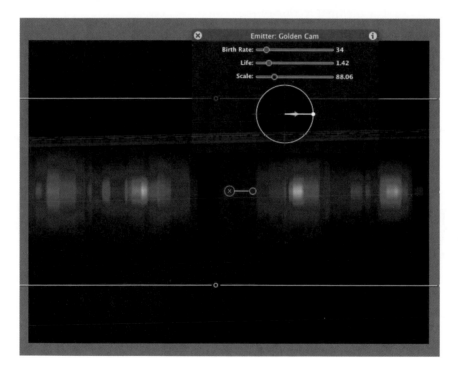

Here is another example of a particle system that could serve very well as an element in a layered composite. Let's look at one more.

19 In the Layers tab (F5), delete the item called Layer.

20 In the Library, drag Reflection into the center of the Canvas.

A little '70s, but potentially useful nonetheless. In the case of all the particle effects, things like color, size, and shapes can be tailored to your specific application. Exactly how you go about doing that will have to wait until a little later in the book, when we delve into the creation of particle systems.

Using the Cellular Generator

In the next few lessons we'll be creating an entire TV station promo from start to finish. For the final section of the promo, we need an abstract background over which the other elements will be layered. We'll create the background in the remaining exercises of this lesson, and along the way you'll learn all about using and customizing properties of Motion's generators.

We'll start with the Cellular generator, a particularly versatile tool for creating all kinds of background textures. It simulates thousands of cells squirming under a microscope. In and of itself, the effect has limited application, but when combined with Motion's other filters it offers many creative possibilities.

1 Press Cmd-Option-W to close all open projects.

> **TIP ▶** Motion allows you to have several projects open at once. This is great if you need to edit multiple pieces at the same time, but it may not always be a good idea. More projects open means more drag on precious system resources, and if you don't keep everything organized, you may find yourself editing the wrong project. Pressing Cmd-Option-W closes all open projects so that when you open a project or start a new one, you're sure that no other open projects are hiding in the background.

2 Press Cmd-O; then navigate to the folder APTS_Motion > Lessons > Lesson02 and open the project **B.CellularGenerator**.

3 Begin playback by pressing the spacebar or clicking the Play button at the bottom of the Canvas.

4 Click the Library tab (or press Cmd-2) and select the Generators icon.

5   Drag the Cellular generator into the center of the Canvas, releasing it
     when it snaps to the Dynamic Guides.

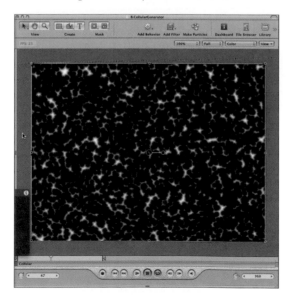

Thousands of tiny cells are now squirming around on your screen. It's a nice start, but we need to do some significant tweaking to fashion this into our abstract background.

In the Dashboard (press F7 to reveal it if it isn't visible), you'll see that you have a handful of controls. The bottom one allows you to choose from several gradient presets to change the color of your cells.

6 Choose the Blue Sky preset from the Gradient menu in the Dashboard.

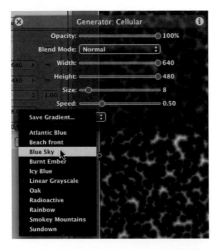

We now have white cells on a blue background. But what if we want to choose our own colors instead of relying on the presets? Unfortunately, the Dashboard doesn't give us any way to do that. In fact, the Dashboard only provides access to *some* of the properties of a selected object, behavior, or filter. For the rest of the controls we need to use the Inspector.

Working in the Inspector

The Inspector is where you make detailed changes to the properties of filters, behaviors, and objects. We use the Dashboard for quick tweaks, but all the fine-tuning happens in the Inspector.

1   Press F7 to close the Dashboard.

2   Press F4 to go to the Inspector tab of the Utility window.

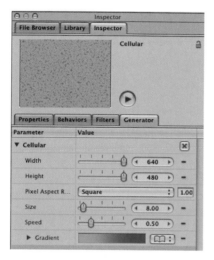

The Inspector has four tabs: Properties, Behaviors, Filters, and object (a contextual tab). The object tab changes depending on what's selected in the Canvas. Right now, we're looking at the Cellular generator, so the fourth tab is labeled Generator. If we had a particle emitter object selected instead, it would be labeled Emitter.

To navigate among the four tabs of the Inspector, simply click the tab header, or use function keys F1 to F4.

3 Press F1 to switch to the Properties tab of the Inspector.

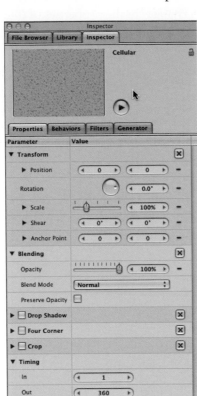

The Properties tab contains all the global properties you can specify about an object. You can do things such as change the scale and position of an object in the Canvas, edit its opacity (transparency), add a drop shadow, and set a corner-pin distortion.

4 Press F2 and F3 to switch to the Behaviors and Filters tabs, respectively.

The Behaviors tab lists the properties for all the behaviors attached to the selected object; the Filters tab does the same for any filters that have been applied to it. In the case of our Cellular generator, we haven't yet applied any filters or behaviors, so those tabs are empty.

5 Press F4 to return to the Generator tab.

> **NOTE ▶** If you've accidentally deselected the generator, just click it again in the Canvas to reselect it.

You'll notice that in addition to the parameters available in the Dashboard, there's a gradient color bar in the Generator tab of the Inspector. We can use this to create our custom gradient.

6 Click the disclosure triangle to the left of Gradient to toggle open its parameters.

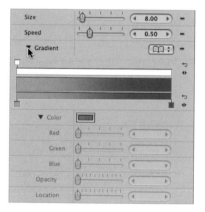

Working with Gradients

A *gradient* is a graduated blending of two or more colors. Gradients are used throughout Motion as a way to define a range of colors. In our case we're using one to define the range of colors between the cells (which take the color of the far-left side of the gradient) and the "petri dish" they're floating in (which takes the color of the right side of the gradient).

There are two parts to a gradient in Motion: the opacity (transparency) and the hue (the actual colors).

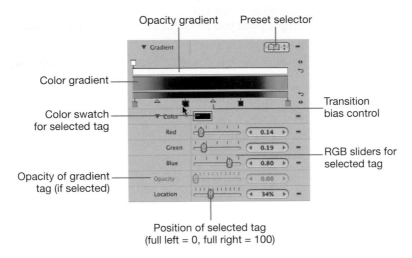

The Gradient parameter contains three bars: a thin white one at the top, a thick center one, and a thin colored bar at the bottom. The bottom bar determines the range of colors that the object will use. In our example, the gradient determines the appearance of the cells compared with their surrounding petri dish. In other situations, the gradient may affect an image in other ways. For example, in the case of particles you can use a gradient to randomly assign different colors to particles as they're born or even have the particles cycle through colors over their lifetime.

The top bar determines the opacity of the gradient. It allows you to set a range of transparencies for the colors you choose. Our example is a grayscale gradient. It currently looks solid white because we haven't adjusted any values for it. Any parts of this gradient that show up as white will be completely solid, while any black parts of the gradient will be completely transparent. In other words, in the Canvas you'd be able to see through those parts of the generator—if we had another object behind it. By default, the opacity gradient shows a solid white, meaning that the full range of colors will be solid. We can always add black or gray areas if we want some of the colors in the gradient to be semi-transparent. We would add the black or gray swatches to the opacity gradient directly above the color in the main gradient we want to make transparent.

Modifying gradients is simple once you learn the basic editing techniques.

1   Click the color tag at the lower left of the color gradient bar to select it.

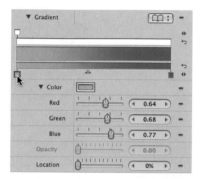

Clicking a color tag loads it into the Color swatch below the gradient. You can then edit its red, green, and blue values and even adjust the position of the tag along the gradient using the Location slider. This is great if you have precise values to enter, but usually you want to select colors visually rather than with sliders.

TIP ▶ Motion uses a range of numbers between 0 and 1 to describe the red, green, and blue values of a color. If you're used to applications such as Adobe Photoshop that use the range 0–255, just be aware that what you're used to calling 255 is what Motion calls 1. To convert a value on a 0–255 scale to a value on a 0–1 scale, just divide it by 255. To convert a value on a 0–1 scale to the 0–255 scale, multiply it by 255.

2   Double-click the color tag at the lower left of the gradient bar to open
    the Colors window, and click the color wheel in the upper-left corner
    of the Colors window to make sure you're in the HSV view.

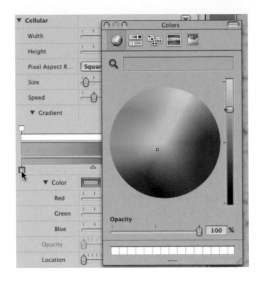

For those of you new to HSV color selection, it works like this:

▶ The angle around the circle determines the hue—reds, blues, greens,
and so on.

▶ The distance from the center determines the saturation of the color.
The closer to the center, the less saturated and more gray the color
becomes; the closer to the outer edge, the stronger and richer the color
becomes.

▶ The vertical slider to the right of the circle determines the value, or
brightness, of the color.

3   Drag around the color wheel to modify the color of the cells in the
    Canvas.

4   Close the Colors window by clicking the gray Close button in the upper-left corner.

Let's add another tag to the gradient.

5   Click the middle of the lower color gradient bar to add another color tag.

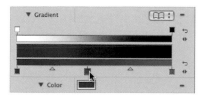

NOTE ▶ You must click the lower color gradient bar to add a color tag, or the upper opacity gradient to add an opacity tag. Clicking the wide, center gradient will have no effect.

If you need to reposition the tag, just drag it left or right. Notice the two triangles on either side of the new tag? These allow you to adjust the bias between the selected tag and its neighboring tags. Drag these if you want the gradient to contain more of one color than the other.

For our purposes, we need only the gradient tags at the far left and far right, so let's delete the one we just added at the center.

6   Click the newly created center tag and drag downward until the tag disappears, and then release the mouse. The tag should disappear in a puff of smoke.

Using Hot Boxes and Sliders

Let's continue to set up the gradient for our intended purpose: creating an abstract background for a TV station promo. In doing so, we'll take a look at different ways to enter values in Motion.

1   Click the left gradient tag to select it.

2   Drag the Red slider to 0.02, the Green slider to 0.00, and the Blue slider to 0.02.

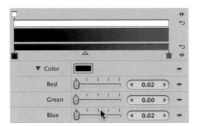

Using the sliders is one method of entering values for parameters. Sometimes a precise value is required, and that's difficult or impossible to dial in with the sliders. In such cases you can use the entry boxes to the right of the sliders, also known as *numeric entry boxes,* or *hot boxes.*

3   Click in the hot box to the right of the Red slider. It should become darker, indicating that the existing number is highlighted.

4   Type *1.00* in the Red hot box. This will replace the existing value of 0.02.

You may have noticed that your pointer changed shape when it was over the hot box. That's because Motion's numeric entry boxes allow for *hot-scrubbing.* By clicking and dragging the pointer over these boxes you can enter values as if dragging a slider. The benefit of this method is that in some cases it allows you to access values beyond the range of the slider presets. For example, a slider might have a range from 1 to 100, but you may want a higher value than that. You could use the hot-scrubbing capability to set the value beyond the slider limit.

5   Click and hold the pointer in the middle of the entry box, and drag it to the left until the value in the box is restored to 0.02, just as we had it set in step 2.

6   Now click the right gradient tag to select it.

7   Using one of the methods outlined above, set Red to 0.40, Green to 0.40, and Blue to 1.00.

Adding a Slit Scan

It's time to bend and twist the Cellular generator into the background we need it to be.

1   Still in the Generator tab of the Inspector, set the Size parameter to around 32.

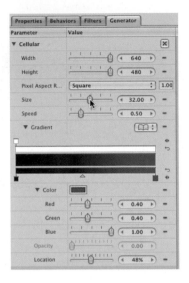

Now for the fun part. It's time to add a Slit Scan filter.

2   Click the Add Filter button at the top of the Canvas and choose Stylize > Slit Scan.

Now that's more like it! The Slit Scan filter takes our somewhat generic lumpy cells and turns them into a cosmordial waterfall. Notice too that the Inspector immediately jumped to the Filters tab when we added the Slit Scan filter.

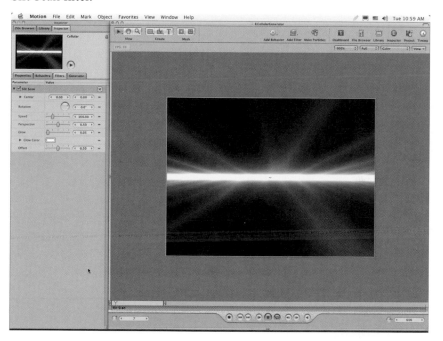

For the exercises in the next few lessons, we want the background to appear to flow from the right, so we'll make some adjustments to the Slit Scan to accommodate our design intent.

3   In the Filters tab of the Inspector, set the Slit Scan's rotation to 90 degrees either by using the dial widget or by manually typing *90* into the hot box.

   NOTE ▶ When using the dial widget to enter angles, be aware that a counterclockwise rotation produces a positive increment in the angle. Most people expect a clockwise rotation to increase the angle positively; in the case of Motion, it's the reverse.

   You'll see that the filter's Center parameter has two hot boxes. The left hot box determines the slit's horizontal offset from the center of the screen.

The right box determines its vertical offset. We want to push it to the right, so we'll just adjust the horizontal offset.

4   Drag in the horizontal (left) Center hot box to push the slit off the right side of the screen (a value of about 350).

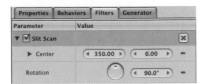

5   Set the Perspective parameter to about 0.20. This shifts the effect back a bit, giving a little more detail in the branches flowing out of the slit from the left.

6   Set the Glow parameter to about 0.10.

7   Click the Glow Color swatch to open the Colors window. Select a medium shade of pink to add a nice highlight glow to our cosmordial soup.

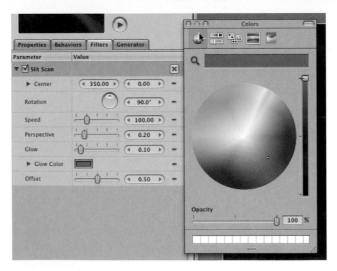

8   Close the Colors window.

We're almost done, but we need to add a blur just to soften some of those edges on the rays branching out from the slit.

9 Click the Add Filter button and choose Blur > Directional Blur.

That softens up the branching nicely, but you'll notice we've introduced a kind of embossing around the edges of the image. That's because the Directional Blur has "pulled in" some black from outside the frame to blur with the rest of the image. Usually this effect is a good thing, because it keeps blurs from cropping at the edge of an object. However, in cases like this one where the entire background is being blurred (not just a small object within the composite), the result is this undesirable embossing.

10 In the Filters tab (F3) of the Inspector, check the box next to Crop in the Directional Blur parameter.

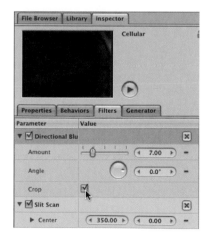

The blur is now cropped at the edges of the Canvas, and no black is pulled in.

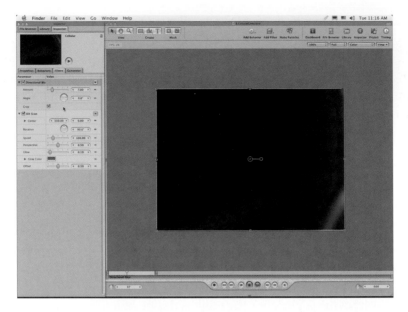

All is well.

Rendering a Generated Object

It's all very well to tinker under the power of Motion's real-time design engine, but at some point you need to render to disk. We'll do this now for the background we've just created, so that in future exercises Motion won't need to calculate the generator and filters we've applied; it will just need to read in a previously rendered movie from the hard drive.

1   Choose File > Export (or press Cmd-E).

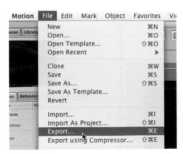

You could also choose the "Export using Compressor" option if you wanted to set up a batch render of several movies. There's no real benefit to using the Compressor export option if you're planning on taking your project to DVD Studio Pro as a motion menu. Instead, you'll simply load the Motion project into DVD Studio Pro as "virtual footage"—see Lesson 14 for more information.

2   From the Export Preset pop-up menu, choose Lossless Movie.

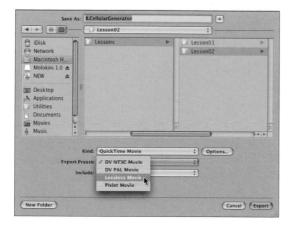

In many cases you can set your filename and click Export. But first, let's take a look at how we can optimize some of the settings.

3   Click the Options button to open the Export Options dialog.

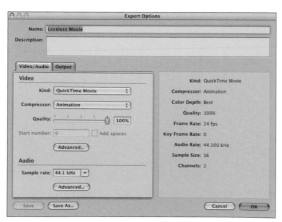

Here you can choose a specific codec and make quick changes to the quality of the render. Animation is usually the best choice for output, since it preserves the alpha channel information. It's also a lossless compressor; leaving the quality slider set to 100% guarantees that the rendered movie will be at the highest possible quality.

4   In the Export Options Video/Audio tab, click the Advanced button to open the Compression Settings dialog.

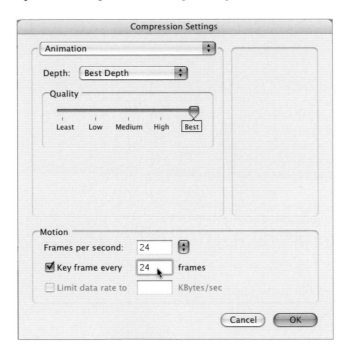

This is where you can change codecs, compression quality, frame rate, and keyframe options. We'll set the keyframing to every 24 frames. This will cause the movie to compress losslessly, saving room on the hard disk.

5   Set "Key frame every" to 24 frames (as in the preceding figure), and then click OK to close the Compression Settings dialog.

6   Click OK again to close the Export Options dialog.

7   Back in the Export dialog, name your movie *CosmordialSoup.mov* and save it to APTS_Motion > Lessons > Lesson02 > Student Saves.

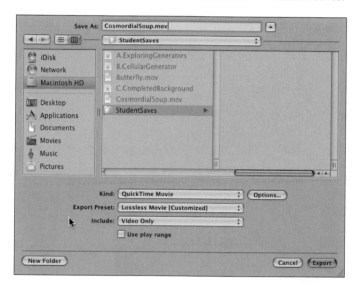

8   Click the Export button.

NOTE ▶ By default, Motion will render out the entire project length. Checking the "Use play range" box will cause Motion to render only the portion of the Timeline between the play range In point and the play range Out point.

An Export render window shows you the progress of the render and displays a thumbnail of the frames being rendered.

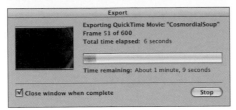

9   When the export is finished, click in the File Browser and navigate to the APTS_Motion > Lessons > Lesson02 > Student Saves folder. Double-click **CosmordialSoup.mov** to play your newly rendered movie.

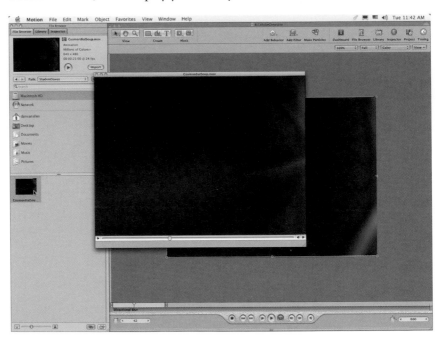

With just a single generator and a Slit Scan filter, we've managed to create an impressive background element. The real-time design engine in Motion makes it possible for you to quickly and visually dial in many simple elements to create unique backgrounds without having to reach for an expensive stock footage library.

What You've Learned

▶ The Library is the central repository for all of Motion's assets, filters, behaviors, and presets.

▶ The Library offers previews of the effects, filters, and behaviors.

▶ Generators can produce sophisticated motion graphics backgrounds.

▶ Motion's particle system can be used to create motion graphics elements as well as the more common fire and fairy dust effects.

▶ The Inspector contains all of the adjustable parameters for objects and their filters and behaviors.

Keyboard Shortcuts

Cmd-Option-W	closes all open projects
Cmd-E	exports a project

3

Lesson Files APTS_Motion > Lessons > Lesson03

Time This lesson takes approximately 45 minutes to complete.

Goals Create custom project settings

Learn about the role of layers and objects in Motion

Navigate the Layers tab

Build a basic multi-layered composite

Manipulate common behaviors and filters via the Layers tab

Lesson 3

Working with Layers and Objects

Motion graphics compositing is all about layering images and movies to create a final, unified montage. Motion offers an elegant system for combining and managing these elements. In this lesson we'll take a look at how to organize and combine these elements using Motion's Layers tab and Timeline views.

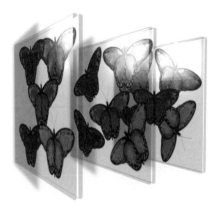

Creating a TV Station ID

Throughout the next few lessons we'll be creating a promo ID for a fictitious television station. Our hypothetical client brief goes something like this:

The new owner of a television station somewhere in Asia wants to rebrand it for a younger, hipper audience. The owner wants to begin the process immediately by announcing a change of name from XBRN to Cinematíve. Your job—should you choose to accept it (and you will, of course, since nobody passes up paying work in this business)—is to create a 30-second station ID depicting the change in identity and firmly embedding the Cinematíve brand in the consciousness of the 238 senior citizens still watching.

The outstanding creatives at the advertising agency contracting you for the work have decided on a butterfly as the universal symbol of rebirth. Seemingly oblivious to the exhausted ubiquity of the butterfly in modern advertising, the agency talent thinks this is the freshest idea they've had since the talking-dog campaign.

In the storyboards, an actress set against a skyline smiles enigmatically and says, "A new beginning," as butterflies burst from her cupped hands. These butterflies then flutter into a surreal landscape and explode in a shower of colors, nicely setting off the Cinematíve logo.

You happily start to calculate the many, many hours you'll be able to bill for this job when the agency rep suddenly mumbles awkwardly, "Now, here's the thing. We've had to revise the budget a little since we first talked and…" Any other day you would have collapsed under the weight of it. But today, you have your fresh new copy of Motion to fall back on.

We'll work backward on this project, building the last half of the piece in the next couple of lessons and then proceeding to the front end. This isn't necessarily how you'd execute the job; it just conveniently introduces and builds up the Motion feature set as we go.

The television station formerly known as XBRN broadcasts in three countries; two of them use the PAL format while the third uses the NTSC standard. One of the countries is also introducing a high-definition (HD) broadcast. To accommodate these formats, we'll design the promo with an aspect ratio of 720x540 square pixels, at 24 frames per second (fps). Later we'll repurpose the content for the high-definition version.

> **NOTE** ▶ For definitions of formats like PAL and NTSC as well as frame rates, see the Glossary in the back of this book.

To preview the final HD version of the project, open APTS_Motion > Lessons > Lesson 3 > **FinalCinemative.mov**.

Building a Multi-layered Composite

Before we get started building our composite, we need to look at the way Motion organizes its elements.

Adding Objects

We're going to explore the Layers tab, which is where layers and objects are organized. Before we do, we need to add some objects to work with.

1   Press Cmd-Option-W to close any projects you might have open.

2   Choose File > New or press Cmd-N to create a new project.

    We want our project to have specific settings, so we'll create a custom project instead of using a standard preset.

3   In the Select Project Preset dialog, choose Custom from the Preset pop-up menu.

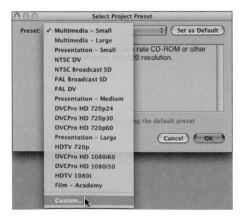

4   In the General tab of the Project Properties dialog, do the following:

▶ Set the Width to 720 and the Height to 540.

▶ Make sure the Pixel Aspect Ratio is set to Square.

▶ Set the Field Dominance to None.

▶ Set the Frame Rate to 24.

▶ Set the Duration to 600 Frames.

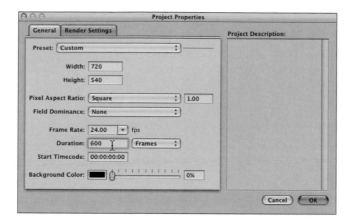

NOTE ▶ Make sure the pop-up menu to the right of the Duration text field is set to Frames. Otherwise you might accidentally create a sequence 600 seconds (10 minutes) long—a little more air time than the Cinematíve people can afford.

5   Click OK to create the project.

TIP ▶ Now's a good time to save the project so that you won't have to re-enter your settings if you decide to start over. It's always wise to save projects incrementally, with names like Cinematíve01, Cinematíve02, and so on. This protects you in case you accidentally mess up something you've spent hours creating, or if your current project somehow becomes corrupt. You can save projects into the Student Saves folder inside each of the Lessons folders.

6 In the File Browser (Cmd-1), navigate to the file **CosmordialSoup.mov**, located in the APTS_Motion > Lessons > Lesson03 folder. Drag it into the Canvas, releasing it when it snaps to the Dynamic Guides.

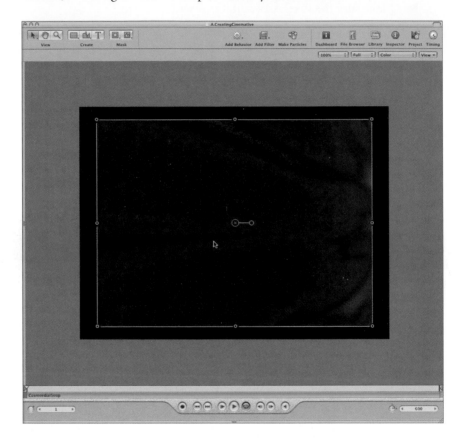

When we created the background in Lesson 2, we did so at only 640x480. Our current project dimensions are 720x540. No problem. We'll just scale up the background to match. Given the "organic" nature of the background, the softening that always comes with scaling things up won't be a problem.

7 Press F1 to jump to the Properties tab of the Inspector. Set the Scale to 115%.

It's now time to start adding other elements to the scene. We'll begin by blocking out the positions of the other objects, and then we'll talk about how to integrate them into the background using blend modes.

8 Make sure you're at frame 1. If you're not, click the Go to Start button at the bottom of the Canvas, or press the Home key.

9 Click in the File Browser (or press Cmd-1) and drag **Boxes.mov** into the Canvas (don't worry about the precise location just yet).

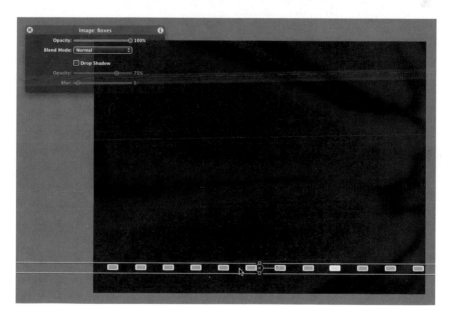

10 Press the spacebar to play.

These little boxes represent a cross between TV sets, paparazzi flashbulbs, and film sprockets, summing up the flavor of the Cinematíve brand. What, you didn't get the symbolism? Don't worry, neither will the audience—just part of life for the misunderstood artist.

Unfortunately for motion graphics designers, TVs don't usually show the whole broadcast image on the screen. The image usually ends up getting clipped around the edges. How much of your image gets clipped out depends on the model of the TV set, but there are basic guidelines that all manufacturers should adhere to. Theoretically, any activity taking place inside the Action Safe area of the screen should be visible, and any text written inside the Title Safe area should be clearly legible.

We need to make sure that our boxes can be seen by anyone watching, regardless of their TV set. So we'll turn on the Safe Zones overlay to help us position the boxes.

11 From the View pop-up menu in the upper-right corner of the Canvas, choose Safe Zones to activate the Safe Zones overlay.

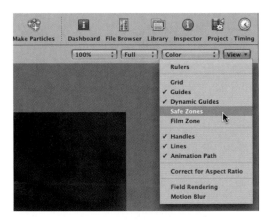

Action and Title Safe areas are now displayed as thin blue overlays. We want to position our boxes between Action Safe (the outer rectangular guide) and Title Safe (the inner rectangular guide) at the bottom of the screen.

12 Drag the boxes so that their tops are lined up with the Title Safe line at the bottom of the Canvas. They should snap into place.

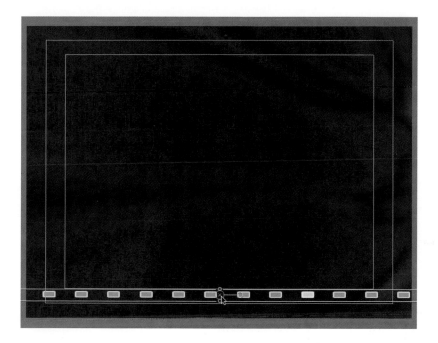

The boxes have snapped to the Title Safe guide, but they don't quite center directly between Action and Title Safe. We'll nudge them down a little.

13 Press Cmd–down arrow three times.

Pressing Command in conjunction with the up, down, left, and right arrow keys nudges the object in the direction of the arrow. To get even finer movements, zoom into your Canvas first (using one of the methods outlined in Lesson 1). Pressing Command and Shift in conjunction with the arrow keys produces a much larger jump in the position of the objects.

Boxes.mov is a very wide movie clip. We've made it that wide so it can pan across the bottom of the screen over the course of the composite. We need to move most of it off frame to the left, ready for the pan to the right during playback.

TIP To find the dimensions of a movie clip or image, select it in the File Browser and look at the information next to the thumbnail at the top of the window.

You can either drag the clip to the left until it snaps to the right side of the screen or enter the value numerically. We'll do the latter.

14 Press F1 to jump to the Properties tab of the Inspector.

15 Set the X Position (the *left* of the two Position boxes) to –302.

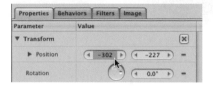

16 If you've paused playback, resume by pressing the spacebar or by clicking the Play button at the bottom of the Canvas.

17 From the File Browser, drag **BigWheel.psd** into the Canvas and position it so that its center is in the upper-right corner of the Action Safe overlay.

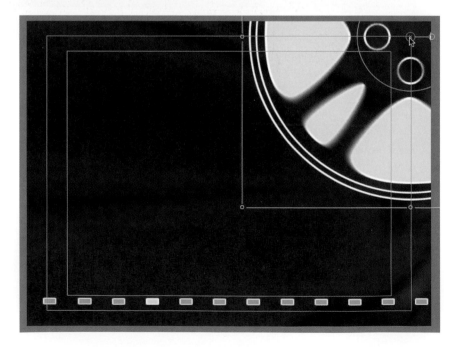

The wheel is a little big—it's overpowering the rest of the image.

18 Go back to the Properties tab (F1) and set the Scale to 85% for BigWheel.

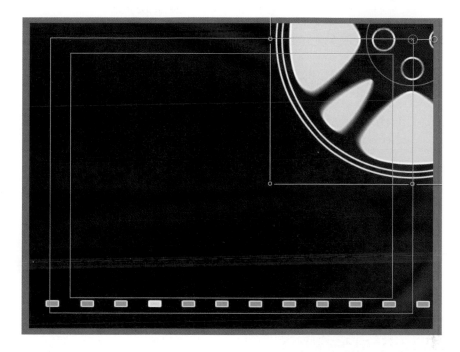

Let's add one more layer before we start. This time, we'll create text instead of importing something from the File Browser.

19 Select the Text tool from the Create buttons at the top left of the Canvas window. Alternatively, press the T key.

20 If the Dashboard isn't active, press F7 to activate it.

21 Click in the Canvas toward the left edge, just above the row of boxes. Don't worry about the exact location; we'll move the text into position later.

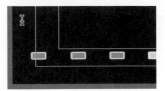

This creates a text object and sets an insertion point in the Canvas in a place ready for you to type text into.

22 Type the following: *Murder.Betrayal.Fortunes.*

We want to create a line of flowing text complementing the boxes at the bottom of the screen, moving in the opposite direction. Right now, the text is a little too big.

TIP ▶ If you accidentally deselect your text in the Canvas and are having a hard time reselecting it by clicking it, press the up and down arrow keys to cycle through all the objects in the Canvas until you reselect the text.

23 In the Dashboard, set the font to Gill Sans Bold and the Size to 18 points.

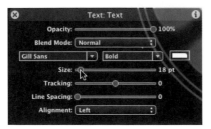

The text is much smaller now. We're going to type more words to create a full scrolling message. However, if we keep typing directly onto the Canvas, eventually we'll reach the right-hand side of the screen and won't be able to see what we're typing. Motion provides a nice alternative for adding text to a text object.

24 Press the Escape key to exit text entry mode.

25 Press F4 to jump to the Text tab of the Inspector (if it's not still open). You'll see a text entry box at the bottom of this tab. Click in the box and add to the existing words to create the following string of text:

Murder.Betrayal.Fortunes.War.Hope.Sacrifice.Desire.Romance.Escape.Lust. Forgiveness.Revenge.Love.Redemption.Passion.Drama.Comedy.Virtue.Fear

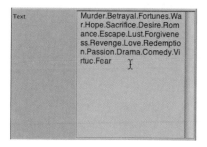

26 Click the Properties tab of the Inspector. Set the X and Y Position values to –360 and –210, respectively.

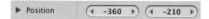

NOTE ▶ When you've been typing in the text field in the Text tab of the Inspector, any hot keys you press will be interpreted as text to be entered into the field. As a result, we needed to click over to the Properties tab, where usually we could have just pressed F1.

The text is now in position, ready to be scrolled to the left.

Understanding Objects and Layers

As we've seen so far, a composite is a combination of movie clips, still images, text, generators, and particles. In Motion, these elements are referred to as *objects*. When objects are added to a composite, they are put into *layers*.

Layers in Motion are a little different from layers in other software (for more extensive coverage of this, see Appendix B, "Motion for After Effects Users"). The distinction can be a little confusing, but the following analogy should help.

Imagine you're working in the entomology wing of a museum, and you're responsible for displaying the 3000 species of butterflies in the catalog. So that patrons of the museum can see both the tops and undersides of the butterflies, you decide to sandwich the specimens between two sheets of glass.

Translating the conceit to Motion, the glass sandwich is a Motion *layer* and the butterflies are Motion *objects*. So you might choose to place five butterflies in one glass sandwich. In Motion terms, you'd have five objects sharing one layer.

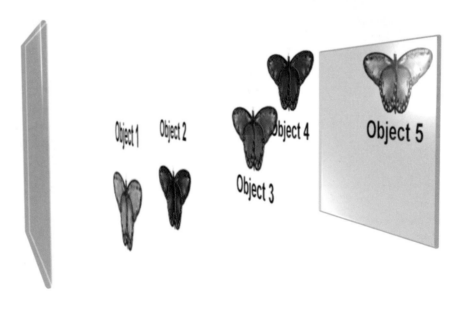

The glass is expensive and the museum's funds are limited, so you're forced to overlap the butterflies to make all five fit inside the same sandwich. Even inside a single sandwich there's an order; some butterflies rest on top of others.

Now if you take three of these glass sandwiches—our Motion layers—and place them on top of each other, you can look through them and see the combined result of all the butterflies from all three layers.

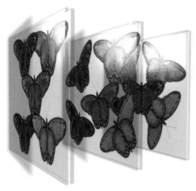

Three separate layers viewed from the side

The three layers viewed from the front (equivalent to a composite of all three layers)

To your enormous embarrassment (you take the appraisal of your entomological peers very seriously), the African blue in your collection has lost its color during cold storage. You decide to take some blue plastic and lay it over the butterfly to tint it the right color. Of course, all the other butterflies in that glass sandwich remain unaffected, since you were careful to cut the blue plastic to the shape of the African blue.

No color correction   Single object in layer color corrected

This is equivalent to applying a filter to one object in a layer—the object's color changes, but the rest of the layer is unaffected.

All of a sudden, a thought comes to you: What if all the butterflies in that glass sandwich were tinted blue? Four new varieties of African blue would be one of the great entomological discoveries of the decade. You quickly push aside thoughts of your fraud being discovered and proceed to tint all the butterflies in that sandwich blue.

This is equivalent to applying a filter to a layer—every object contained within that layer will be affected by the filter.

In Motion, you can get even more detailed than this—you can put layers inside of layers. This is referred to as *nesting*, and it gives you even more creative possibilities.

The main point to come away with is that when we talk about *layers* in Motion, we're referring to containers (our glass sandwiches) that hold the objects of a composite. When we talk about *objects*, we're referring to movie clips, still images, particles, generators, and text—the basic building blocks of a composite (the butterflies in the preceding example).

Navigating the Layers Tab

Now we'll do some work on our objects in the Layers tab.

> **TIP** ▶ If you've fallen behind, feel free to open the project **B.NavigatingLayersTab** to catch up.

1   Press F5 to open the Layers tab. The Canvas slides to the right to make way for the Project pane, which contains the Layers tab.

Here you can see all the objects for the composition assembled in a single layer, called (of all things) Layer. The objects in each layer are listed in order; the top object overlays the others, and so on.

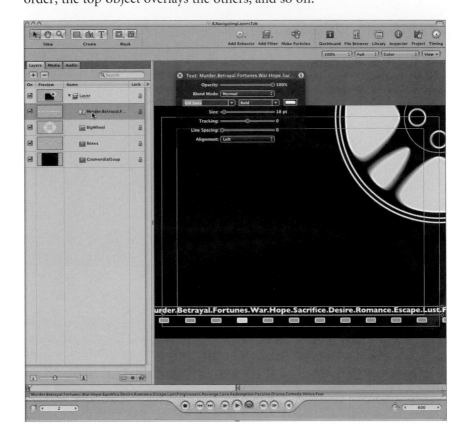

TIP You can also open and close the Project pane by dragging the dividing line between the Project pane and the Canvas.

The Layers tab is the primary place for making adjustments to the order of layers and objects. Use the Layers tab to do the following:

▶ Shuffle the order of objects in a given layer

▶ Shuffle the order of a layer with respect to the other layers in the composite

▶ Select a specific layer, object, filter, or behavior

▶ Enable or disable layers, objects, filters, and behaviors

▶ Replace an object's media with different media (swap clips)

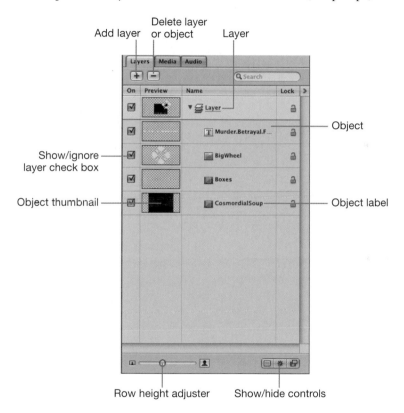

Notice that the Layers tab has no timeline. There is a Timeline view that duplicates most of the Layers tab's functions.

2 Press F6 to reveal the Timing pane.

If you're familiar with such applications as Adobe After Effects, you may wonder why you should bother with the Layers tab when you have all the functionality in the Timeline. The answer comes in the form of the mini-Timeline.

The timeline is the center of the universe in other applications, because it's where you make adjustments to an event's beginning and end—and in motion graphics (to borrow a cliché), timing is everything. One of the frustrations with conventional timeline-based systems is that as you approach 20 to 30 objects in your composite, it rapidly becomes difficult to locate the specific object or effect you're trying to adjust in the midst of all the clutter.

When you select an object or effect in the Layers tab, its timing bar is displayed in the mini-Timeline. It's as if Motion has gone to the trouble of searching through all the timing bars in the main Timeline and pulled out just the one you want to see.

So between the Layers tab and the mini-Timeline, there's little need to deal with the clutter of the main Timeline view. The exception is when you want to compare or align more than one object or effect in time. In that case, you need to use the main Timeline view to see more than one timing bar.

3   Press F6 to close the Timing pane. In the Layers tab, click and hold either the Boxes thumbnail or its text label. (Clicking in an empty space in the row will select the layer but not allow you to move it.) Drag it down and hold it just over the bottom border of the CosmordialSoup label.

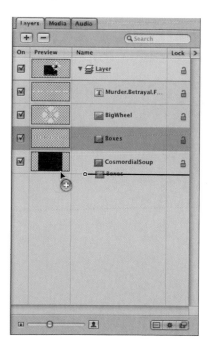

You'll see a black line with a hollow circle to its left. This is called the *position indicator*. There are two insertion positions for each border line.

TIP ▶ If you get tired of holding your pointer over the line while you read all of this, just drag your pointer back over the Boxes row and release. If you accidentally moved the Boxes row, press Cmd-Z to return it to the original state.

4 With your pointer still over the border line at the base of CosmordialSoup, gently drag from side to side.

The position indicator jumps between two positions. In the first position, "Move object into new layer," the hollow circle at the left of the position indicator aligns with the Layer label, and a round green plus symbol is visible (signifying that a new layer will be created) just below the pointer. In the second position, "Move object in existing layer," the hollow circle aligns with the object label.

 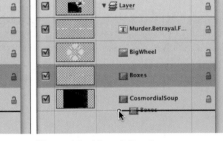

Move object into new layer   Move object in existing layer

Choosing the "Move object into new layer" option will reposition the object in a new layer, which is created to contain the object. Choosing the "Move object in existing layer" option will move the object within its current layer, and no new layer will be created.

5   Release the pointer in the second position, "Move object in existing layer." Boxes will now appear below CosmordialSoup in the Layers tab, and the boxes will have disappeared in the Canvas.

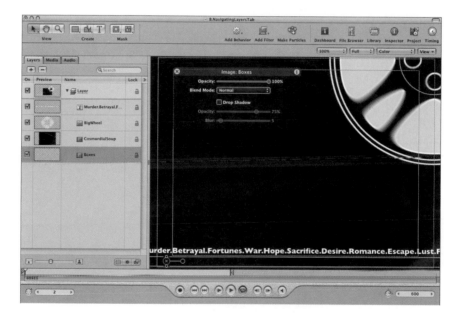

The Boxes object now appears below the CosmordialSoup object in the Canvas. Because the CosmordialSoup object is completely opaque (solid), we can't see through it to the Boxes object, so the boxes are hidden from view.

6 Click in the space between the thumbnail and the label of our text object ("Murder.Betrayal…"), and drag down into the BigWheel row. Both objects are selected, but neither moved.

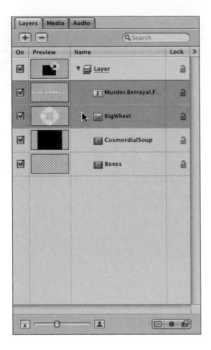

7 Click and hold the pointer over the thumbnail or label for either object, and drag down to the lower border line of CosmordialSoup.

Notice in this case that there is only one position for the position indicator. New layers can be created only at the very bottom of the Layers list, not in the middle of a layer.

8 Release the mouse. All three layers are now beneath CosmordialSoup and, as a result, hidden from view in the Canvas.

9 Drag CosmordialSoup below the other three objects. Choose the "Move object into new layer" position (the position that appears as a green plus symbol below the mouse pointer), and release the mouse.

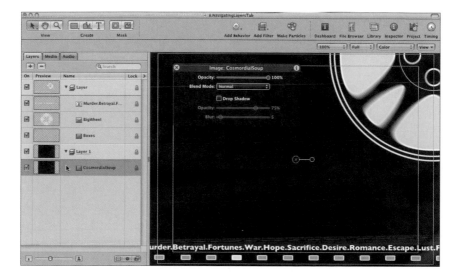

CosmordialSoup is now below the other objects, so they appear in the Canvas. This time CosmordialSoup is in its own layer, since we just created one in the last step. The layer is given the name Layer 1.

10 Double-click the label for Layer 1 to make it editable. Type *Background* and press Return.

11 Click the check box to the left of BigWheel. BigWheel disappears from the Canvas. The object is treated as if it doesn't exist as part of the composite.

12 Click BigWheel's check box again to reactivate it.

13 Click the check box to the left of Layer.

All three objects on top of CosmordialSoup disappear, because they live in the layer we've just ignored. Obviously CosmordialSoup is still in the Canvas, since it lives in its own layer called Background. Organizing common elements into their own layers is a great way to quickly hide them with a single click.

One of the most frustrating things when designing is to have an object set perfectly in the Canvas and then to accidentally move it while trying to select another object. To prevent this, it's good practice to lock down the layers you've finished editing.

14 Click the padlock icon to the right of CosmordialSoup. The CosmordialSoup object is now locked down, and its position and other parameters can't be changed without first unlocking its padlock.

15 Click the padlock to the right of Layer. This time, all objects contained within the layer are locked.

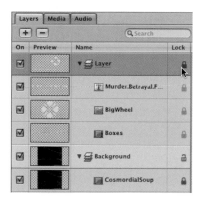

If you have the Timeline view open, you'll notice that these locked layers and objects appear with diagonal hatching. That's because locking a layer prevents it from being moved in time as well as in space.

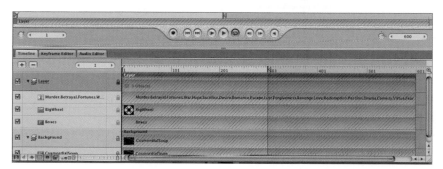

Working with Filters and Behaviors in the Layers Tab

The Layers tab also allows you to enable and disable filters and behaviors. We'll take a quick look at how to do these things in the following exercise.

Let's say we want to give the BigWheel even more blur than it has currently, to simulate the motion blur it would have if rotating quickly.

TIP ▶ If you've fallen behind, feel free to open the project **C.WorkingWithFilters** to catch up.

1   In the Layers tab, select BigWheel in the Layer.

2   Click the Add Filter button and choose Blur > Radial Blur.

You'll be disappointed to discover that nothing happens. That's because we locked the layer that contains the BigWheel object.

3   Click the padlock to the right of Layer to unlock the layer, and then repeat step 2. This time a Radial Blur is added to BigWheel.

We also want the wheel to spin, so let's add a behavior to do that.

4   Click the Add Behavior button and choose Basic Motion > Spin.

5 In the Dashboard (F7), drag around the outside of the circle to make one full revolution of spin.

Let's add a couple of more behaviors before we work with them in the Layers tab.

6 Select the Boxes object in the Layers tab, and then click the Add Behavior button and choose Basic Motion > Throw.

7 Press F2 to jump to the Behaviors tab of the Inspector.

Notice the small *disclosure triangle* just below the Increment label. Whenever you see one of these triangles, there's a hidden menu of parameters ready for the opening.

8 Click the disclosure triangle underneath Increment to expand the hidden menu.

9 Set the X Throw Velocity to 23 and leave the Y set to 0. These values will guarantee that our row of boxes completes its journey from left to right over the course of our composite.

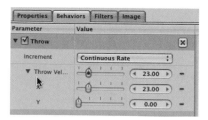

TIP ▶ If you don't care about a precise speed for your Throw but want to make sure an object moves horizontally or vertically only, you can still use the Dashboard to set up the motion. While dragging the pointer around the circle in the Throw Dashboard, press Shift to constrain the motion to 45-degree angles.

10 Select the Murder.Betrayal.Fortunes… text object in the Layers tab, and apply a Throw behavior to this as well.

11 In the Behaviors tab, click the disclosure triangle below Increment and set X to −26 and Y to 0. This will move the text to the left as the animation plays.

You may need to tighten up the preview range to make sure that everything caches happily (depending on how much RAM you have available in your system).

12 Stop playback (press the spacebar), and then drag the playhead in the mini-Timeline to 90. Press Cmd-Option-O to set the play range Out point to the current frame, 90.

13 Click Play to begin previewing. Remember that you'll need to wait until Motion has cached all the media into RAM (one full run through the preview range) before you start seeing real-time playback.

Now that things are moving, it's obvious that the radial blur on the wheel is inappropriate. The wheel's just not moving fast enough to warrant that kind of motion blur.

14 Click the check box to the left of Radial Blur in the Layers tab. The Radial Blur filter is now deactivated and the BigWheel no longer looks blurred in the Canvas.

Things can get very crowded very quickly in the Layers tab. Sometimes you just want to look at the objects and layers without having to wade through the behaviors and filters attached to them. Motion includes show/hide buttons to toggle the visibility of behaviors and filters on and off.

15 In the lower-right corner of the Layers tab, click the middle of the three buttons. It's the Show/Hide Behaviors button, represented by the gear icon.

All behaviors are now hidden in the Layers tab. The behaviors haven't been disabled; they're still causing your objects to animate in the Canvas. They've just been hidden to reduce clutter.

16 Click the button to the right of the Show/Hide Behaviors button. This is the Show/Hide Filters button, and when you click it you'll see the Radial Blur filter disappear from the Layers tab, hidden just like the behaviors.

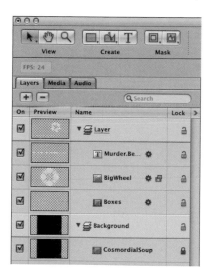

The first button in the row of three is Show/Hide Masks. We haven't used any masks yet, so this button will currently affect nothing in our Layers tab.

17 Click the behaviors and filters show/hide buttons to reveal all behaviors and filters again.

You may have noticed these same filter and behavior icons at the far right of the BigWheel row. These are enable/disable toggles.

18 Click the gear icon to the right of the BigWheel row label.

A red strikethrough appears through the behavior icon (the gear) and the wheel stops spinning in the Canvas. Notice also that the Spin is grayed out in the Layers tab. These buttons next to the object's label enable or disable all effects of their kind for that object. In this case we only had one behavior attached to BigWheel; if we'd had three or four, they would all have been disabled when we clicked this icon. If there were masks applied to an object, a mask enable/disable icon would also show up.

19 Click the same gear icon to enable behaviors again.

20 Click the Radial Blur row to select it. Press Delete. The unneeded filter is now deleted from the composite.

As you've seen, navigating around the Layers tab is remarkably simple. The same functionality is available in the Timeline (F6), but the availability of the mini-Timeline makes this far less important than in other applications. Before you revert to your old ways, spend the next few lessons resisting the urge to reach for the Timeline, and try to get a feel for using the Layers and mini-Timeline in Motion.

What You've Learned

► Safe zones can be used to align objects in the Canvas.

► Objects can be snapped to guides in the Canvas or nudged incrementally.

► Layers are containers for objects.

► Composite objects and layers can be reorganized in the Layers tab.

► Text can be entered directly into the Canvas or in the Text Inspector.

► Filters and behaviors can be hidden, ignored, and deleted in the Layers tab.

Keyboard Shortcuts

Cmd-N	creates a new project
Cmd–left arrow, right arrow	nudges the selected object
T	enters text entry mode
Escape	exits text entry mode
Shift–drag any Dashboard circle control	constrains angle to 30- or 45-degree increments

4

Lesson Files APTS_Motion > Lessons > Lesson04

Time This lesson takes approximately 30 minutes to complete.

Goals Create a composite using a standard Motion template

Work with template elements

Create a custom template

Using Templates

Stripping the postproduction industry down to its most basic, you'll find there are two kinds of gigs: the ones that pay well and the ones that don't. (There are also the ones fueled by your life passion, but they usually lead to mortgaging your house, driving your marriage to the breaking point, and developing severe dissociative disorders, so let's ignore them for the sake of simplicity.) For the ones that don't pay well, it's a struggle to find the time or energy to build a motion graphics composite with any degree of style or sophistication. On the other hand, the work going out the door has your name on it and acts as a calling card for other potential clients who might see it. What's an impoverished designer to do?

The answer is *templates*. Templates allow you to quickly throw together a polished design simply by dragging and dropping custom footage into a prebuilt composite. Change a couple of titles and voilà!—an instant masterpiece. You can create your own templates or use the ones that ship with Motion. Either way, templates let you generate a stylish product for the thrifty client without breaking a sweat. That way you can spend more time on those multimillion-dollar contracts you've been meaning to get around to.

Using Motion's Templates

Let's start by taking a look at how to use the templates that ship with Motion. Imagine the following scenario: You've been asked to come up with a promotion for a local child-care center. It's really just a group of local parents, and they need a break. Your heart goes out to them, but you've just landed some real, paying work that needs to be done in the same time frame. Rather than toss these parents out on the street, you turn to a trusty template and save the day (and earn yourself a sizable helping of free babysitting).

1   Press Cmd-Option-W to close any open projects.

2   Choose File > Open Template.

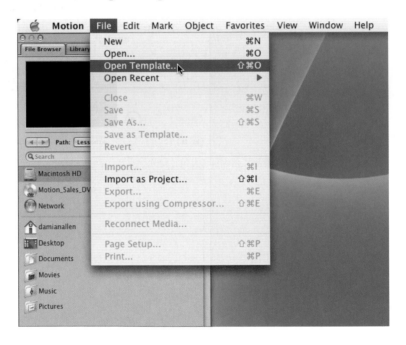

The Template Browser window opens, allowing you to choose from several collections of templates.

NOTE ▶ Motion ships with two install DVDs. The second DVD contains the template content. If your Template Browser appears blank, it means you didn't install the templates from the second DVD.

3   Select Curves from the Collection scrolling list at the left side of the Template Browser.

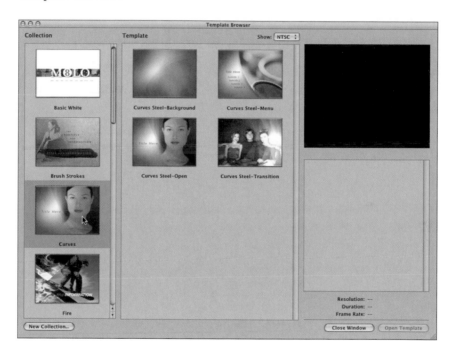

There are four templates in the Curves collection.

4 Click the Curves Steel-Open item in the center Template pane.

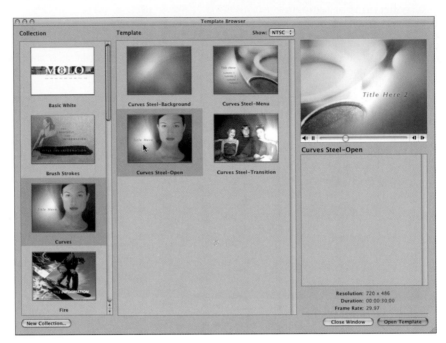

The preview window in the top right of the Template Browser shows you how the template looks. By browsing through the various collections and clicking the template icons you can quickly preview the templates and choose one to suit your purpose.

Notice the Show pop-up menu at the top of the browser; it allows you to choose templates formatted for PAL, NTSC, or HD. For this exercise we'll work with the NTSC setting.

NOTE ▶ Motion ships with only PAL and NTSC presets. If you select the HD option, the template preview window will appear blank.

5   Double-click Curves Steel-Open to open the template.

6   Open the Layers tab by pressing F5.

The template is neatly organized into four layers. The ones we care about arc the Text and Replace Here layers.

7   Click the disclosure triangles at the left of the Text and Replace Here layers to reveal their contents.

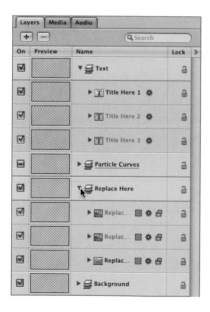

This template allows you to transition between three elements, each with its own title. Let's customize the template for our purposes.

Modifying the Text

We'll start by customizing the text. We'll type in the three core principles of the child-care center, one for each shot in the sequence.

> **TIP** ▶ If you've fallen behind, feel free to open the project
> **A.TemplateOpened** to catch up.

1   Move the playhead to frame 80.

It's much easier to change the text when you can clearly see it, so we've moved to a frame where *Title Here 1* appears onscreen.

> **NOTE** ▶ If your Current Frame field is displaying timecode, click the clock icon to its left to switch back to frames.

2   In the Canvas, double-click in the text *Title Here 1* to select it. The letters should all change to white on black to indicate that they're selected.

3   Type *Discovery* and then press Escape to exit text entry mode.

4   Move to frame 300. This is where you can clearly see *Title Here 2*.

5   Now select the text *Title Here 2* and change it to read *Understanding*, and then press Escape to exit text entry mode.

6   Move to frame 520. Change the *Title Here 3* text to *Purity*. Once again, press Escape to exit text entry mode.

Now that the text has been modified, all that's left to do is add custom images.

Changing the Media Content

The parents at the child-care center want to emphasize individual care, so they've chosen one child to appear in the commercial. Unfortunately, the three shots they've given you (two stills and a movie clip) look completely different.

> **TIP** ▶ If you've fallen behind, feel free to open the project **B.TextModified** to catch up.

1   In the File Browser (press Cmd-1 to jump there), navigate to APTS_Motion > Lessons > Lesson04.

2   Double-click **MSA01.tif** to open it in a preview window.

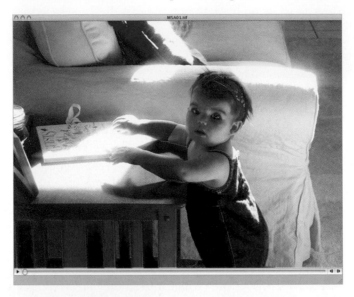

It is a nice, stylized image with warm orange tones.

3   Close the preview window and then double-click **MSA02.tif**.

This shot is a more neutral digital photograph and lacks the stylization of the first image.

4   Close the preview window and then double-click **MSA03Matted.mov**.

5   Press the spacebar to begin playing the clip in the preview window.

This is a nicely affected 8mm film–style clip, again remarkably different from the other two shots.

6   Close the preview window.

The great news about the template is that it color-corrects all the footage to the same color scheme, so there's no need to worry about the different styles of the shots. This is about as close to plug and play as motion graphics gets.

7   In the Layers tab (F5), make sure the Replace Here layer is still expanded.

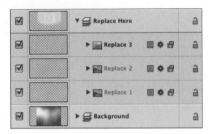

8   Drag **MSA01.tif** from the File Browser and drop it onto the Replace 1 item in the Layers tab (the bottom of the three objects).

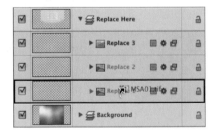

Make sure you see the curved arrow over the Replace 1 object before you release the mouse; otherwise you might add **MSA01.tif** to your comp instead of replacing the Replace 1 object. If you make a mistake, just press Cmd-Z to undo and try again.

9   Move to frame 80.

You should now see the image **MSA01.tif** in the Canvas. You should also see it listed in the Layers tab in lieu of the Replace 1 object.

10 Drag **MSA02.tif** onto the Replace 2 object in the Layers tab (the middle of the three Replace objects) to swap out the footage.

11 Drag **MSA03Matted.mov** onto the Replace 3 object in the Layers tab (the top of the three Replace objects) to swap out the footage.

If you like, you can now render out the final movie. You should find that the two stills and the movie clip all integrate nicely with the style of the template, even though the originals looked quite different. Alternately, double-click **FinalTemplateMovie.mov** in the File Browser to launch a preview of the final version.

Accessing Template Elements

Even if you turn your nose up at the idea of prebaked designs, you can still take advantage of some of the elements that are used to create the templates. There are some very nice fire, water, satin, and light clips that would blend well into all kinds of projects. Let's take a look at how you can get your hands on them.

1   In the Library (press Cmd-2 to jump there), click the folder labeled
Content.

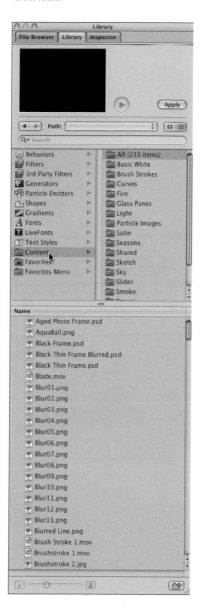

2 Click the Fire subfolder, and then select **Fire Crawl.mov** from the list of clips in the lower pane.

You're instantly treated to a preview of the QuickTime movie of crawling fire. Take some time and click through the different preview categories to examine the many movie clips available. They provide great background and matte elements, regardless of whether or not you use the templates.

Creating Your Own Templates

OK, so you're in the competitive market of bad cable commercials. You want to use quick, easy templates. Problem is, the design firm down the street also owns a copy of Motion. If you want to distinguish yourself, you can't use the standard templates. The solution? Build your own, of course.

To simplify, we'll load in a project from which we can create a template. Normally, however, you'd build the project from scratch.

1   Close any open projects (Cmd-Option-W).

2   Press Cmd-O.

3   Navigate to APTS_Motion > Lessons > Lesson04, and double-click **NastyCableAd**.

4   Press the spacebar to begin playback.

You should be looking at that cable TV ad classic, the fire-sale commercial. Assuming that about half of your clients are probably into fire sales, this could *really* save some time if it were a template.

5 Press the spacebar to pause playback. Choose File > Save as Template.

The Save Template dialog opens.

Notice that the Collection menu is grayed out. That's because we currently only have the template collections that ship with Motion. These can't be altered, so we'll need to create a new collection of our own.

6 Click the New Collection button. Type *Low Budget Cable Ads* into the New Collection dialog that appears, and then click Create.

7 Name your template *Crazy Fire Sale* and then click Save.

The Export dialog appears, telling you that Motion is rendering the preview movie of your template for the Template Browser.

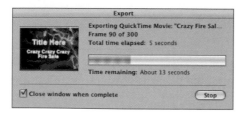

8 When the render is finished, press Cmd-Option-W to close all open projects.

9 Choose File > Open Template.

10 In the Collection scrolling list of the Template Browser, click the Low Budget Cable Ads item.

Instead of a pretty collection icon, you'll see a generic folder icon.

11 Click the Crazy Fire Sale icon in the Template pane.

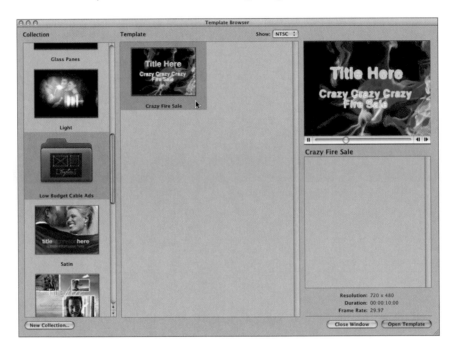

And there you have it, your very own template ready to go—and such a useful template at that. Strange that the Fire Sale template didn't ship with Motion as a preset ...

TIP Templates are a great way to create custom safe areas. For example, if you're designing in HD with a mind to down-res to standard definition as well, you might want to set up guides (View > Guides > Add Vertical/Horizontal Guide) for your 4:3 safe zones. You could then save the project as a template so that you always have the guides ready to use in production.

What You've Learned

▶ Templates save time by providing a quick, customizable way to produce elegant motion graphics composites.

▶ You can customize templates by replacing text in the Canvas and dragging new media into the Layers tab.

▶ Media used in the standard Motion templates is also available in the Library tab for individual element use.

▶ You can make a template out of any Motion project by choosing File > Save as Template.

5

Lesson Files	APTS_Motion > Lessons > Lesson05
Time	This lesson takes approximately 90 minutes to complete.
Goals	Navigate through the Timeline via markers
	Learn the basic structure of particle systems
	Customize the basic properties of particles
	Learn about the life cycle of particles
	Use the still-proxy method for particle design
	Work with parameter behaviors
	Understand the use of random-seed values
	Apply an attractor behavior using a null image

Particles and Parameter Behaviors

Particles are often considered a peripheral part of motion graphics—more a plug-in than a central feature. However, as you become familiar with particles in Motion, you'll find yourself using them in almost every project you create. In this lesson we'll take a look at creating particles from footage, still images, and presets. We'll also explore the relationship between particles and emitters, along with the various particle parameters ripe for the tweaking.

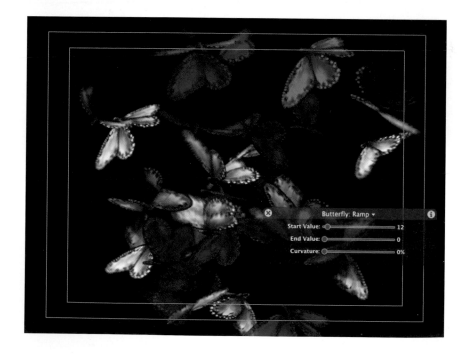

Building Particles from a Movie Clip

In Lesson 3 we began creating a promo ID for a fictitious TV station, Cinematíve. Part of the project involves butterflies bursting from a young woman's hands and then exploding into a plume of colors. We'll use the same butterfly we were experimenting with in Lesson 1, but this time we'll make use of advanced particle parameters to get the exact performance we're looking for.

1   Launch Motion if it is not already open; if it is open, press Cmd-Option-W to close all open projects.

2   Open the project **A.ButterflyMedley**, located in the APTS_Motion > Lessons > Lesson05 folder.

   Markers have already been added to the project to help us time when the butterflies should emerge and "depart this world." We'll look at how to create and edit markers in Lesson 11.

3   Press F6 to open the Timing pane.

   You'll see three markers in the Timeline: one green, one blue, and one red. The green one shows the moment in time when we want the butterflies to emerge from the woman's hands.

   To snap the playhead to a marker, press the Shift key as you scrub the pointer along the Timeline.

   TIP To jump from one marker directly to the next, press Cmd-Option and either the left or right arrow key.

4   Press Shift and place the mouse over the play range line of the mini-Timeline or over the ruler section of the main Timeline view.

5 Drag the pointer left and right to scrub. Release the mouse when the play-head snaps to the green marker labeled Butterflies Emerge.

6 Drag **Butterfly.mov** into the Canvas and snap it to the center guides (be careful not to use the similarly named **Butterfly.pct**).

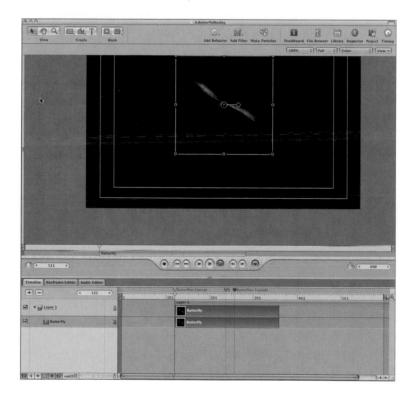

7 Press Cmd-Option-I to set the play range In point.

8 Press Shift and scrub in the Timeline until the playhead snaps to the red Butterflies Explode marker.

9 Press Cmd-Option-O to set the play range Out point.

The playback range now encompasses the main events for the butterflies.

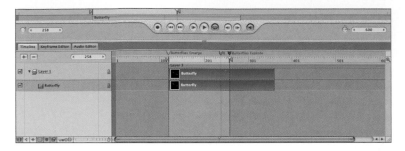

10 Press Shift-Home to jump to the play range In point.

11 Click the Make Particles button at the top of the Canvas. The butterfly movie turns into a particle system.

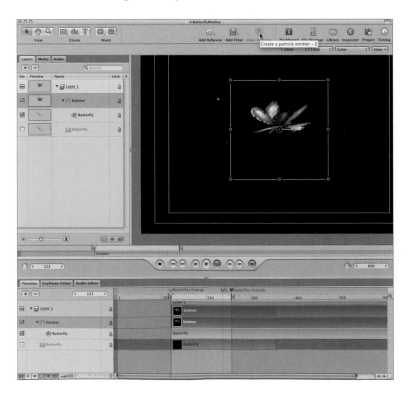

Notice what's happened in the Timeline and the Layers tab (press F5 to open if necessary): Two new objects have been added to the Layers tab, one called Emitter and one called Butterfly. Butterfly is a *sub-object* of the Emitter object. Notice, too, that the original Butterfly object has been turned off. That's because it's now acting only as a *reference* for the particle system; it's no longer an actual object in the composite.

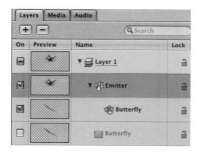

The *emitter* is the object that creates the particles. The sublayer with the name Butterfly is called a *particle cell*. Particle cells are the particles created by an emitter object. Think of the emitter as a volcano and the particle cells as the molten rock flying out of it.

What makes this whole arrangement interesting is that emitters can have more than one particle cell attached to them. Imagine trying to simulate an exploding brick wall—you'd have bricks flying everywhere. You'd also need to add dust from the disintegrating bricks. You'd need smoke particles to simulate the combustion that caused the explosion. You might even need flame particles for a particularly volatile explosive charge.

All of these particles are distinct in the way they look and the way they travel through air, but they all come from the same original explosion. In Motion-speak, they all belong to the same emitter. If we were to create this

simulation in Motion, our particle system might look something like that
in the following figure:

In the case of our butterflies, we need only one type of particle, so we'll
leave things where they are. But before we begin playback, we need to
reduce the number of particles being emitted. Usually, particle systems are
designed with very small images or movies as particle cells. In our case, we
have a fairly large butterfly clip, so the default number of particles is going
to be too much to play back in real time over the whole play range.

NOTE ▶ If your computer has only the minimum hardware requirements
for Motion, you may have a difficult time adequately playing back the butterflies. If so, you can use the still-proxy method described later in this lesson to
maintain real-time playback during the design stage. Try the following playback steps with the fully animated butterflies first, and then fall back on the
still-proxy method if necessary.

12 Close the Timing pane if it's still open (by pressing F6).

13 Make sure the Emitter object is selected, and set the Birth Rate to about 3
in the Dashboard (press D or F7 to show the Dashboard if it's hidden).

The Birth Rate refers to the number of particles born each second. A rate
of 3 per second isn't a lot of butterflies, and it's a manageable number
while we're designing. We'll increase the number once we've finished

tweaking the particle system's parameters. (In fact, we'll ramp up the number to create an initial explosion of a whole lot of butterflies and then taper off to just a few.)

14 Begin playback of the Timeline by pressing the spacebar.

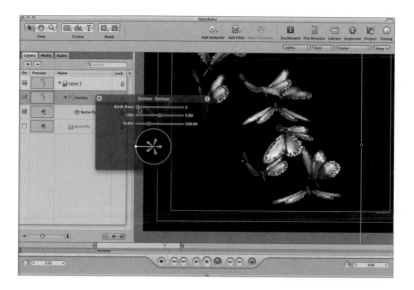

Notice a couple of things here: First, the butterflies are popping into existence, which is a little weird. Second, new butterflies are being born in front of existing ones. We're trying to give the illusion that the butterflies are exploding from someone's hands and flying toward the camera, so new butterflies should be appearing *behind* the older ones.

We can fix both of these problems, but first we need to adjust the emitter's duration to match the butterflies' time onscreen.

15 Stop playback.

16 Press Shift-End to jump to the play range Out point.

17 Make sure that Emitter is still selected, and press O to set the layer Out point.

The emitter now ceases to exist at frame 258—right on the red marker.

TIP ▶ It's always a good idea to trim your footage to the place where it's no longer needed onscreen *before* applying behaviors. That's because behaviors set themselves to the length of the clip they're applied to. So if, for example, your title flies off the screen at frame 60 never to return, set its Out point to 60.

Refining the Particle System

Once a basic particle system is set up, there are many ways to customize the look and behavior of the particles.

1 In the Layers tab (F5), make sure that Emitter is selected.

2 Press F4 to open the Emitter tab of the Inspector.

When you first see the Emitter tab, you might feel a little intimidated. Don't panic—once we start working with it, all the parameters will make sense.

NOTE ▶ When a particle system has only one particle cell (as in our example), Motion conveniently combines the parameters for the emitter and the particle cell into the Emitter tab of the Inspector. If you were to add more particle cells, you would see only a few master controls specific to the emitter; the rest of the controls would then be found in the Inspector for each particle cell object.

The first thing we want to do is make sure that older butterflies are drawn on top of newer ones to give the appearance that the butterflies are coming toward the camera.

3   Toward the top of the Emitter tab of the Inspector, go to the Render Order pop-up menu and choose Oldest Last.

The older particles are now rendered after all the other particles and therefore appear in front.

Adding a Splash of Color

Now it's time to keep the butterflies from popping onto the screen. We can also vary their colors at the same time.

TIP ▶ If you've fallen behind, feel free to open the project **B.AddingColor** to catch up.

1   From the Color Mode pop-up menu located about halfway down the Cell Controls parameters in the Emitter tab of the Inspector, choose Pick From Range.

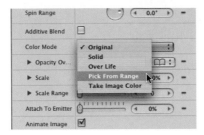

You'll see a color gradient appear, labeled Color Range. This allows us to indicate a range of colors for the butterflies. In this mode, Motion randomly selects a color from the chosen range each time a particle is generated.

Notice the other options in the Color Mode menu; one of the most useful is Over Life. In this mode, particles start their life tinted the color at the left side of the range gradient, and by the end of their life they're the same color as the gradient on the right. That's great for things like flame particles, which might start their lives "hot" and cool off as they move away from the explosion.

2   Click the disclosure triangle to the left of the Color Range label to reveal the gradient edit controls.

Remember the background we created for our composite? To complement it, let's try to keep the butterflies in the indigo blue part of the spectrum. Also, since the original butterfly object is powder blue, choosing white will create some of the butterflies with that original color.

3   Click in the gradient and create multiple colors, drawing on indigo blues in the color wheel. Alternatively, you can use the values in the following figure.

TIP ▶ If you're not sure how to do this, see the "Working with Gradients" exercise in Lesson 2.

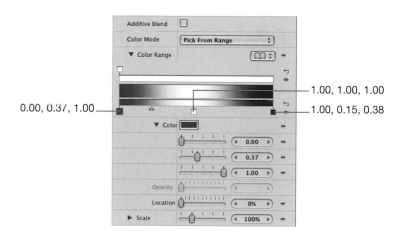

0.00, 0.37, 1.00 ⎯⎯

⎯ 1.00, 1.00, 1.00

⎯ 1.00, 0.15, 0.38

The opacity gradient bar above the main gradient determines the opacity of the butterflies over their lifespan; as the particles grow older, they move from the opacity settings at the left of the gradient to the settings at the right. We want to make sure our butterflies don't just pop onto the screen, so we'll create a gradient change to fade each butterfly in from invisible to opaque over the beginning of their lives.

4   Click in the opacity gradient bar to create a new tag just to the right of the original one.

5   Click back on the original opacity tag at the far left.

6   Drag the Opacity slider to 0.

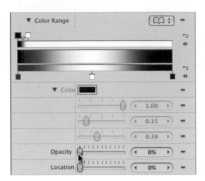

If you resume playback, you'll now see that the butterflies fade in as they're born and continue to be opaque throughout the rest of their days.

Putting English on the Ball

Currently the butterflies fly outward in a smooth, straight motion. But if you look carefully, you'll notice that they are all moving at the same angle. It's true that they rotate as they fly, but that's because the butterfly rotates in the original movie clip we used for the particles (that is, the rotation is built into the animation). To add more individuality to each butterfly, we'll apply a custom rotation to the particles.

About a third of the way down the Emitter tab of the Inspector you'll notice four parameters with rotation dials. You can quickly set angles by adjusting the dials with your pointer.

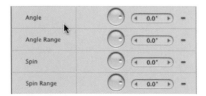

Dragging to rotate a dial counterclockwise produces positive values; dragging clockwise produces negative values. You can even specify multiple revolutions by "winding" the dial full circle several times in either direction.

1   Drag the Angle Range rotation dial counterclockwise just slightly, until the numeric entry box to its right reads approximately 30 degrees.

Did you notice how the rotation of the butterflies starts to scatter as you rotate the dial? The Angle Range determines the possible angles that particles can have at birth. As with the Pick From Range option in the Color section, particles can now be born oriented anywhere from the initial angle of the source footage to an offset of 30 degrees.

The plain-vanilla Angle parameter just above Angle Range sets all the particles to a specific start angle. We don't need to use it here. If you found that all your particles were upside down for some reason, you could set this to 180 degrees and they'd all right themselves.

2   Set the Spin Range to 30 degrees.

3   Set the Spin to 360 degrees.

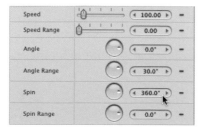

Looking in the Canvas, you'll see that the butterflies are now in a rather nasty death roll. The Spin parameter determines how fast the butterflies rotate as they emerge from the emitter. We don't want all the butterflies to spin at the same rate, and certainly not in a death roll, so we'll set Spin back to its default of zero.

4   Set the Spin back to 0 degrees.

5   Set the Spin Range to 30 degrees.

Like the Angle Range, the Spin Range sets a range of spin rates each butterfly might take on. Some butterflies may spin as much as 30 degrees per second, while others may not spin at all.

So, just to be clear: Angle (and its close relative Angle Range) determines the initial rotated position of a particle when it's born, while Spin (and Spin Range) determines how fast a particle rotates.

Changing Scale

The phrase goes, "All creatures great and small," not "All creatures of pretty much exactly the same size." In nature, any population of animals comes with varying sizes. You've got your giants and your minis, with the average folk living out their average lives in between.

Our butterflies are all the same size—very unnatural. Time, then, to uneven the score.

> **TIP** ▶ If you've fallen behind, feel free to open the project **C.ChangingScale** to catch up.

1   Locate the Scale Range parameter toward the bottom of the Emitter tab of the Inspector. Set it to a value of 20.

Particles will now be born with a size difference of up to 20 percent from the original movie clip. As you probably guessed, the Scale parameter just above this determines the default scale for all the butterflies.

We also need to do something about the particles' size over their lives. If we want to create the illusion of the butterflies' bursting forward, we need them to start their lives small and grow big as they move toward the camera. We'll use the Scale Over Life behavior, just as we did in Lesson 1 when we were playing around with the butterflies.

2   In the Layers tab, select the Butterfly particle cell.

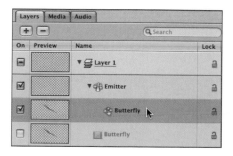

Remember, the Scale Over Life behavior affects particles—not their emitters—and so it needs to be applied to the particular particle cell it affects. In this case we have only one particle cell, the butterflies.

3   Click the Add Behavior button at the top of the Canvas and choose Particles > Scale Over Life.

4   In the Behaviors tab (F2) of the Inspector or in the Dashboard, set the Increment Type to Birth and Death Values, the Scale At Birth size to 20%, and the Scale At Death size to 250%.

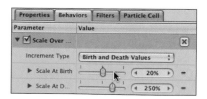

The butterflies should now move much more realistically toward the camera.

Birth, Death, and the Transitory In-Between Called Life

No doubt you've noticed by now that many of the parameters associated with particles are linked to their "lives." There are two important parameters we've yet to look at: Birth Rate and Life.

Modifying the Birth Rate Parameter

The *birth rate* of a particle determines how many particles are born every second. Our current birth rate of 3 means that three particles are born every second.

TIP ▶ If you've fallen behind, feel free to open the project **D.ScaleApplied** to catch up.

1 In the Layers tab, select the Emitter object.

2 In the Emitter tab of the Inspector (F4), set the Birth Rate to 1.00.

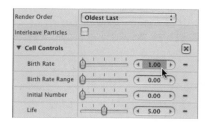

3 Resume playback by pressing the spacebar if you stopped it.

As you watch the animation, you'll now see that only one butterfly emerges every second.

4 Set the Birth Rate Range to 1.00.

Now the butterflies are born erratically—on *average* one is born every second, but sometimes two are born close together, and other times a second goes by with no births.

5 Set the Birth Rate Range back to 0.00. Set the Birth Rate back to 3.00.

In our project, we want the butterflies to initially explode out of the woman's hands in large numbers, with only a few trickling out afterward. This takes more-advanced animation, and we'll get to it shortly. First, we need to turn to a meaningful discussion of life itself.

Changing Life

Alas, the life of a particle is an ephemeral one. The good news is that Motion's advanced tool set allows us to prolong their lives, if only for a few precious seconds. Then again, maybe you had a nasty episode with a swarm of butterflies as a child, in which case you'll want to trim down the few seconds they've already been given.

1   Locate the Life parameter toward the top of the Emitter tab of the Inspector and set it to a value of 1.00.

2   If you've stopped playback, resume it by pressing the spacebar.

As if in a flashback to the opening scenes of *Logan's Run,* the butterflies wink out of existence only a second after their birth. Notice also that they rapidly scale from small to big. That's because the Birth and Death values we set in our Scale Over Life behavior are set for the start and end of a particle's life. Now that the butterflies only live for 1 second, they scale from the Birth value of 20% to the Death value of 250% in that brief time.

For the final movie, our butterflies need to be onscreen for a little over 5 seconds, so if we set their lifetime to 6 seconds, we can guarantee that the first butterfly to be born will still be around when it comes time to obliterate them in a shower of colors.

3   Set the Life to a value of 6.00. The butterflies now live throughout their time "onstage."

Using the Still-Proxy Method

Motion can do some pretty amazing things in real time, but at some point everybody hits a wall, no matter how fast the hardware. A great way to regain the interactivity of your animation while building particle systems is to use a still proxy in place of an animated movie.

NOTE ▶ The processor calculates the trajectory of particles. If you have a slower processor in your system, the still-proxy method described here probably won't speed things up—the bottleneck on a slower machine for working with particles is more likely to be the CPU than the graphics card.

A still proxy is a single still image you substitute for the particle that is the source of your movie. Because there's only one frame for Motion to think about, it can do a lot more in real time. In our case, we can replace the animation of the butterfly with a single still frame.

1 In the File Browser (Cmd-1), locate the image **Butterfly.pct** in the APTS_Motion > Lessons > Lesson05 folder.

2 Drag **Butterfly.pct** into the Layers tab and position it over the thumbnail of the ghosted Butterfly clip. (That's the layer that was deactivated when we converted it to a particle system at the beginning of the lesson. It now exists as a reference for the particles.)

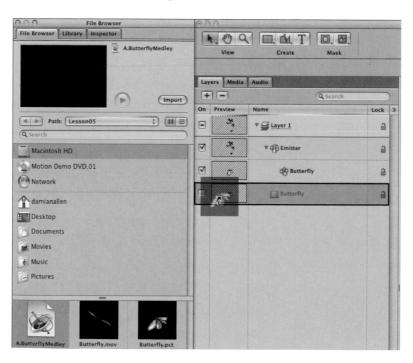

Notice how the pointer has turned into a curved arrow. This indicates that you're about to replace the current footage with another piece of source media.

3   Release the mouse button. The butterfly movie is replaced with the **Butterfly.pct** still.

If you now play back the particle simulation, you may find that the performance is dramatically improved. You can go ahead and tweak your design as much as you like.

When you're done, it's time to restore the original animated butterfly footage. You follow exactly the same process, this time using **Butterfly.mov** to replace the still image.

4   Drag **Butterfly.mov** from the File Browser and drop it onto the thumbnail of the ghosted Butterfly object in the Layers tab.

5   Press Cmd-R to generate a cached RAM preview of the particle system ready for real-time playback.

Using Parameter Behaviors

Our butterflies have come a long way, but it's important that they match up with the script. The script calls for the butterflies to explode out of the woman's hands. Right now they're *streaming* toward the camera. We need them to initially burst out in great numbers, with just a few stragglers to follow.

We need a way to control the birth rate of the butterflies; we want it to be high at first to create lots of butterflies and then taper off to a trickle. Those of you with a motion graphics background may already be thinking, "The behavior thing is cute, but now we need to reach for good old-fashioned keyframes." We *could* keyframe the birth rate, but that would cause us to miss out on one of the most powerful features in Motion: *parameter behaviors.*

Parameter behaviors are ways to quickly assign value changes to any parameter you can see in the Inspector. Usually in motion graphics work you want things to speed up, slow down, oscillate, wriggle around, and so on. In Motion, all you need to do is apply a parameter behavior and the software figures out the rest.

Parameter behaviors don't apply just to movement. Let's say you want something to flicker in and out of existence. You can simply apply a Randomize parameter behavior to the object's Opacity parameter, and all of a sudden the object is flickering.

I could go on, but the easiest way to get a handle on what a parameter behavior does is to try one out.

> **TIP** ▶ If you've fallen behind, feel free to open the project **E.UsingParameterBehaviors** to catch up.

1   Make sure you have the Emitter object or the Butterfly particle cell selected. In the Particle Cell tab of the Inspector (F4), change the Birth Rate parameter to 0.00.

   If you're playing back right now, you'll see absolutely nothing. Obviously—there are no particles being born.

2   Ctrl- or right-click the Birth Rate label to access the contextual menu.

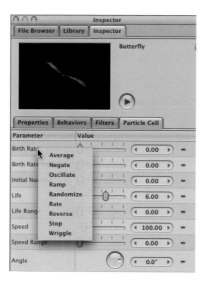

TIP ▶ True to Apple's philosophy of simplicity, Motion works with the traditional single-button Macintosh mouse. Nonetheless, if you're planning to do a lot of production work on your Macintosh, go get yourself a fine-looking two- or three-button optical mouse. They're about as affordable as a super-sized meal at McDonald's, and they make motion graphics work a lot easier.

The list that appears reveals the available parameter behaviors. Don't be intimidated by the geeky mathematical names—the behaviors are actually quite simple to use.

3　Choose Ramp.

Motion automatically jumps to the Behaviors tab of the Inspector, where you'll find a new behavior called Ramp (along with the Scale Over Life behavior we added earlier).

The geeky name simply comes from the shape this behavior would make if you graphed it out over time. It allows you to start with one value and gradually increase or decrease to another value. When you look at that on a graph (and, in fact, in Motion's Keyframe Editor), it angles up or down, depending on whether you want the values to increase or decrease, like a ramp.

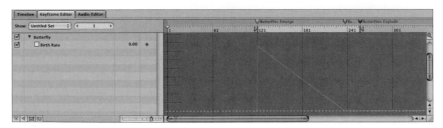

A typical Ramp curve

In our example we want lots of butterflies initially and then fewer over time to the point where no butterflies are born at all. That is, we want to *ramp down*.

4 Press F4 to jump to the Particle Cell tab of the Inspector.

If you look at the Birth Rate parameter, the only thing that tells you the behavior's been activated is the gear icon appearing to the right of the numeric entry box ◄ 0.00 ► ✳ .

5 Press F2 to jump back to the Behaviors tab of the Inspector.

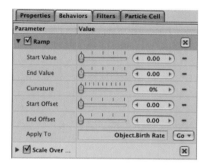

Notice at the bottom of the Ramp section a parameter called Apply To, with the term *Object.Birth Rate* in its text box. This tells us that the birth rate of the current object is being controlled by this behavior.

6 Set the Start Value to 12.00.

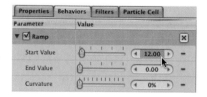

7 Resume playback of the Timeline. You should now find a plethora of butterflies swarming your screen. Depending on your system, they may also be causing a lag in playback (if so, see if the still-proxy method, described earlier in this lesson, helps speed things up).

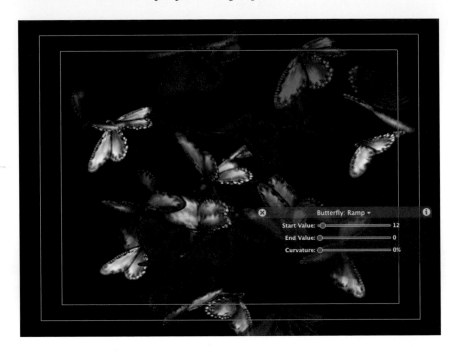

8   Press F4 to jump back to the Particle Cell tab of the Inspector.

Take a look at the Birth Rate parameter. As the Timeline plays, you should see the Birth Rate values drop from 12 to 0. That's what a Ramp does—it begins with its Start Value (which we set to 12) and slowly drops its value over time until it reaches its End Value (which we left at the default of 0).

The Ramp starts when we want it to, but we need it to finish a little earlier. We want the last butterfly to emerge just before the big bang at the end of the play range. Since the End Value of our Ramp is still set to 0.00, the particle system will stop birthing new butterflies wherever the Ramp behavior ends in the Timeline.

9   Make sure the Ramp behavior is still selected (if not, select it in the
Layers tab).

10   Click in the Current Frame field and type *238* to jump to that frame.

11   Press O to set the Out point of the Ramp behavior.

If you look at the playback, you'll see that no butterflies are born after
frame 238.

We're getting closer, but it's still not a "burst." There's another parameter
in the Ramp behavior called Curvature. It determines the acceleration or
deceleration of the ramp from the Start Value to the End Value. When it's
set to 100, the object moves like a boulder rolling down a hill. At first it
barely moves, and then its speed starts to increase dramatically.

In our case, setting the Curvature to 100% will cause the birth rate to stay
high longer and then taper off quickly toward the end.

12   Set the Curvature to 100%.

In the playback, the butterflies now seem a little too crowded. Let's pull
back on our initial Birth Rate.

13   In the Ramp parameters (F2), reduce the Start Value to 10.00.

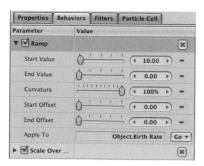

That's better. It's still crowded but not quite as chaotic.

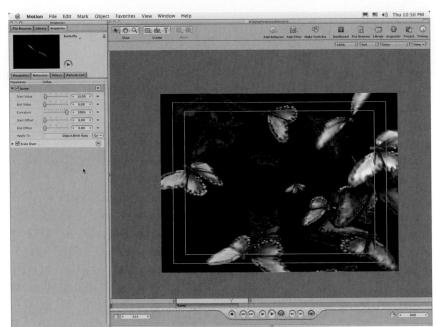

Modifying the Butterflies' Movements

The butterflies are exploding out from the center of the image, which is a good thing. However, unlike other types of particles, butterflies are self-propelling. That is, in addition to being propelled by the explosion, these butterflies can move themselves, which is presumably what they're trying to do by flapping their wings.

In this exercise we'll stop the movement generated by the emitter and give a random motion to each butterfly, creating the sense that every butterfly is powered by its own energy and volition.

Generating a Random Seed

If while watching the animation you notice several of the butterflies flapping their wings in almost exactly the same sequence, you'll need to make an adjustment. Otherwise, the duplicate motion may pull viewers out of the moment.

The good news is that it's easy to do. Simply click the Generate button next to Random Seed in the Particle Cell or Emitter tab of the Inspector; Motion will create a new random distribution of sequence timing for the butterflies being emitted.

Keep clicking until you're satisfied that the butterflies all seem to be flapping individually. For more information on the random seed, see the exercise "Modifying the Random Seed" in the next section of this lesson.

TIP If you've fallen behind, feel free to open the project **F.ModifyingMovement** to catch up.

1   In the Layers tab (F5), select the particle cell called Butterfly.

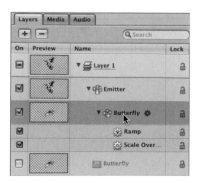

2 In the Particle Cell tab of the Inspector (F4), set the Speed to 0.00.

The butterflies now go absolutely nowhere. They do, however, still seem to move toward the screen, due to our Scale Over Life behavior.

3 Click the Add Behavior button at the top of the Canvas and choose Simulations > Random Motion.

You might now see a little lateral motion, but not much.

4   In the Behaviors tab (F2) of the Inspector, set the Amount for the Random
Motion behavior to 400.00.

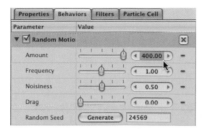

The butterflies now have minds of their own. The behavior is applied to
each particle individually. The Random Motion behavior's job is, obviously, to create random motion. While the animation's playing, try to keep
track of just one of the emerging butterflies. You'll probably notice it moving one way and then another. Its movements are graceful; it's not erratically jumping around as if the motion were random from one frame to
the next. In fact, you can adjust how frequently the butterfly changes
direction with the Frequency slider.

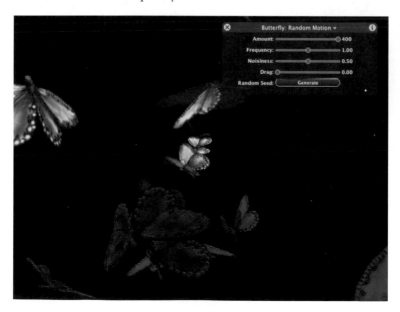

This may be more realistic (then again, what's realistic about blue, indigo, and violet butterflies exploding out of someone's hands?), but we've created another problem: Half of our butterflies are escaping off the edges of the screen.

What we need to do is to give the butterflies an initial strong, explosive velocity, and then slow them down as they distance themselves from the epicenter of the explosion. We can do this with a little parameter called Drag.

5   In the parameters for Random Motion, set Drag to 0.7.

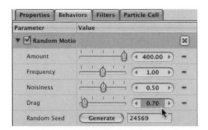

The butterflies now experience "wind resistance" that slows their escape from the center.

Creating an Implosion

The butterflies are supposed to end their lives by exploding in a dizzying shower of colors. Essentially they're playing the role of rocket fuel for the explosion. In order for them to explode, though, we need to gather them all into the center of the explosion.

> **NOTE ▶** If you'd like to preview the final movie, take a look at APTS_ Motion > Lessons > Lesson03 > **FinalCinemative.mov**. Remember, however, that the final movie is the high-definition version of the promo— right now we're working in standard definition.

Modifying the Random Seed

No, a random seed isn't someone's eccentric offspring; it's the parameter that determines what kind of random numbers Motion will generate. Random numbers in Motion aren't strictly random. That is, they don't change every time you turn on your computer. Think of random seeds as being different lists of random numbers in a book. So if you use a seed of 5, Motion will refer to page 5 of its random-number list when creating random values. If you choose a seed of 20, Motion will look at page 20 instead, and so on. The lists never change; page 20 will always show exactly the same list of random numbers.

Throughout Motion you'll find parameters that rely on random-number sequences. In our case, we're using one random-number sequence to determine which frame in the butterfly loop animation is used as the start frame for each butterfly (in the particle cell parameters), and we're using another random-number sequence to determine in which direction each butterfly will move (in the Random Motion behavior).

We're about to carefully choreograph the motion of the butterflies, so we need to make sure that what you see onscreen is the same as how we've set things up in the book. By using the same random seeds, we're guaranteeing that everyone's butterflies will be flapping the same way and moving in the same directions.

1 At the bottom of the Particle Cell tab of the Inspector (F4), set the value for Random Seed to 1.

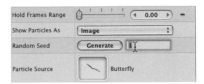

2 Click the Behaviors tab, and in the parameters for the Random Motion behavior set the Random Seed to 20.

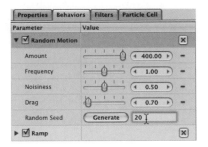

NOTE ▶ Do *not* click the Generate button. That will generate a new random seed, overwriting the value you just entered.

You now have specific random seeds set for the way the particles are generated and the way they move.

Creating an Attractor Null

We need something to draw the butterflies into one place, and an Attractor behavior does this perfectly. The catch is that the Attractor behavior needs to be attached to an object.

> **TIP** If you've fallen behind, feel free to open the project **G.CreatingAttractor** to catch up.

1   Open the Layers tab (F5).

2   Press Shift-Home to jump to the beginning of the play range.

3   In the File Browser (Cmd-1), locate **Null.png** in the APTS_Motion > Lesson05 folder.

4   Drag **Null.png** over the bottom of the ghosted Butterfly layer's border (in the Layers tab) until you see the position indicator line up with Emitter, and then release.

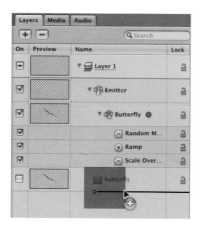

We've now added a new object called Null. This is a still, 10x10-pixel image. It doesn't matter what image we use—it could just as well be a picture of your dog—we're using it only as a reference. We'll hide it later.

5 In the Properties tab (F1) of the Inspector, set the Position of the Null object to −200, 133.

This positions the Null object at the epicenter of the explosion. Now it's time to add the behavior.

6 Click the Add Behavior button at the top of the Canvas and choose Simulations > Attractor.

7 Resume playback.

The butterflies are now flocking to the Null object—not exactly what we had in mind, but it's a start. We need the butterflies to flock at the end of their onscreen appearance. Also, we need the butterflies to shrink, as if they're being drawn away from the camera as they're absorbed as fuel for the impending big bang.

8   Stop playback and then move the playhead to frame 225.

9   Press I to set the Attractor's In point to frame 225.

10 Press Shift-End to jump to the play range Out point.

11 Press O to set the Attractor's Out point to match the play range Out point.

The butterflies are now unaffected by the Attractor until frame 225. Since the Attractor has much less time to influence them, it's no longer strong enough to fully draw the butterflies into its center.

12 In the Behaviors tab of the Inspector, set the Attractor's strength to 400.00 and the Drag to 5.00.

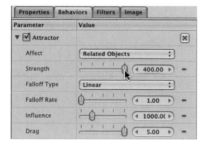

The higher Strength value pulls the butterflies in, and the Drag value of 5 damps their movement and keeps them from overshooting their target in their enthusiasm to explode. All we need to do now is shrink the butterflies.

13 In the Layers tab (F5), uncheck the On box for Null.

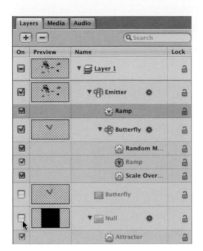

If you're still playing back your preview, you'll notice that nothing has changed. That's because even though you deactivated the object called Null (causing it not to show in the Canvas), its Attractor behavior continues to be active. That's why you could have used a picture of your dog for the job; after the On box is unchecked, the only thing that matters is the Attractor behavior attached to it.

Applying Shrinkage

We now need to shrink the butterflies down into the implosion. Emitter itself has a scale parameter. When you scale down an emitter, you scale down all the particles that belong to it—perfect for pulling a bunch of butterflies into a central location.

1 Cease playback and again move the playhead to frame 225.

2 In the Layers tab select Emitter.

3   In the Properties tab (F1) of the Inspector, right-click or Ctrl-click Scale and choose the Ramp parameter behavior.

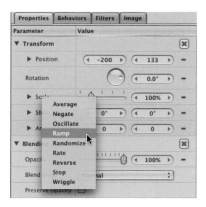

4   Press I to set the In point for the Ramp you've just added.

5   In the Behaviors tab (F2) set the End Value to −100%.

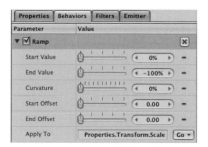

Ramp behaviors add their values to whatever their "host" parameter was initially set to. Scale was set to 100% before we applied the Ramp. Because we want to scale down the butterflies from this initial scale value of 100%, we've left the Start Value at 0% and put the End Value at −100%. This means that at the beginning of the Ramp behavior, a value of 0% from the Ramp will be combined with the 100% (100 + 0 = 100) value of the Scale parameter, leaving the butterflies at normal size. By the end of the Ramp behavior, the Ramp value drops to –100%. This is combined with the Scale parameter's original 100% to create a net scale of 0% (100 – 100 = 0). As a result, the butterflies should scale from full size at frame 225 to invisibly small at the end of the play range.

6   Resume playback.

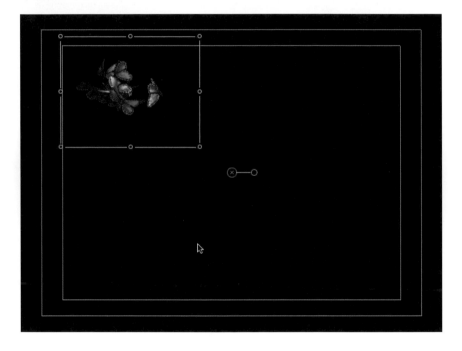

You've just successfully annihilated a couple dozen innocent butterflies. I wouldn't mention this to your therapist.

What You've Learned

▶ Particle systems consist of an emitter and one or more particle cells.

▶ Parameter behaviors are useful for changing values over time without keyframes.

▶ Random-seed values are used to determine what list of random numbers Motion will draw from.

▶ Behaviors can be applied to particle cells to affect each particle individually.

Keyboard Shortcuts

Cmd–Option–left/ right arrows	jumps to last marker/next marker
Shift-drag	snaps to markers in the Timeline
I	sets the In point of the selected object to the current frame
O	sets the Out point of the selected object to the current frame
Shift-Home	jumps to the start of the play range
Shift-End	jumps to the end of the play range

6

Lesson Files

Bonus Files

Time

Goals

APTS_Motion > Lessons > Lesson06

SmokeMaker.motn

BrightSmoke.mov

This lesson takes approximately 60 minutes to complete.

Design a sprite-based particle system

Create multiple particle cells attached to a single emitter

Work with particle proxies

Create an alpha matte

Lesson **6**

Advanced Particle Design

We now need to generate the explosion for the butterflies in the previous lesson. And if there's one thing particles are good at, it's blowing stuff up. In this lesson we'll take a look at how to create more-advanced particle systems using sprites and multiple particle cells. You'll also discover how to create your own particle presets.

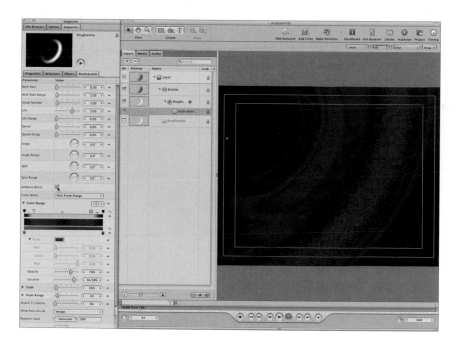

Working with Sprites

Up to now, we've been using movie clips as the source for our particle systems. The problem with movie clips is that they take up a lot of space in the computer's memory. That's fine if you want to animate a dozen or so butterflies flopping about the screen, but what if you want to generate hundreds or even thousands of particles? In that case you use *sprites*.

Sprites are simple graphic images that, when emitted from a particle system, blend to create the illusion of such elements as steam, water, and sparks. They're usually small and muted in color (often grayscale), allowing for dramatic modifications of their color and size in the particle-engine settings.

Let's see an example.

1   Press Cmd-Option-W to close any open projects, and then navigate to the folder APTS_Motion > Lessons > Lesson06 and open the file **A.Explutterfly**.

2   In the File Browser, navigate again to the APTS_Motion > Lessons > Lesson06 folder.

3   Click **RingParticle.tif** to load it into the File Browser preview pane.

That's a sprite. Not very inspiring, is it? Believe it or not, it's going to be the basis for our primary butterfly explosion. It's only 64x64 pixels, but Motion will scale it up to be much larger as it's emitted. The good news is that it will be anti-aliased as it grows, so it will keep nice, soft edges.

TIP The sprite's size is 64x64 pixels for a reason. Computers are binary machines, and as a result they work better with things that fit into their storage scheme of bits and bytes (8 bits to a byte). So when designing particle sprites, create them in a memory-friendly dimension such as 8x8, 16x16, 32x32, 64x64, 128x128, or 256x256. These are the most efficient sizes for Motion to use and will help keep your particles flowing in real time.

4 Drag **RingParticle.tif** into the Canvas and release it anywhere.

5 In the Properties tab of the Inspector (F1), set the Position to –200, 133.

TIP You can press Tab to cycle through numeric entry boxes in the Inspector.

This matches the position we set for the Null object in the previous lesson—the point into which the butterflies were "imploded."

6 Click the Make Particles button at the top of the Canvas to turn the RingParticle object into a particle system.

7   Resume playback (press the spacebar).

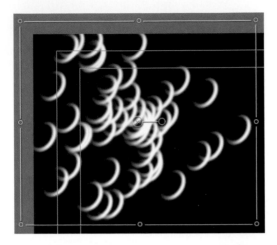

Not a particularly inspiring explosion, unless you wanted to simulate someone tossing toenail clippings into the couch (no, probably not). That's because in this case we designed the sprites to stay fixed in one place, but they should scale outward, creating the effect of exploding rings.

8   About halfway down the Emitter tab of the Inspector (F4), set the Speed to 0.

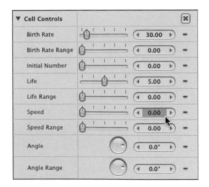

9 Near the bottom of the Emitter tab, set the Scale to 20%.

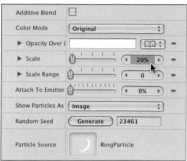

The result so far is truly uninspiring. Fear not—we'll see things change in just a moment.

10 Select the RingParticle particle cell in the Layers tab (F5); click the Add Behavior button at the top of the Canvas and choose Particles > Scale Over Life.

11 In the Behaviors tab of the Inspector, set the Scale Rate to 2000.

Now we're starting to get somewhere. We've still got a lot more tweaking to do, but now the sprite looks much more like the remnants of a super-nova than the remnants of a pedicure.

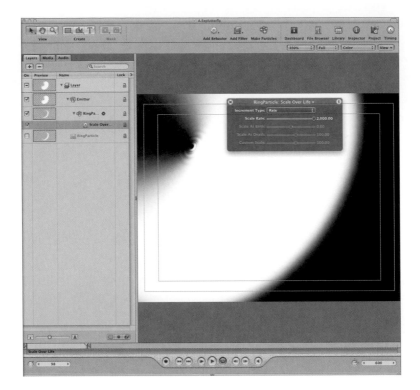

12 At the top of the RingParticle parameters in the Particle Cell tab of the Inspector (F4), set the Birth Rate to 0, the Birth Rate Range to 2, the Initial Number to 3, and the Life to 7.

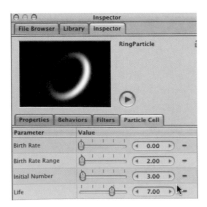

Setting the Initial Number to 3 means that three rings will be born right at the start of the particle emitter (frame 1). Setting the Birth Rate to 0 means that no particles will be created after those first three are born. At least that *would* be the case, but since we set the Birth Rate Range to 2, we could have as few as zero or as many as two particles born each second. Also, with a Life of 7 seconds, we've been more than generous with each ring's screen time (each ring will "live" for an entire 7 seconds from the time it's born until the time it dies).

NOTE ▶ The Life parameter of a particle is unrelated to the start point of the emitter. An emitter might start at frame 1 in the Timeline, but a given particle might not be born until 3 seconds have elapsed. In that case, the 7-second countdown from birth to death for that particle would begin at 3 seconds into the Timeline, *not* at the frame where the emitter started (frame 1). That is, the particle will die 10 seconds into the project, exactly 7 seconds after it was born.

To make sure that what you're seeing on your screen is the same as what was created for the book, let's synchronize our random seeds as we did in Lesson 5.

13 At the bottom of the Particle Cell tab of the Inspector, set the Random Seed value to 200.

Time to add a little more excitement to the supernova.

14 Toward the bottom of the Particle Cell tab, set the Scale Range to 20.

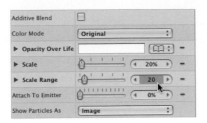

Because we've created a range of possible sizes for the rings at the moment they're born, some scale up faster than others. It makes sense—if you take a tall person and a short person and double their height through some bizarre genetic modification experiment, the tall person will grow by a much greater amount than the short person.

The effect this produces in the animation is of some rings' having more explosive energy and "overtaking" other rings born before them.

Finally, let's add a splash of color and change the opacity of the rings as they age.

TIP If you've fallen behind, feel free to open the project **B.AddingColor** to catch up.

15 Choose Color Mode > Pick From Range.

16 Click the Color Range disclosure triangle to edit the gradient.

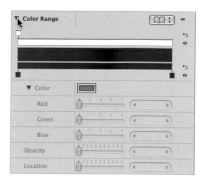

NOTE ▶ If you're not sure how to edit the gradient, see Lesson 2 for more details.

17 Click the lower-left color tag. Set its Red, Green, and Blue values to 0.98, 0.00, and 1.00, respectively.

0.98, 0.00, 1.00 ───

─── 0.00, 0.00, 1.00

18 Click the lower-right color tag. Make sure its Red, Green, and Blue values are set to 0.00, 0.00, and 1.00, respectively.

19 Create tags for the Opacity gradient as illustrated in the following figure. The values of the two inner tags should be set to 70%, and the outer two set to 0%. Remember, you can set the opacity only by dragging the Opacity slider below the gradient bars.

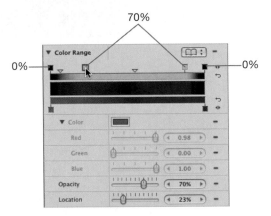

One last tiny detail to attend to: You may have noticed just above the Color Mode and Color Range parameters an unassuming little check box labeled Additive Blend. When this is checked, particles that cross over each other are added together, resulting in brighter patches where they intersect. This is often desirable in particle systems simulating some kind of illumination; when two glowing particles occupy the same space on the screen, that part of the screen becomes brighter.

20 Check the Additive Blend box.

You should now be able to see strong bright areas where the rings overlap.

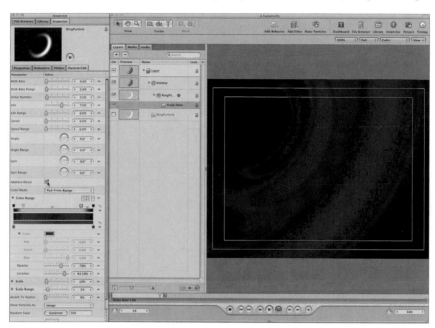

Adding a Second Particle Cell

We mentioned briefly in Lesson 5 that an emitter can have more than one particle cell attached to it. Our supernova rings are nice, but any good explosion has a strong initial nucleus, with some debris to boot. So we'll add two more particle cells to the emitter to create a bit of bang and sizzle.

> **TIP** ▶ If you've fallen behind, feel free to open the project **C.AddingAnotherParticle** to catch up.

1 Press Home to set the playhead back to frame 1.

2   In the File Browser (Cmd-1), locate **Blur11.png** in the APTS_Motion > Lessons > Lesson06 folder and drag it into the bottom of the Layers tab (F5) until the position indicator lines up with the ghosted RingParticle layer.

NOTE ▶ Remember, as you drag the layer in, the position indicator can either line up with the layers in the menu and create a new layer for the footage you're importing, or line up with other objects and include the new object in the existing layer. In this case we want the latter.

You should now have a big fuzzy shape in the middle of your Canvas. By default, when you drag an object into the Layers tab, it's automatically positioned in the middle of the composite. Where it appears in the Canvas doesn't matter; we're only using it as a reference to create particles, so its onscreen position doesn't make any difference to the final effect.

NOTE ▶ Did you forget to set your playhead to frame 1 before adding the footage? If so, your footage In point will be set to the frame where the playhead was parked when you added the footage. Don't sweat it—just press Home to jump to the start of the Timeline, and then press Shift-[to snap the active object (in this case Blur11) to the newly positioned playhead. To make sure your footage always comes in at frame 1, choose Motion > Preferences and choose Create Objects At > "Start of project." This isn't recommended, as in real-world projects you'll often be working 2 or 3 minutes into your Timeline, and it would be incredibly tedious to have to drag the clips all the way from frame 1 every time you import them.

3   Uncheck the box next to Blur11 in the Layers tab to deactivate it. The Blur11 particle cell should now be ghosted, just like its neighbor RingParticle.

Since we're just using Blur11 as a reference, there's no need to leave it turned on. If we did, we'd have two things appearing onscreen: the original object Blur11 at the center of the Canvas, and the particles generated from Blur11, which we're about to introduce.

4   Drag the ghosted Blur11 particle cell onto the Emitter above it and release the mouse button.

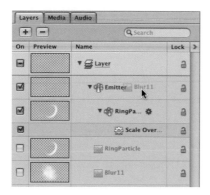

5   Resume playback.

A new particle cell called Blur11 is created and can be seen billowing wildly in the Canvas, positioned at the center of the emitter.

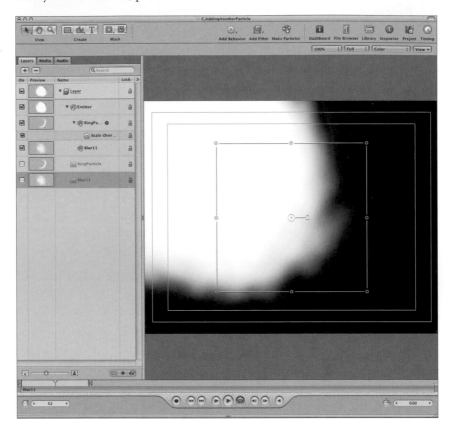

Now we want to work on our new friend Blur11, so let's temporarily turn off the RingParticle cell.

6   Uncheck the box for the RingParticle cell to deactivate it.

7   Select the Blur11 particle cell.

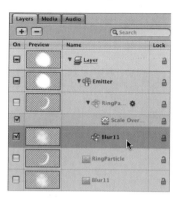

8   In the Particle Cell tab of the Inspector (F4), set Life to 2, Life Range to 2, and Scale to 5%.

You're now looking at some very strange popcorn. Hang in there—this really will look cool in a moment.

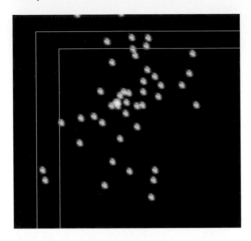

9 Choose Color Mode > Over Life, click the Color Over Life disclosure triangle, and set the color and alpha gradients to the values indicated in the figure below:

10 If you stopped playback, resume it.

The popcorn is now extremely difficult to see, and rather purple. We're about to make these particles much bigger, so we've reduced their opacity to make sure they don't "build up" too much when they overlap.

It's time to make sense of this whole creation.

11 With the Blur11 particle cell still selected, click the Add Behavior button at the top of the Canvas and choose Particles > Scale Over Life.

12 In the Behaviors tab of the Inspector, set the Scale Rate to 2000.

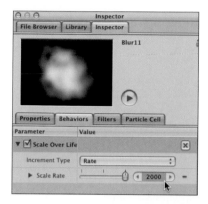

Now that's more like it—a plume of smoke rather than a kettle of popcorn.

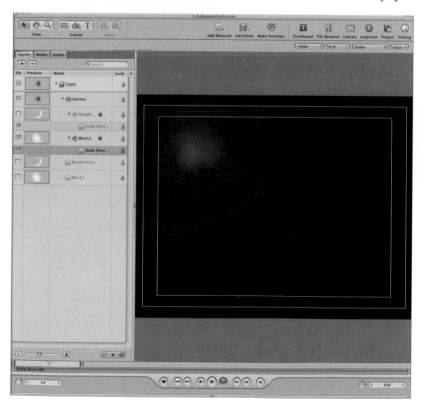

Particle systems are deceptively complex. Our particle cell looks like a mass of tiny smoke particles coalescing in the atmosphere, but it's really just a bunch of simple little sprites overlapping and scaled to create the effect.

13 Back in the Particle Cell tab of the Inspector (F4), set the Initial Number to 30.

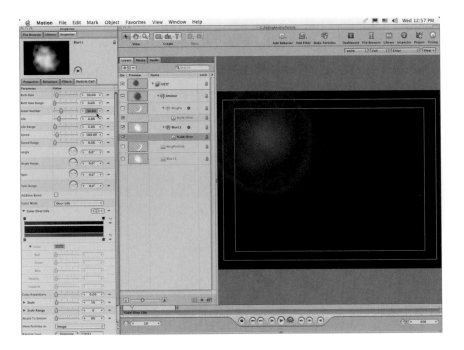

This starts us off with a nice big bang. Our particle system looks pretty good. There's only one problem—it's moving out predictably and evenly in all directions, but our supernova rings are angled down and to the right. We'll fix this with a couple of behaviors.

Modifying Particle Behavior

It's time again to apply some custom behaviors to the particles to break up the monotony of their performance. Real life is full of turbulence and unpredictability; there's a whole branch of mathematics dedicated to this chaotic activity. To add realism, we need to incorporate behaviors that eliminate some of the symmetry and smoothness of computed calculations.

> **TIP** ▶ If you've fallen behind, feel free to open the project **D.BehaviorModification** to catch up.

1   In the Layers tab, make sure the Blur11 particle cell is selected; click the Add Behavior button at the top of the Canvas and choose Simulations > Random Motion.

2   In the Behaviors tab of the Inspector, set the Amount to 300, the Frequency to 2, and the Noisiness to 1.

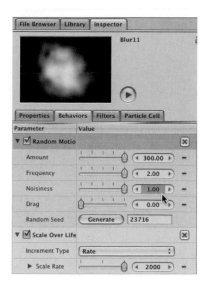

The particles now move out with more random trajectories.

3 Click the Add Behavior button and choose Basic Motion > Throw.

The shape of the RingParticle creates the illusion that the explosion has depth and is traveling toward the bottom-right corner of the screen. To reinforce this illusion, we'll skew the direction of the explosion's other elements using the Throw behavior.

4 In the Dashboard (D or F7), set the direction of the Throw to the lower right.

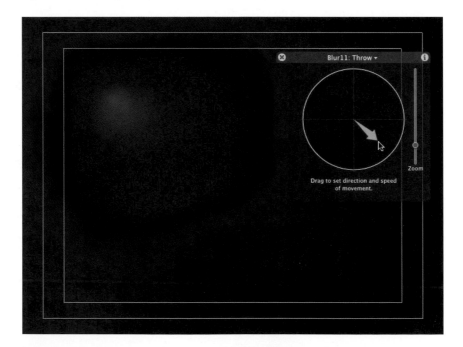

The direction's not bad, but the particles seem way too insubstantial toward the end of their lives.

5 If you had stopped playback, resume it.

We've now got a nice little dust explosion to form the core of our effect. Let's bring back the rings.

6 In the Layers tab (F5), check the box for the RingParticle particle cell to reactivate it.

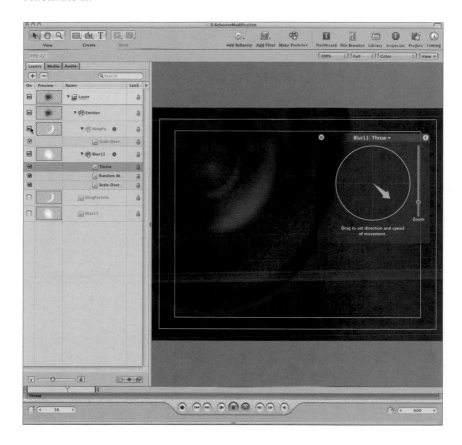

NOTE ▶ Feel free to experiment with different parameters in these behaviors and particle cells. The precise values provided in this exercise weren't derived using a slide rule and sophisticated Fourier transforms. They were derived by playing with the particle system in real time and tweaking the values until it looked the way we wanted it to look.

Using Particle Proxies and RAM Preview

If animated particles are slowing down your real-time playback, you have a couple of options. The first one is to set your particles to a proxy mode. This is different from the still-image proxy method discussed in Lesson 5. Let's see how it works.

> **TIP** ▶ If you've fallen behind, feel free to open the project **E.ParticleProxies** to catch up.

1   Select the Blur11 cell and click the Particle Cell tab of the Inspector (F4).

2   Near the bottom, choose Show Particles As > Wireframe.

So that you can see what's going on, we'll temporarily change the opacity of the particles.

3   In the Color Over Life gradient, click the tag at the far left of the opacity gradient and drag the Opacity slider from 15% to 50%.

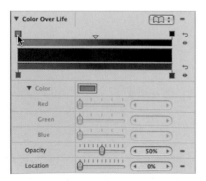

4   If you had stopped playback, resume it.

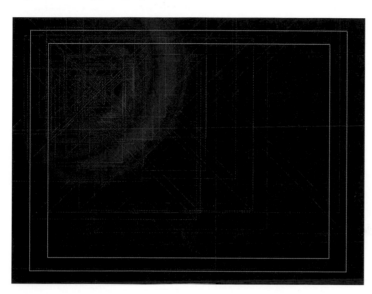

In this mode you see bounding boxes in place of animated particles. This can be a cool effect in itself if you're going for a geometric feel. You have two other proxy modes here, Points and Lines. (I'll leave you to figure out what they look like.)

Although these modes don't provide a faithful representation of the actual particles' look and feel, they do give you real-time feedback as to their positions, overlap, and general motion.

5   Set the Opacity of the left opacity tag back to 15%.

6   Return the Show Particles As menu to Image.

The second way to regain performance is to generate a RAM preview. Unlike regular playback, a RAM preview renders out the entire play range and stores it in your computer's system memory. When you play back the Timeline, everything plays back in real time. That's because all the calculations have been done in advance, and all Motion needs to do is play back the rendered movie. The downside is that as soon as you make a change to any element in the composite, you'll need to re-render before you can see a real-time preview again.

7   Choose Mark > RAM Preview > Play Range.

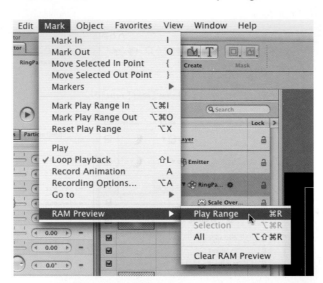

Notice that you can choose to render a selection or all of the Timeline (assuming you have enough free RAM to do that). You can also choose Clear RAM Preview. This is useful if you've rendered a large RAM preview that's occupying most of your system's RAM. Once you're done watching the preview, you might want to release that RAM to be used elsewhere.

While Motion creates the RAM preview, it displays a dialog that tells you how long the render will take.

8   Resume playback to watch the preview in real time.

This is fine, but what happens if you want to make changes to the RingParticle cell? As soon as you make a change, your RAM preview will need to be re-rendered. If you try to make the modifications in the normal mode, it will be hard to judge speed and timing because the FlashPart cell is slowing down the playback. The solution is to use the Solo mode we explored in Lesson 1.

9   With playback still running, select the RingParticle cell in the Layers tab.

10 Press Ctrl-S to solo the RingParticle object.

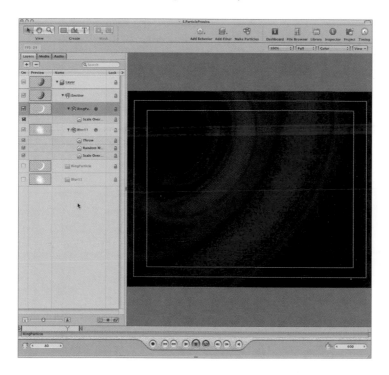

Everything *except* the RingParticle object disappears from the screen, and the composite can play back in real time again. Notice how the activation check boxes for all the other layers are ghosted.

You can now make real-time adjustments to the RingParticle object. When you're satisfied, you can unsolo the layer to reunite it with its comrades.

> **TIP** Even though we've selected only one object here, you can also select several objects and solo them as a group.

11 Press Ctrl-S to unsolo the RingParticle object.

Blending Dust

For a final touch of style, let's add some atmospherics to the explosion. Assuming that the initial bang threw dust across our surreal universe, we should see the smoky haze illuminated by our expanding rings.

> **TIP** If you've fallen behind, feel free to open the project **E.ParticleProxies** to catch up.

1 Pause playback and press Home to move to frame 1.

2 In the File Browser drag **BrightSmoke.mov** from the Lesson06 folder and position it above Layer in the Layers tab; release the mouse button when you see the position indicator appear.

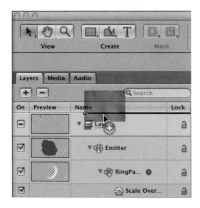

Dragging the footage above the existing layer creates a new layer for the added footage. This helps us keep our particles organized in one group and our smoke in another.

NOTE ▶ BrightSmoke.mov was also created using Motion's particle system. Check out the project **SmokeMaker.motn** if you want to see how it was made.

3   Double-click the label for Layer and rename it *Particles*.

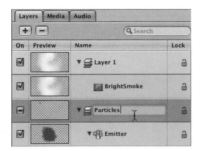

4   Double-click the label for Layer 1 and rename it *Smoke*.

TIP ▶ Once you have more than one layer, it's a good idea to start giving them intuitive names. It's all very simple right now, but if you have 20 or 30 layers, a title like Layer 19 isn't a particularly useful indication of a layer's content.

5   Select the Smoke layer in the Layers tab, and press F1 to jump to the Properties tab of the Inspector.

6 Set the Blend Mode to Stencil Alpha.

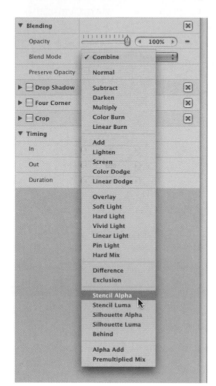

We'll be taking an in-depth look at blend modes in Lesson 7. To satisfy your curiosity, though, let's talk about what Stencil Alpha does. Remember those paper or plastic stencils you used in grade school—you know, the ones shaped like letters that you positioned over a piece of paper and scribbled inside to make titles for your class project? They caused your scribbling to appear on the paper only inside the cutaway areas of the stencil.

What we've done is use the alpha channel of the Smoke layer to cut a hole in the Particles layer, *stenciling* the particles so that they show up only where there's smoke. That's why when you play back the composite, you see a nice, smoky look to the image.

7 Play back the composite.

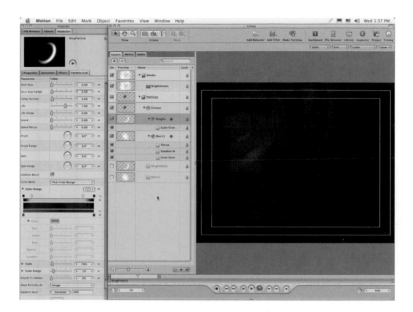

With just a little work, we've turned two average-looking sprites into a veritable supernova. In the last two lessons we've covered most of the controls in the Particle Cell tab of the Inspector. Go ahead and click back onto one of the particle cells and look at its properties in the Inspector (F4). You should find that the many intimidating controls now all make sense to you.

What You've Learned

- ▶ Sprites are simple graphic images blended together to create the illusion of many particles.

- ▶ Scale Range can be used to vary the speed of particles scaled by the Scale Over Life behavior.

- ▶ The Over Life color mode allows particles to change their color as they get older.

- ▶ Particle emitters can contain several cells.

- ▶ Particles can be set to wireframe, line, and point proxy modes to speed up the preview of complex particle systems.

- ▶ The Stencil Alpha transfer mode can be used to mask off areas of underlying layers.

7

Lesson Files	APTS Motion > Lessons > Lesson07
Time	This lesson takes approximately 30 minutes to complete.
Goals	Learn how to apply blend modes
	Adjust text styling and color
	Modify the properties of media

Using Blend Modes

Blend modes are the secret of modern motion graphics design—of modern graphic design in general, for that matter. Think of blend modes as defining the kind of material an object or layer is made from. To use an analogy, imagine building materials such as plastic, glass, and wood. If you were to paint a design on plywood, you'd see the design but not what's behind it. Plywood is opaque, so if you hung up the design in a window, the light coming through from the window would be blocked out; all you'd see would be the painting.

Now imagine taking the same design and creating a stained glass window out of it. This time, when you put it in the window, not only would you see the design, but you would also see the light shining through it. In fact, the image would look different depending on what kind of light shone through it. At midday the image might look well lit but uninspiring, while at dusk the deep reds and ochers of the setting sun might create a dramatic, reverential tone in the image.

So the final image you see as you stand in front of the stained glass design is a *blend* of the design itself and the light passing through it. This is similar to the way blend modes work: They take your design and turn it into something like stained glass, which interacts with the objects behind it. Aesthetically, different blend modes cause different effects. Some blend highlights; others stencil the image beneath; still others keep the form of an object or layer but take on the colors of the background layers.

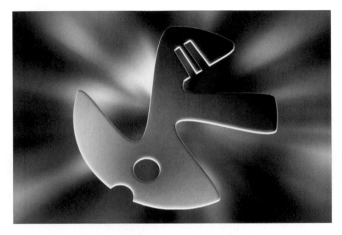

The Normal blend mode

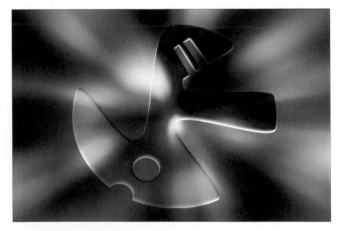

The Overlay blend mode

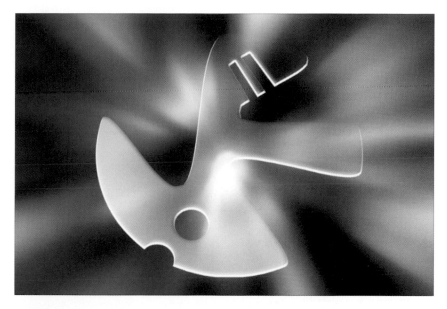

The Screen blend mode

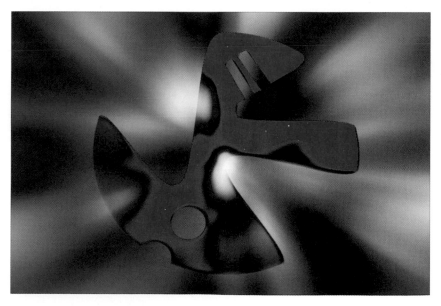

The Color Burn blend mode

The Subtract blend mode

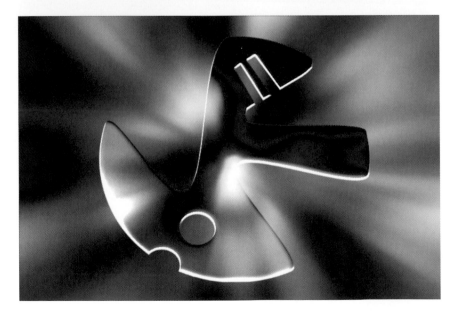

The Vivid Light blend mode

Blend modes are a fundamental element in modern motion graphics design. The subtle use of these different modes allows designers to incorporate many layers of imagery into a single, cohesive composite without that jarring contrast you might see in, for example, a child's collage of magazine cuttings.

One of the great ways to design with blend modes—whether you're a new designer or an experienced one—is simply to experiment, trying the various modes and observing the results. Nonetheless, an understanding of exactly what the modes do will dramatically improve your ability to create and prepare elements for certain effects.

Blending Objects

You may have noticed at the end of Lesson 3 that the objects in our composite were positioned and moving nicely, but they contrasted dramatically with the background. Now we'll apply different blend modes to integrate them more naturally.

1   Press Cmd-Option-W to close any open projects.

2   Navigate to the folder APTS_Motion > Lessons > Lesson07 and open the project **A.BlendModes**.

   NOTE ▶ To optimize real-time performance, the CosmordialSoup background layer was re-rendered to include the 115% scaling we performed in Lesson 3. If you're continuing to work with your own version of the project carried through from that lesson, that's fine—the result will be the same.

3   Select the BigWheel object either by clicking it in the Canvas or selecting it in the Layers tab (press F5 to reveal the Layers tab if it isn't visible).

   TIP▶ Sometimes it's hard to select objects in the Canvas because they overlap with other layers. Use the up and down arrow keys to cycle through the layers if you can't select them. If you look at the Layers tab as you do this, you'll see the objects highlighted there as well.

4   Make sure the Dashboard is active (press F7 if it isn't).

Notice the two main controls in the Canvas: Opacity and Blend Mode. These are the most important controls for each layer.

5   In the Blend Mode pop-up menu choose Overlay, and resume playback.

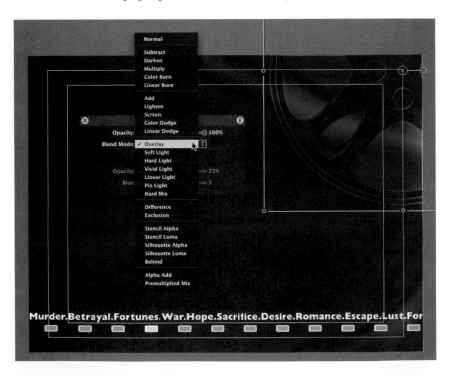

Overlay is a great blend mode to use for stenciling grayscale images over a background. Bright pixels in the image are screened over the background, creating accentuated highlights, while dark pixels are multiplied against the background, causing more subdued tones. Overlay mode works best with objects that have a range of pixel brightness; areas with gradients are ideal.

Another mode with a look similar to Overlay, but with slightly less contrast, is Soft Light.

6 Change the Blend Mode to Soft Light.

Using Soft Light, BigWheel stands out too prominently. Let's dial it back a little.

7 Set the Opacity of the layer to 25%. BigWheel now sits nicely in the background.

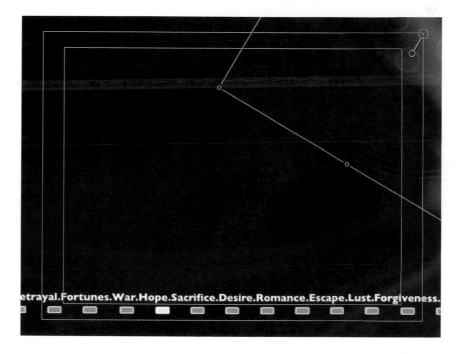

Next, let's get to work on the boxes.

8 In the Layers tab (F5), click the Boxes object to select it.

9   In the Dashboard, choose Blend Mode > Overlay.

Overlay works nicely with the Boxes object, creating some strong contrast variation based on how the branches of the CosmordialSoup object overlap different sections of boxes over time.

10 Select the Murder.Betrayal.Fortunes. object.

11 Choose Blend Mode > Color Dodge.

And…absolutely nothing seems to change. That's because this particular blend mode, Color Dodge, has no effect when it's applied to a pure white object. We need to modify the color of the text to see an effect.

12 Press F4 to open the Text tab of the Inspector.

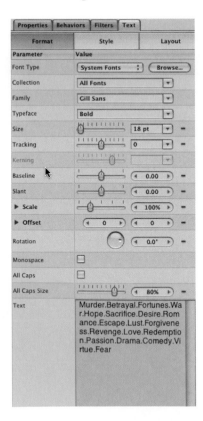

Notice that the Text tab of the Inspector has three panes: Format, Style, and Layout. We'll go into detail about text in Lesson 13, but for now we simply want to change the color of the text, and that's done in the Style pane.

13 Click the Style button to access the Style options.

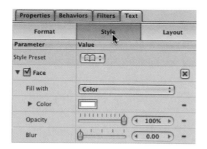

14 Right- or Ctrl-click the Color swatch in the Face parameters.

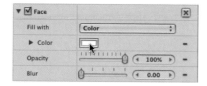

Up until now, to choose a color, you've double-clicked to bring up the Mac OS X Colors window. Right- or Ctrl-clicking a color swatch is another great way to quickly choose a color. A whole host of color choices is available just by dragging the eyedropper around in this contextual pop-up color window. The HSV color wheel we've been using in the standard Colors window still tends to be a more intuitive way to choose a specific range of colors, but if you're looking for a quick way to choose an arbitrary color, right- or Ctrl-clicking is a great time-saver.

15 Move the eyedropper around inside the color palette and watch the results in the Canvas.

As you move the eyedropper, you'll see that the Color Dodge blend mode now has a much more dramatic effect.

16 Choose a color that complements the background. If you like, use RGB values close to 125, 0, 162, and then click the red Close button to close the window.

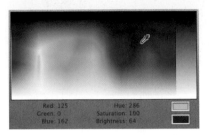

NOTE ▶ The RGB color values in the contextual color palette are in the 0–255 range. When you close the window, these values convert to Motion's 0–1 range. In this instance, that's 0.49, 0, 0.64. You can click the disclosure triangle next to the Color parameter to see these.

Now the Color Dodge causes the text to interact nicely with the background.

Creating a Title

It's time to turn to turn to the task of creating the title for our fictitious TV station, Cinematíve.

TIP ▶ If you've fallen behind, feel free to open the project **B.CreatingTheTitle** to catch up.

1 Make sure the Dashboard is visible (F7).

2 Press Home to move to frame 1 and press T to select the Text tool.

3 Click in the lower middle of the Canvas to position the insertion point.

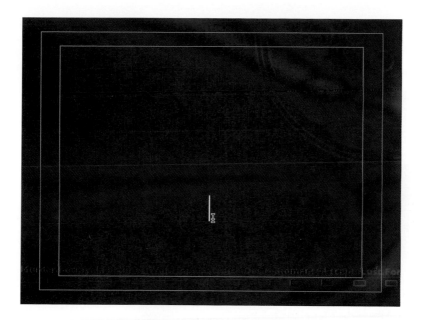

4   In the Dashboard, choose Alignment > Center.

5   Type *cinematíve*. To create the accented *í,* press Option-E before you
    type *i.*

    Why is the *c* in *cinematíve* lowercase? Because some marketing guru
    decided that the company would seem much hipper if its name appeared
    lowercase in this promo, and you have no choice but to buy into it.

6   Set the font to Gill Sans, the style to Bold, and the Size to 64 pt.

7 Press Escape to exit text entry mode.

The text is centered in its own text box, which is roughly in the middle of the frame, but we now need to align the text to the dead center of the Canvas.

8 Drag the text horizontally until it snaps to the yellow Dynamic Guide. (If snapping is turned off, press N to turn it back on.)

9 In the Properties tab (F1) of the Inspector, set the vertical position of the text to −120.

Now it's time to add a little style, courtesy of blend modes.

10 In the Dashboard, set the Blend Mode to Overlay.

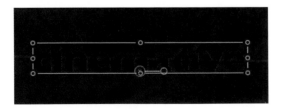

It's an interesting effect, but it's a little too subdued for the client's all-important title. We'll take advantage of the way overlay works by setting different brightness levels for the outline and face of the text.

11 In the Text tab of the Inspector (F4), click the Style button.

12 In the Style pane, check the text Outline box.

The outline is a thin border around the edge of the text. It's off by default, and since most text is solid, there's no need for a border. Adding outline to a text is a quick way to add a touch of style to text effects.

The default color for the outline is red (to help you see the effect of applying it), which is almost never the color you want to use.

13 Drag the Color swatch in the Face parameters onto the Color swatch for Outline and release.

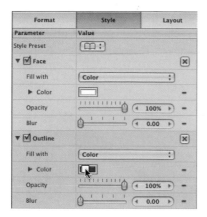

This is a great way to quickly copy a color from one parameter to another.

14 In the Face parameters, set the Opacity to 49%.

Setting the Face opacity darker than the outline creates a nice contrast and yields different interactions with the background. The text is still a little too dark—it needs to stand out, since it's the company name. We'll use an old motion graphics trick to solve the problem.

15 Press Cmd-D to duplicate the layer.

Simple things are often the most effective. Doubling up the layer results in a stronger, bolder font for our promo ID.

To clean up, let's group the two text objects into a single layer.

16 In the Layers tab (F5), Shift-click to select both the cinematíve and cine-matíve copy layers.

17 Choose Object > Group (or press Cmd-Shift-G) to group them.

18 Rename the grouped layer *CineText*.

19 Click the disclosure triangle to the left of CineText to hide its contents.

Adding a Logo

The centerpiece of the composite is the Cinemative logo. In fact, it's a butterfly that turns into the cold corporate logo as its comrades explode, but let's dwell on the positive aspects right now, shall we?

> **TIP** ▶ If you've fallen behind, feel free to open the project **C.AddingTheLogo** to catch up.

1 Move the playhead to frame 83.

2 In the File Browser (Cmd-1), navigate to the folder APTS_Motion > Lessons > Lesson07.

3 Drag **Bfly2Logo.mov** into the center of the Canvas (or to the bottom of the Layers tab).

4 Press Cmd-Option-I to set the play range In point.

5   Move to frame 336. Press Cmd-Option-O to set the play range Out point.

The logo is just a little too large, so we'll resize it.

6   In the Properties tab (F1) of the Inspector, set the Scale to 65%.

7   In the Canvas, drag the logo up so that it sits comfortably just above the text. (You can take advantage of the Dynamic Guides to center the logo horizontally and snap its bounding box to the base of the text.)

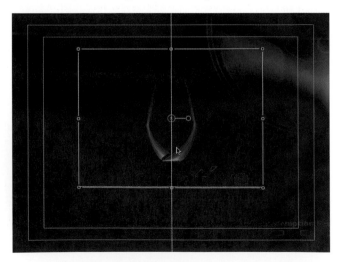

The logo is now sitting happily above its accompanying text.

Changing Media Properties

If you look carefully at the logo, you'll notice it has a dark, jaggy outline. This is a telltale sign of incorrect alpha interpretation.

Without going too deeply into the boring details, images with alpha channels can come into Motion either *premultiplied* by their alphas or not premultiplied. If they're not premultiplied, they're referred to as *straight*. There's some math behind all this, which we unfortunately (or fortunately) don't have time to get into. For now, let's live with the fact that images with alphas can come either premultiplied or straight, and leave the true meanings of these terms a blissful mystery.

> **TIP** ▶ For those of you hungry to understand the truth behind these terms, you'd be well served to read Ron Brinkmann's *The Art and Science of Digital Compositing* (Morgan Kaufmann, 1999).

For each imported image containing an alpha channel, Motion needs to know if it's straight or premultiplied in order to correctly composite it into the scene. Whenever you bring an image into your project from the File Browser, Motion makes an intelligent guess as to its state. Most of the time it gets it right; in the case of the logo, it guessed wrong. We therefore need to manually go in and change the alpha's type.

> **TIP** ▶ A dark ring around the edges of an object is a good indicator that it's being interpreted as straight when it's actually premultiplied. If the background around an object seems to lighten when it's dropped into a composite, that's a likely indicator that it's being interpreted as premultiplied when it's actually straight.

1   In the Layers tab, select BFly2Logo.

2   Press Shift-F.

This is a great keyboard shortcut to access media properties. Notice how Motion has jumped from the Project pane (which contains the Layers tab) to the Media tab of the Inspector. The Media tab lists the footage upon which the objects in the Layers tab are based.

3   While watching the logo in the Canvas (you may want to zoom in on it), change the Alpha Type to Premultiplied-Black.

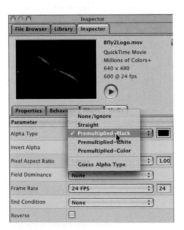

It's a subtle change, but you should see the black border disappear from around the logo.

4   If you zoomed in to look, press Option-Z to turn to 100% zoom level, or Shift-Z to enter Fit in Window mode.

Notice the other options available in the Media tab of the Inspector. You can change things like the pixel aspect ratio (to compensate for nonsquare-pixel footage, such as D1), the field dominance of interlaced footage, and the frame rate (the speed at which the clip will play back). You can even set up the footage to freeze or loop from the last frame using the End Condition parameter.

Adding the Explosion and Sound

You'll be combining all the elements we've been working on into one final piece in Lesson 10, but for now let's at least add the explosion to balance the screen weight of the wheel on the right side of the Canvas.

> **TIP** ▶ If you've fallen behind, feel free to open the project **D.AddingExplosion** to catch up.

1   Move to frame 257.

2   If you're still looking at the Media tab of the Inspector from the previous exercise, click back to the Layers tab (or press Cmd-4).

3   From the File Browser (Cmd-1), drag **Explode.mov** into the Layers tab and release it when its position indicator is lined up below the Boxes object.

4   In the Dashboard (F7), set the Opacity of Explode to 65% and the Blend
Mode to Screen.

Screen is a great blend mode when you want to composite an element that
has a black background over other objects, while building up the overall
brightness. Another advantage is that it doesn't require an alpha channel
for the composite.

You may have been wondering why everything happens at specific frames.
It's because there's a soundtrack that ties in to the visual elements. Let's
add the sound in preparation for the final render.

5   Return to frame 1.

6   Drag **Soundtrack.aiff** from the File Browser into the Canvas.

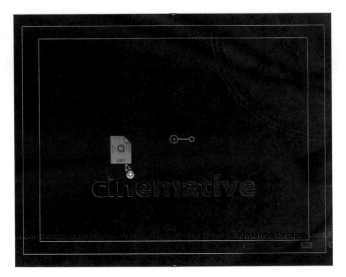

Let's go ahead and render out the story so far. First we'll set the play range
so that it covers only the completed section of the Timeline. We're currently missing the greenscreen elements that belong at the front of the
project, so it's pointless to include those frames in our test render.

7   Go to frame 121 and set the play range In point (Cmd-Option-I).

8   Go to frame 600 and set the play range Out point (Cmd-Option-O).

9 Choose File > Export.

10 In the Save As dialog that appears, choose Lossless Movie as the Export Preset.

11 Check the "Use play range" box.

Since the front end of the project is incomplete, there's no need to render the entire Timeline. When this box is checked, the render will be limited to the play range we just established—frames 121 through 600.

12 Click the Options button.

13 In the Export Options dialog that appears, choose MPEG-4 Video from the Compressor pop-up menu and then click OK.

14 Back in the Save As dialog, name your test movie, choose APTS_Motion > Lessons > Lesson07 > Student Saves as the location, and then click the Export button.

Once it's rendered, you can open it up and take a look. With the last half of the project completed, we can now focus on the greenscreen elements for the beginning of our Cinematíve promo ID.

What You've Learned

▶ Blend modes change the way overlapping objects combine together in the Canvas.

▶ Right- or Ctrl-clicking a color swatch opens a pop-up color palette.

▶ Duplicating objects can quickly make them look brighter and bolder.

▶ The interpretation of a clip's alpha channel can be adjusted in the Media tab of the Inspector.

8

Lesson Files

Time

Goals

APTS_Motion > Lessons > Lesson08

This lesson takes approximately 20 minutes to complete.

Setting up Gestures in the Motion preferences window

Using a pen and tablet to control the Motion interface

Drawing Gestures

As we mentioned way back at the beginning of the book, there are two kinds of compositing software: the programs that cost millions of dollars and the ones that don't. One of the things that separate the two types—aside from real-time performance—is their interface design.

High-end systems are typically driven by graphics tablets that use a pen (also known as a *stylus*) instead of a mouse to move the onscreen pointer. Special symbols known as *gestures* can be quickly drawn on the tablet to perform basic interface functions like opening and closing windows, panning, and zooming. A well-trained artist can execute these gestures smoothly and in swift succession, allowing for a speed that's hard to match using only mouse clicks and keyboard shortcuts.

In addition to the other user interface innovations we've seen so far, Motion implements a comprehensive set of gesture-based commands for controlling the interface by stylus and tablet. We'll take a look at how to set up gestures in Motion using a Wacom tablet, one of the most common and reliable graphics tablets on the market.

Activating Gestures

Gestures are activated using the Gestures pane of Motion's preferences window.

1   Choose Motion > Preferences (Cmd-,).

2   In the upper-right corner of the Preferences window, click the Gestures button.

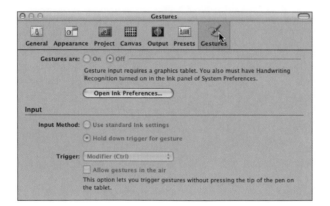

Notice that by default the "Gestures are" options are grayed out. That's because gestures rely on Mac OS X's built-in handwriting-recognition software, called Ink. Before we can start using gestures in Motion, we need to turn on Ink in System Preferences. Motion provides a nice shortcut to the Ink System Preferences pane so that you don't have to go hunting for it yourself.

NOTE ► You must have a tablet connected to your Macintosh to perform the following step. If a tablet isn't connected, Ink settings will not be available in System Preferences.

3 Click the Open Ink Preferences button to access the Ink System Preferences.

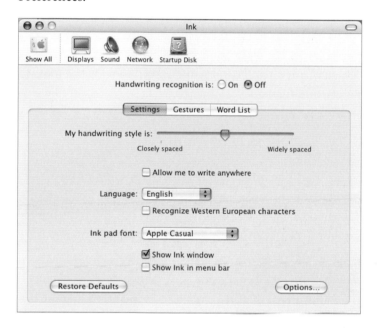

4 Set "Handwriting recognition is" to On.

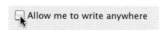

5 In the Settings tab, uncheck the "Allow me to write anywhere" box.

Allow me to write anywhere

"Allow me to write anywhere" sounds like a good idea, but it means that strange little pseudo–legal pads appear onscreen every time you drag the pen. We only want to activate Ink so that Motion can access it; we're not planning to write text on the screen with it.

6   Tap the red Close button to close the Systems Preferences window.

> **TIP** ▶ If you're new to using a pen and tablet, it's important to under-
> stand that tapping on the tablet is the equivalent of clicking the mouse.
> So instead of clicking the mouse button, you tap the pad, and instead of
> clicking and dragging with the mouse, you press and drag with the stylus.
> Also, the tablet usually maps to the screen, so the top right of the tablet
> corresponds to the top right of the screen, the bottom right of the tablet
> to the bottom right of the screen, and so on. This is unlike the action of
> a mouse, whereby you often lift and scroll to keep moving the mouse
> pointer in a certain direction.

▶ **Choosing a Graphics Tablet**

A common question that arises is, What size tablet should I buy?
If you're going to use the tablet only to create gestures, a low-cost,
4x5-inch tablet may be perfect. However, most people prefer using
a 6x8-inch tablet, since it provides a more comfortable work area.

Now, if you go to any large postproduction facility, you'll usually see two
or three large Wacom tablets stacked in a corner somewhere. That's
because someone insisted that a large tablet was the best thing the boss
could buy to increase productivity. That person got the tablet and set it
up, only to discover that there was no room left on the desk for the
computer keyboard. And after a couple of weeks trying to share desk
space with the keyboard and the tablet, the person gave up and tossed
the tablet in the corner, never to use it again.

The moral of the story: Don't get more tablet than you can handle. If
you're a traditional artist moving into the digital world, by all means
buy a big tablet. But if you're just planning to use it for gestures and as a
mouse substitute in other apps, a 6x8-inch tablet may be plenty big. And
keep in mind that a graphics tablet and stylus are not *required* for creating gestures in Motion.

As soon as you close the System Preferences window, you're back in the Gestures pane of the Motion preferences window.

7   For "Gestures are," click On.

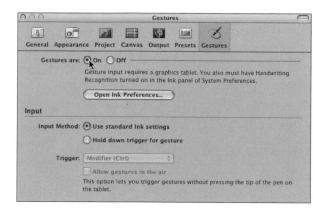

Next you need to choose how you want to input gestures. You have three main options: "Use standard Ink settings," "Hold down trigger for gesture," and "Allow gestures in the air." They work as follows:

▶   "Use standard Ink settings"—All you need to do is draw the gesture symbols on the screen, and Motion will automatically register the motion and perform the requested task. However, should you want to simply drag an object around in the Canvas, you'll need to press and hold the pen to select the object you want to move, pause briefly, and then drag to move the object. If you simply tap with the pen and try to move the object without pausing, Motion will think you're trying to initiate a gesture instead.

▶   "Hold down trigger for gesture"—When you use this option, gestures will be generated only if a modifier trigger button or key is pressed in conjunction with the movement of the pen. If the pen is pressed without the designated modifier's being held down, the movement will be treated as a standard mouse movement instead of a gesture.

The modifier can be a key on the keyboard or one of the buttons on the side of the pen. The pens usually come with a rocker switch located right where your fingers grip them—pushing toward the nib of the pen triggers button one, pushing toward the top of the pen triggers button two. The default trigger is the Control key. It works well, assuming that the keyboard is close to the pen.

NOTE ▶ If you plan to use one of the pen buttons as a trigger, you must set that button to be ignored in the tablet's preferences (for Wacom tablets this is found in Applications > Wacom). It's also a good idea to set your tablet's preferences so that the other button functions as a right click. That way, you can use it to access Motion's contextual menus.

▶ "Allow gestures in the air"—With this option selected, you don't actually need to press on the tablet. As long as the modifier key is depressed, simply hovering the pen over the tablet will trigger the gestures. If that's your kind of thing, then more power to you.

It's up to you to decide which method you prefer. With standard Ink settings, you run the risk of drawing gestures when you're trying to move objects and sliders (remember, in this mode you need to press, then briefly pause to tell Motion that you're moving something rather than gesturing). With a modifier button or key, it requires a bit more coordination to press the modifier at the same time as you initiate the gesture.

8 Set Input Method to "Use standard Ink settings" and close the Preferences window.

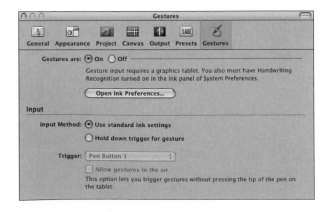

Now let's try out a few gestures.

Working with Gestures

Let's open a project and take it for a spin. For this exercise we'll be working with no trigger. Once you've got a feel for it, you might want to go back to Motion's preferences and try working with a trigger to see which method you prefer.

1   Close all open projects by pressing Cmd-Option-W.

2   Press Cmd-O to open **A.GestureTest**, located in the folder APTS_Motion > Lessons > Lesson08.

This is a project made up of elements from the Cinematíve closer.

3   In a single pen stroke, press and drag in the Canvas to create the following caret shape, and then lift the pen:

If you drew your gesture correctly, your project should now be playing back (remember, it may take a couple of times through the Timeline to cache the elements and achieve reasonable playback).

Notice how an "ink" line is temporarily drawn to show you what you've written on the screen.

4   Draw a straight stroke directly down the screen, and then lift the pen.

Playback should halt.

5   Draw a stroke from left to right (like a minus sign).

The playhead should move forward one frame.

6   Draw a stroke from right to left.

The playhead should move back to the previous frame.

7   Draw a clockwise circle.

The Canvas zooms in.

8   Draw a counterclockwise circle.

The Canvas zooms out.

By now you should be getting the idea. Just by drawing simple symbols on the tablet it's possible to perform most of the basic interface functions in Motion. But what if you just want to use the pen like a regular mouse to, say, drag and select objects?

9   Press down on one of the solid parts of the wheel in the top right of the
    Canvas. Pause for a moment, and then drag it down and to the left to relo-
    cate it.

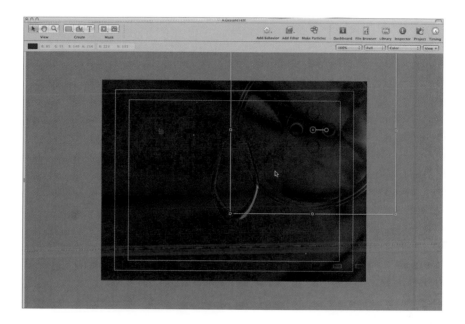

    If you paused long enough, the wheel should have moved down and to the
    left. If not, Motion would have thought you were drawing a gesture, and
    the gesture "ink" would have appeared on the Canvas.

10 If you succeeded in moving the wheel, press Cmd-Z to undo the move,
    restoring the wheel to its correct location.

11 Practice step 9 again, experimenting with pauses of different durations to
    get a feel for how long you need to hold before dragging.

    So far we've looked at only a handful of gestures for driving Motion. The
    following section reveals all the gestures available to you.

Exploring the Gestures Dictionary

Shown below are diagrams for all the gestures built into Motion for driving the interface. The best way to get familiar with gestures is to immerse yourself in them. It's a good idea to set aside a couple of hours to explore each one in turn and then try to use them for an entire project, to begin moving them from conscious memory to "muscle memory."

So enjoy, and just think of all the medical bills you'll be avoiding by rescuing your mouse hand from carpal tunnel syndrome.

Playback Control Gestures

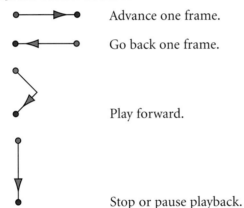

Advance one frame.

Go back one frame.

Play forward.

Stop or pause playback.

General Navigation Gestures

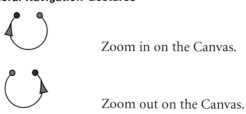

Zoom in on the Canvas.

Zoom out on the Canvas.

Select the Zoom tool.

Select the Pan tool.

Set the Canvas to Home (100%).

Fit the Canvas in the window.

Show/hide the Timing pane.

Show/hide the Project pane.

Show/hide the Inspector.

Show/hide the File Browser.

Show/hide the Library.

General Commands

 Undo.

 Redo.

 Delete the selected object.

 Choose the Select tool.

 Show/hide the Dashboard.

 Copy.

 Paste.

Timeline Navigation and Editing Gestures

Go to the start of the play range.

Go to the end of the play range.

Go to the start of the project.

Go to the end of the project.

Go to the start of the currently selected object.

Go to the end of the currently selected object.

Group.

Ungroup.

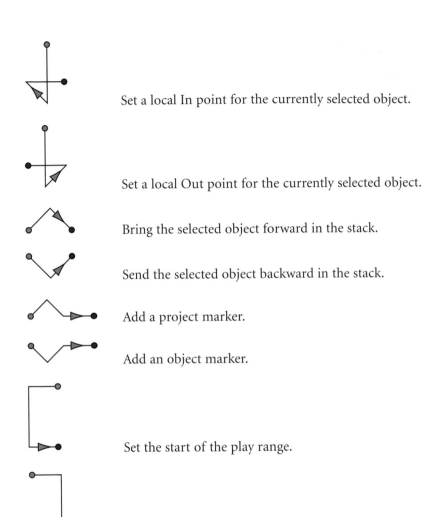

Set a local In point for the currently selected object.

Set a local Out point for the currently selected object.

Bring the selected object forward in the stack.

Send the selected object backward in the stack.

Add a project marker.

Add an object marker.

Set the start of the play range.

Set the end of the play range.

What You've Learned

- ▶ Gestures are shapes drawn with a stylus that can be used to control the Motion interface.

- ▶ Gestures require Ink to be activated in the Mac OS X System Preferences.

- ▶ You can set a button or press a key to trigger gestures, or activate gesture detection whenever you move the stylus.

9

Lesson Files   APTS_Motion > Lessons > Lesson09

Time   This lesson takes approximately 45 minutes to complete.

Goals   Learn how to generate a key in Motion

Refine a key with the parameters in Primatte RT

Apply a Matte Choker

Create a garbage matte using the masking tools

Apply a Zoom Blur effect

Keying

So far we've been quite happily layering objects on top of each other in our composites. That's because for the most part the objects we've been compositing have had alpha channels that tell Motion which parts of an object should look opaque and which parts should be transparent. A problem arises when you want to composite an image without an alpha channel. In such situations you need to create one. One way to do this is by "pulling a key."

Look at the following photograph. We want to composite the woman in the image over another background. So how does Motion know which parts of the image to keep and which parts to throw away? With a *matte*, also known as a *key*, we can tell Motion what to use and what to discard.

Creating a key is like cutting holes in a piece of cardboard and then laying it over the top of a photograph. The only parts of the photograph you'll see are the ones showing through the holes. The following figure is a key for the photograph on the preceding page: The white area corresponds to the part of the image we want to keep; the black area corresponds to the part we want Motion to cut away, so that we can replace it with a different background.

NOTE ▶ There's often confusion when talking about mattes, keys, and alphas. Use of the term *matte* developed in the film world, while the term *key* initially referred to a video process. Both words effectively mean the same thing. An *alpha* is simply a matte that's been "attached" to an image or a movie file. It's given a special channel, called (believe it or not) the *alpha channel*. It sits alongside the red, green, and blue channels, which contain the color data of the image.

Creating a good key is an art unto itself, and it tends to be associated with visual-effects compositing rather than motion graphics. Applications like Apple's Shake therefore provide greater flexibility and finesse for completing greenscreen and bluescreen shots. Nonetheless, Motion ships with some capable keyers, and the real-time performance of these keyers actually offers a level of interactivity unavailable in many visual-effects-oriented software applications.

Pulling a Key

Pulling a good key entails a tradeoff: You want a solid contrast between the foreground black and background white while also preserving a nice feathered edge on the foreground so that it blends smoothly with the new background (the one that's replacing the green or blue you're removing). For this exercise, we'll be using Primatte RT, a sophisticated yet easy-to-use plug-in that comes bundled with Motion.

Preparing a High-Definition Project

Before we start keying, we need to make sure the project is set up appropriately for the footage we're using.

1   Press Cmd-Option-W to close any open projects.

2   Press Cmd-N to open the New Project dialog.

The footage we'll be using was shot with a Panasonic VariCam on the DVCPRO HD format, so we'll need to choose a project to match.

3   From the Preset pop-up menu, choose DVCPRO HD 720p24, and then click OK.

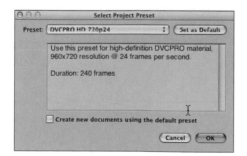

NOTE ▶ If the Select Project Preset dialog fails to appear, close the project that was created automatically and press Cmd-Option-N. At some point in the past you must have checked the "Create new documents using the default preset" box in the Select Project Preset dialog. Pressing Cmd-Option-N opens the dialog so that you can choose a different preset.

4   In the File Browser, navigate to the folder APTS_Motion > Lessons > Lesson09. Drag **NewBeginningBG** into the Layers tab, or drag it into the Canvas and snap it to the center guides. *(BG* stands for *background.)*

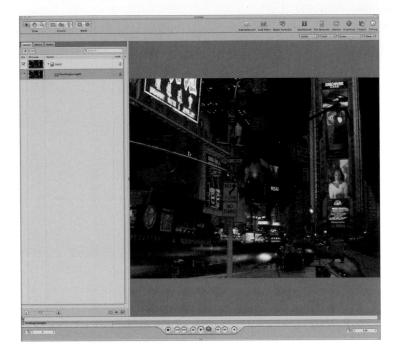

5   Make sure that Correct for Aspect Ratio is checked in the View menu at the top right of the Canvas.

The DVCPRO HD 720p24 preset assumes a size of 960x720. That's because it scales the image horizontally by a factor of 1.33 before display-ing it. This is referred to as *anamorphic footage*. It means that the pixels of the stored image are nonsquare. (For more information on nonsquare pixels, see Appendix A.) Once Motion stretches the footage for display, the *effective* screen resolution is 1280x720.

TIP ▶ If you're working with 720p HD footage created natively at 1280x720, you'll need to create your own custom preset in Motion's preferences. See "Creating, Editing, and Deleting Presets" in the Motion user guide.

Let's face it: HD is big. Even 720p—the humbler version of HD—has an effective screen resolution of 1280x720. So there's a good chance you won't be able to fit the whole image on your screen, especially with the Layers tab visible.

6   In the upper-right corner of the Canvas, change the Zoom level to 50%.

7   Drag **NewBeginningFG** from the File Browser into the Canvas and release when it snaps to the center guides. *(FG stands for *foreground*.)*

TIP To make it easier to read the names of files, you may want to click the List View button at the top of the File Browser.

8   Shift-drag the playhead until it snaps to the end of the NewBeginningFG bar in the mini-Timeline.

The playhead snaps to frame 60. Shift-dragging the playhead is a good way to quickly get to the start or end of a clip.

9   In the bottom-right corner of the Canvas, set the project duration to 60.

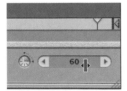

You could have simply set the play range Out point to 60, but in this case we know our footage finishes at frame 60, so why not set the project to exactly that length?

10 Begin playback.

When the Timeline has played through once, the two pieces of footage should be cached, and you'll be able to watch the composite in real time. (However, right now you'll be able to see only the greenscreen—the background will be fully obscured.)

Applying Primatte RT

Primatte RT is a surprisingly capable keyer, given the simplicity of its interface. It presents you with a grand total of three sliders to adjust when you're pulling a key. One of the things Primatte RT does to help with the process is automatically analyze the background to determine the color you're trying to key out. We know the shot we're looking at is a greenscreen, but Primatte RT needs to determine that it's a greenscreen and not, say, a bluescreen.

> **TIP** ▶ If you've fallen behind, feel free to open the project **A.FootageAdded** to catch up.

1 Make sure that NewBeginningFG is selected in the Layers tab, and then click the Add Filter button at the top of the Canvas and choose Keying > Primatte RT.

Congratulations—you've pulled a key! The woman looks as if she's contracted an alien flesh-eating virus, but at least the green background is gone.

When you applied the Primatte RT filter, it analyzed the frame and determined that green needed to be keyed out. However, at frame 1 only a small portion of the screen is green—the rest is filled with our talent and the studio background around the screen. To help Primatte RT generate the most accurate key, we should find a frame with more green to analyze.

2   Stop playback and set the playhead to frame 10.

Frame 10 shows a much larger area of green screen, so it'll give Primatte RT the best chance of determining the correct color to key out.

3   In the Dashboard (press F7 to reveal it if it's hidden), click the Green button for Auto Sample.

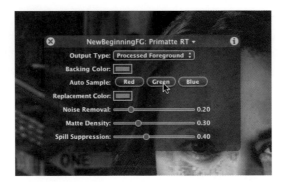

You may notice only a subtle change in the image, but the new Auto Sample values should help when we start to finesse the key.

Now, about that alien flesh-eating disease our talent has contracted: It's the cumulative result of parts of the image being keyed out by mistake, and overzealous spill suppression. We'll fix both of these problems in turn.

4   Resume playback.

Primatte RT is a real-time keyer—let's take advantage of the fact. Now that you're viewing the full playback, you can see all kinds of problems. It looks like that virus has spread to her teeth. We could start adjusting the three sliders—Noise Removal, Matte Density, and Spill Suppression—but there's a better way to see what we're doing.

5   In the Dashboard, set the Output Type to Matte.

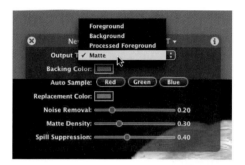

The Matte Output Type lets you see the black-and-white matte (that is, the key) that Primatte RT has generated. For the composite to work correctly, the foreground should appear pure white (unless it includes something semi-transparent, such as a raincoat, in which case you'd expect some gray values in the matte), and the background should appear opaque black. The Matte Output Type is a useful diagnostic tool, since problems with the matte can sometimes hide in the background that you're adding to the shot.

In the current example, our foreground matte is looking anything but opaque. Wherever you see gray, the background will partially show through (that's the source of our flesh-eating disease).

6   Drag the Noise Removal slider all the way to 0.

It appears we've made things worse. Now the background is no longer an opaque black. If we leave this as is, some of the original greenscreen will be added to the final composite, which is not good. We'll fix that in a moment, but first let's fix the gray in the woman's face.

7   Drag the Matte Density slider to the left until the foreground becomes opaque white (a value of around 0.23).

The Matte Density increases the contrast of the matte, making the whites whiter and the blacks blacker.

You will still see two black specks where the woman's eyes should be. These are the specular highlights on the eyes, which have accidentally been keyed out. Fortuitously, the background going in behind her is dark enough to hide this problem, so we can ignore it. (If you had to fix it, you would need to create what's called a *holdout matte* to prevent the specular highlights from being keyed.)

8   Drag the Noise Removal slider back to the right until most of the noise around the foreground has dropped to black (a value of around 0.17).

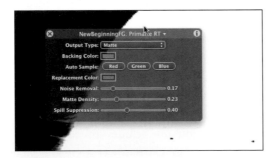

The Noise Removal slider removes pixels from the matte that are close to the original backing color.

9   Change the Output Type to Processed Foreground.

OK, so no flesh-eating disease, but the magenta's a touch strong. What's happened here is that Primatte RT has been a little too eager to remove the green spill and has pushed the colors in the opposite direction.

Whenever you shoot bluescreen or greenscreen images, some of the blue or green lighting inevitably spills over onto the subject you're trying to key. As part of the keying process, it's essential to remove this excess color from the image. In our case it's green spill, and Primatte RT has automatically removed it, albeit to an extreme degree.

10 In the Dashboard, drag the Spill Suppression slider to the left until the color of the foreground looks appropriate (a value of around 0.25).

The Spill Suppression now looks much more natural. You may notice, however, that the contrast of our talent is much flatter than the contrast of the background. That's because the gamma of the greenscreen footage doesn't match the gamma of the background. (Different film and video formats have different response curves to compensate for variations in output devices—well, that's the short story, anyway.)

11 Click the Add Filter button at the top of the Canvas and choose Color Correction > Gamma.

The woman now blends much more naturally into her background.

12 In the Dashboard (F7), set the Gamma to about 0.7.

Treating the Edges

One of the biggest problems in pulling a key is to have the edges convincingly blend with the background. As mentioned at the start of the lesson, visual-effects compositing applications such as Apple's Shake provide far more sophisticated methods for finessing bluescreens and greenscreens. Nonetheless, Motion has a few tricks we can employ to clean up the edges.

One thing we have going for us is that the composite is surreal. We're not trying to suspend disbelief in the audience and convince it that this woman is standing in the middle of a real street. The background is obviously fantastic (meaning "of or pertaining to fantasy," not that it would nicely match your mother's chiffon scarf), and so an audience might forgive here a composite that would look disconcerting in, say, a gritty cop show.

Choking the Matte

If you look at the right side of the woman, you'll see a faint ring of noise around her hair. This is a result of a color shift in the greenscreen background close to the edges of the subject. A common solution to this problem is to *choke* the matte. Choking is the process of trimming away pixels around the edges of an image to remove unwanted pixels.

NOTE ▶ Choking a matte necessarily destroys some edge detail, especially in cases like this, where there are lots of fine, loose strands of hair. More-sophisticated keying techniques (using multiple keys) can remedy many edge problems without the need to choke the matte, but such techniques are beyond the scope of this lesson.

TIP ▶ If you've fallen behind, feel free to open the project **B.KeyedAndClrCorrected** to catch up.

1   Select NewBeginningFG in the Layers tab (F5).

2   Click the Add Filter button at the top of the Canvas and choose Matte > Matte Choker.

As soon as you apply the Matte Choker filter, you should see a change in your image. The Matte Choker chews away at the edges of the matte, cutting away the border pixels of the foreground image.

3   In the Dashboard (F7), move the Edge Thin slider all the way to the right.

As you drag the slider to the right, you're trimming off, or "choking," more of the pixels at the edge of the matte. The result is far too extreme, and the default value of 0 seems preferable.

4   Press Cmd-Z to undo the change to the Edge Thin, reverting its value to 0.00.

The Matte Choker helps "sell" our problematic edge, but now take a look at the woman's hair on the left side of the image. As you play back the sequence, you'll notice that the edges of her hair have been unnaturally darkened. If you look at her exposed ear, you may even see speckling where the Matte Choker has caused holes to emerge in the matte.

5　Toggle the Matte Choker on and off in the Layers tab to view the affected and unaffected versions of the composite.

In this case, the cure seems worse than the ailment; we can fix one side of our composite at the expense of the other. There's always a solution, of course, and we'll get to it a little later in the lesson. First, let's make sure the Matte Choker is on.

6　Toggle the Matte Choker on in the Layers tab.

Creating a Garbage Matte

No doubt you've noticed that at the beginning and end of our clip, the "studio" (all right, the computer lab) in which the shoot took place is visible. Obviously, the lab isn't supposed to be in the shot, so we need to remove it, leaving just the woman in the center and the cityscape behind her. To remove the lab from the composite, we'll create what's called a *garbage matte*. Garbage mattes are used to cut away the unwanted "garbage" from a shot.

In Motion, garbage mattes can be created using layer masks. There are four types of layer masks: rectangular, elliptical, Bezier, and B-spline. (The first two are simple preset shapes made from Bezier points, but let's not worry about that right now.)

Layer masks are mattes that tell Motion which parts of an object to keep and which parts to throw away. Now that we've carefully pulled our key, we can use a layer mask to quickly cut away the garbage around it.

> **TIP** ▶ If you've fallen behind, feel free to open the project **C.Choked** to catch up.

1   Select NewBeginningFG in the Layers tab.

2   Click the Rectangle Mask tool in the top-left corner of the Canvas.

> **NOTE** ▶ In the following exercises, be careful to choose the Mask tools, not the Create tools. Both types of tools can be used to build shapes, but shapes made with the Create tools can't be applied as layer masks. They'll simply be separate objects in the Layers tab.

3   Stop playback and press Home to return to frame 1 in the Timeline.

4   In the Canvas, drag from the upper left of the woman's head down to below her right hip and then release. This is called a *marquee drag*.

> **TIP** ▶ You may want to zoom out to see the gray space around the composite.

The room around the woman should have disappeared, revealing the NewBeginningBG cityscape behind it. We've basically told Motion, "Keep the stuff inside this box. Anything outside the box is garbage." Because we applied the layer mask to our NewBeginningFG object, only the foreground was affected. The NewBeginningBG clip is still intact.

The rectangle would work fine for this shot, but for the sake of demonstrating workflow, let's use the free-form shape tools to finish the job.

5 In the Layers tab, select Rectangle Mask.

Notice that the mask has been added as an extra element underneath NewBeginningFG. It's just like a filter or behavior; it belongs to the NewBeginningFG object.

TIP ▶ Notice the small square that appears to the right of the NewBeginningFG label. It allows you to enable or disable a mask for the object, and it works just like the filter and behavior enable/disable buttons.

6 Press Delete to remove the Rectangle Mask from the object.

TIP ▶ To access the Elliptical Mask tool (also known as the Circle tool), click and hold the Rectangle Mask tool button.

7 Reselect NewBeginningFG, and then click the Bezier Mask tool to select it.

Bezier shapes are made by creating a bunch of points and then joining them to make a closed shape. Don't worry—you'll see in just a moment.

8 Click in the gray space below and to the left of the woman to create a point.

> **TIP** You may want to zoom out to see the gray space around the composite.

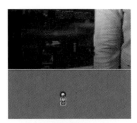

9 Click again just above and to the left of her shoulder to create another point.

It would be nice to create a single point above her head, but if you draw a straight line to that point, it might actually cut part of her head off. Instead, we'll create a Bezier point. To create a Bezier point, simply click and drag the mouse instead of clicking and immediately releasing.

10 Position the pointer just above the woman's head; then click and drag outward to the left to create a curve to the new point.

11 Click to create another point just above and to the right of her other shoulder.

12 Click to create another point just below and to the right of the woman in the gray space outside the Canvas.

13 To close the curve and create the shape, click your starting point.

TIP ▶ When creating shapes, you may find the snapping lines to be more of a hindrance than a help. Pressing N will deactivate snapping; pressing it again will reactivate snapping when you're done adjusting your shape. You can also turn snapping on and off in the View menu. A checkmark next to the command indicates when snapping is on.

Using a Bezier shape, we're able to create a closer fit to the actual contours of our talent. We could have added more points to make the shape fit even closer. In that case, however, we would risk cutting off some of her hair as it flows outward in future frames, so we're better off with a looser shape.

Let's take a look at a few other features of Bezier shapes.

14 Save the project as **A.GarbageMatteCreated** in the APTS_Motion > Lessons > Lesson09 > Student Saves folder.

> **NOTE** ▶ If you want to check your work, we've created **D.GarbageMatteCreated**, a saved file at this point for you to return to.

15 Click the Bezier point above the woman's head.

The lines emerging from either side of the point are called *Bezier handles*. They enable you to adjust the slope of the curve going into and out of the point.

16 Click and drag around the hollow circle at the end of one of the Bezier handles.

The handle pulls in and out, adjusting the slope of the curve as it does. As it moves up or down, it adjusts the angle of the curve coming into it.

17 Option-click the end of one of the handles and drag it.

This time both handles pull in and out, even though you're adjusting only one of them.

18 Cmd-click and then drag the end of one of the handles.

This time the angle of the curve is changed only for the handle you're adjusting. The other handle remains fixed.

19 Cmd-click and drag the handle again.

The two handles are once again uniformly adjusted.

20 Option-click a part of the shape outline where there is no point.

A new point is created.

21 With the new point still selected, press Delete.

The new point is deleted. You can click or marquee-drag through several points to select them, and then press Delete to remove them from the shape.

22 Right- or Ctrl-click one of the straight points to the side of the shape. Choose Smooth from the pop-up menu.

The straight, or *linear*, point has now been converted into a *smooth* point—that is, a point with Bezier handles. Alternately, you can use this menu to convert smooth points to linear points.

OK, now that you've made a mess, it's time to create the garbage matte for real.

23 Press Cmd-Option-W to close the project. When prompted, choose Don't Save.

24 Open the project you saved to the StudentSaves folder in step 14, **A.GarbageMatteCreated**.

NOTE ▸ If you did not create the file, either open **D.GarbageMatteCreated** in the APTS_Motion > Lessons > Lesson09 folder, or rebuild the matte using steps 7–13.

Notice that after you've reloaded the project, the shape now has the standard scale handles around the edges. If you tried, you'd be unable to edit individual points on the curve. That's because when Motion opens a project, it defaults to the Select/Transform tool, the tool you use most commonly in Motion to select objects and move them around the Canvas. If you want to edit the points on your shape, you'll need to use another tool, the Adjust Control Points tool.

25 Click and hold the mouse on the Select/Transform tool at the top left of the Canvas, and choose the second tool from the bottom—the Adjust Control Points tool.

The individual points of the curve are available again for editing.

26 Resume playback.

Keyframing the Garbage Matte

You'll notice that we have a major problem with our garbage matte. It's fine at frame 1, but as the camera zooms in over subsequent frames, it becomes too cramped for our star, who receives an unintentional haircut. We need the garbage matte to expand outward as the camera zooms in, and then to contract when the camera zooms back out. We can do this by *keyframing*.

Lesson 12 will explore the concept of keyframes in great detail, but for now you can just think of them as snapshots in time. We'll create snapshots of the size of the mask at different frames and let Motion interpolate the mask between those snapshots. The snapshots will be created using the Record Animation mode.

> **TIP** ▶ If you've fallen behind, feel free to open the project **D.GarbageMatteCreated** to catch up.

1   Make sure the Mask is selected in the Layers tab.

2   Stop playback and move the playhead back to frame 1.

3   Click the Record button at the bottom of the Canvas to activate it. It should illuminate red.

When Record Animation mode is activated, any changes to the properties of an object, filter, mask, or behavior will create a keyframe (that is, a "snapshot") at that position in time. This is a quick way to create keyframes as you work.

NOTE ▶ The hot key for turning the Record Animation mode on and off is A. Unfortunately, this is also the hot key for switching to the Select tool in Final Cut Pro. If you're a Final Cut Pro user, be careful that you don't turn on Record Animation and set keyframes when you really mean to switch to the Select/Transform tool (press Shift-S).

You could start dragging the individual points of the shape outward as the camera zooms in, but it's easier just to scale the whole shape out instead. To do this, we need the standard Select/Transform tool.

4   Press Shift-S, the hot key to activate that tool.

If you were still using the Adjust Control Points tool from the previous exercise, you'll see the icon change back to the Select/Transform tool icon in the top left of the Canvas.

5   Move to frame 10.

6   Press Option-Shift and drag outward one of the hollow scaling circles on the mask's bounding box. Stop when you're satisfied that the mask shape is big enough to avoid clipping the woman's hair or shoulders.

7   Scrub through the Timeline from frames 1 through 10.

You'll see that the shape automatically grows from the original position you set up at frame 1 to the new size we just set at frame 10.

8 Move to frame 13 and resize the shape outward again. (It should almost fill the frame.)

Now, from frame 13 through 46, the camera stays zoomed in at the same position. Assuming your shape is wide enough (pay careful attention to the hair in the lower left of the Canvas to make sure that some of it isn't cropped by your shape at certain frames), there's no need to add keyframes during this time.

After frame 46, the camera zooms out again. We need to anchor the size of the mask at frame 46 so that Motion knows not to change the shape between frames 13 and 46. We can then continue to keyframe the size of the shape after that point.

9   Move to frame 46.

10   Option-Shift-drag one of the scaling circles outward very slightly, release the mouse, and then Option-Shift-drag it right back to where it started. (Don't worry if it's not precisely in the same location.)

What we've done here is *jiggle* the point—we really haven't altered the scale of the shape. We changed it, but then we immediately changed it back. What this does is force Motion to set a keyframe there for the shape's size. Now when we change the shape at later frames, the shape won't change between frames 13 and 46.

We're about to shrink the matte again as the camera zooms out. If we hadn't jiggled the point, the shape would begin shrinking from frame 13, since that would be the last keyframe recorded. This would start to crop our image. Now that there's a keyframe at frame 46, that's where the scaling down will begin.

11   Move to frame 59 and resize the matte down so that all of the garbage is removed from the frame. Pay careful attention to the bottom edges of (what used to be) the computer lab to make sure they are cleanly cropped out.

12 Resume playback.

The matte should now entirely eliminate the garbage around the edges of the greenscreen, without cropping away any of our talent. If you see any problems with your matte, simply locate the problem position in time and then make adjustments to the matte to fix it. The adjustments should be automatically keyframed to solve the problem.

13 Click the Record button to turn off the Record Animation mode, or press A.

Fixing the Choke Problem

When we applied the Matte Choker earlier, we noted that it fixed one side of the image while damaging the other. We can use another layer mask to solve the problem.

> **TIP** If you've fallen behind, feel free to open the project **E.MaskAnimated** to catch up.

1 In the Layers tab, select Layer and press Cmd-D to duplicate it.

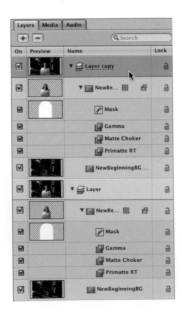

We now have two identical versions of the composite.

NOTE ▶ Make sure the Record Animation mode is off from the previous exercise.

2   Select the Rectangle Mask tool.

3   Rename Layer copy *No Choke*, and Layer *Choke*.

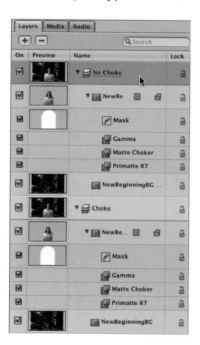

4 With No Choke selected, draw a mask around the left side of the Canvas using the Rectangle Mask tool, passing through the center of the woman's nose.

5 Press F4 to jump to the Mask tab of the Inspector.

6 Set the Feather to around 27.

7 Uncheck the box to the left of Choke to toggle its visibility off.

We've masked off the right half of the woman in our copied layer, called No Choke.

8   Uncheck the box for the Matte Choker filter attached to the New-BeginningFG copy object that's part of the No Choke layer.

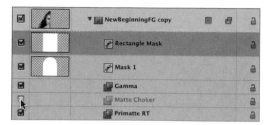

The choke is no longer active, and therefore not adversely affecting the hairline on the left side of the composite.

9   Turn the visibility of the Choke layer back on.

Now you have the best of both worlds: The left side of your image is unaffected by the Matte Choker, while the right side of the image has the choker applied—exactly where it's needed. Because we set the Feather of the Rectangle Mask to 27, there's a soft transition from the unchoked version to the choked version.

Adding a Zoom Blur

The shot you've just keyed was created with a technique called *ramping*, in which the speed of the footage changes over time. It's equivalent to adjusting the crank of a 35mm film camera. As a result, the zoom in and zoom out look stilted—the natural blur that would occur from such a fast zoom isn't visible in the shot. No problem. We'll add our own blur.

The blur should affect the entire shot, so we'll need to apply the filter to a master layer containing everything.

TIP   If you've fallen behind, feel free to open the project **F.ChokeFixed** to catch up.

1   Click the disclosure triangles to the left of No Choke and Choke to hide the contents of both layers.

2   Press Cmd-A to select both layers.

3   Choose Object > Group (or press Cmd-Shift-G).

Both layers are grouped inside a new, master layer.

4   Make sure that Layer is selected in the Layers tab, click the Add Filter button at the top of the Canvas, and choose Blur > Zoom Blur.

This effect is applied to the entire Canvas, so you don't want Motion pulling black from outside the frame for the blur. We'll fix this in Zoom Blur's properties.

5   Press F3 to open the Filters tab of the Inspector. Check the Crop box.

6 Move to frame 1. Press A to turn on the Record Animation mode (or click the Record button at the bottom of the Canvas).

7 In the Dashboard (F7), drag the Amount slider to 0.

The zoom is well on its way by frame 5, so let's add a keyframe with the blur on at that frame.

8 Move to frame 5 in the Timeline, and drag the Amount slider to 3.

By frame 9, the camera's flying in.

9 Move to frame 9 in the Timeline, and drag the Amount slider to 5.

The camera starts to slow down at frame 11.

10 Move to frame 11 in the Timeline, and drag the Amount slider to 3.

The camera comes to a jarring halt at frame 13.

11 Move to frame 13 in the Timeline, and drag the Amount slider to 0.

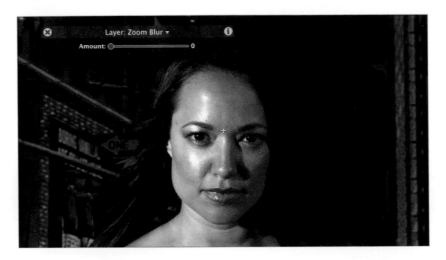

12 Resume playback.

The motion now looks much smoother. Let's add the keyframes for the journey back out.

13 Move to frame 46.

14 Drag the Amount slider to a value other than 0.

15 Drag the Amount slider back to 0.

There's that jiggle again, forcing a keyframe with a value of 0 at frame 46.

16 Set the following keyframes:

Frame	Amount
49	3
54	5
57	3
60	0

17 Turn off Record Animation mode (press A).

That's a wrap. Render a RAM preview and take a look.

What You've Learned

▶ A key is used to tell Motion which parts of an image should be visible and which parts should be transparent.

▶ The Gamma filter can be used to correct the contrast of video content from different sources.

▶ The Matte Choker filter can trim away unwanted pixels from the edges of a key.

▶ Layers can be duplicated to localize effects to a certain area of the image.

▶ A Zoom Blur simulates the motion blur resulting from a camera's zooming into or out of a scene.

Keyboard Shortcuts

N	toggles snapping on/off in the Canvas
Shift-S	selects the Select/Transform tool
A	toggles Record Animation on/off
Cmd-A	selects all

10

Lesson Files APTS_Motion > Lessons > Lesson10

Bonus Files APTS_Motion > Lessons > Lesson10 > BonusFiles

Time This lesson takes approximately 60 minutes to complete.

Goals Assemble the final Cinematíve project

Perform basic nonlinear edits using the Motion Timeline

Automate a lens-flare effect

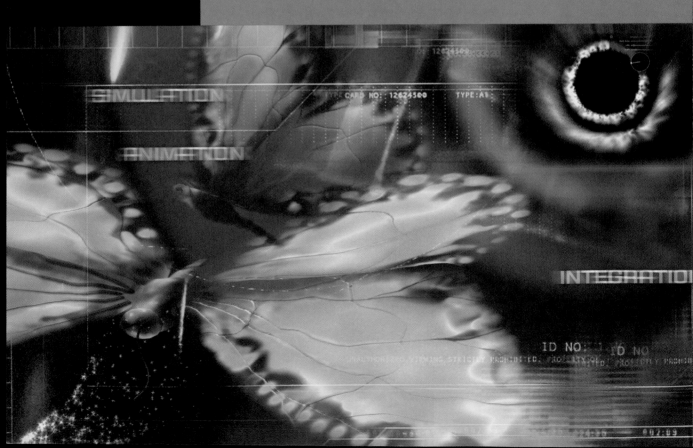

Nonlinear Editing

Until now, we've been working with the standard definition of the Cinematíve project. In this lesson we'll be assembling the final project in HD. One of the great things about Motion's behavior-based approach to animation is that it makes repurposing content very easy. In keyframe-based systems, trying to track down every last keyframe that needs tweaking is truly tedious.

For this lesson, we've gone ahead and formatted the previous projects for HD, but you're welcome to go back and make the changes yourself. If you'd like to look at the final version before we begin, open APTS_Motion > Lessons > Lesson10 > **FinalCinematíve.mov**.

Normally you'd edit a large project using a nonlinear editor such as Final Cut Pro HD, but in this case the edits are relatively minor, so Motion is more than capable of taking care of them.

Assembling the Video

Motion makes some rudimentary editing tools accessible via the Timeline. Let's set up a project and take a look.

1   Press Cmd-N to start a new project.

2   In the Select Project Preset dialog that appears, choose DVCPRO HD 720p24 from the Preset pop-up menu and click OK.

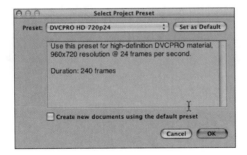

3   Click the Duration icon (the clock) to the left of the Duration field at the lower right of the Canvas.

This switches from displaying time in frames to displaying time in SMPTE timecode—that is, to showing the time in hours, minutes, seconds, and frames, with each unit separated by a colon.

4   Click in the Duration field and type *30.00;* then press Return.

When you press Return, Motion converts your 30.00 into the timecode 00:00:30:00. Your project length is now exactly 30 seconds. Changing to timecode instead of using a frame count makes it a lot easier to set a project length of 30 seconds. Otherwise you would have to pull out the calculator and multiply 24 by 30, and who wants to do that?

> **TIP** ▶ As you've just seen, you type only as many numbers as you need when entering timecode. Since we wanted a 30-second project, there was no need to enter hours or minutes, so we only typed *30.00.* Also, even though timecode is written with colons between the unit measurements, using a period when entering the values is easier (no shifting required).

5   Make sure you're at frame 1 (if not, press Home).

6   In the File Browser, navigate to APTS_Motion > Lessons > Lesson10 and drag **NewBeginning.mov** into the center of the Canvas.

You've just added the first clip to the project. It's now time to add the soundtrack.

7   From the File Browser, drag **CinematíveSoundtrack.aif** into the Canvas.

8   Play back the project from frame 1.

You'll notice that the woman's mouth is moving, but there's no sound. That's because we need to add an overdub audio file for her lines.

9   Move back to frame 1 (Home), and from the File Browser drag **NewBeginningVO.wav** into the Canvas.

10   Play back the project again.

Our talent has found her voice. It's now time to perform the first edit. We'll do it in the Timeline.

11   Press F6 to open the Timing pane, and make sure you're looking at the Timeline tab.

The Timeline tab consists of two sections—the layers list to the left, and the Timeline itself. The layers list is a mirror of the Layers tab we've been working with up to now. The Timeline contains tracks for every object and layer in the project.

Notice that there are currently two seemingly identical tracks in the Timeline—one for Layer and one for NewBeginning. The way the Timeline is laid out can be a little confusing at first. The track for a layer contains icons and labels for the topmost object in the layer. Right now we're seeing NewBeginning's icon and label because it's the only object currently in Layer. As we add more clips, you'll see other labels listed in the Layer track alongside NewBeginning.

When performing basic edits such as insert and overwrite, use the Layer track as the point of insertion—Motion will figure out which clips inside that layer need to be adjusted to correctly perform the edit.

We're now going to insert our next clip at timecode 2:07, or 2 seconds and 7 frames in.

12 Move the playhead to timecode 00:00:02:07 by typing *2.07* into the Current Frame field, located at the bottom left of the Canvas.

13 From the File Browser, drag **Quirky.mov** onto the Layer track in the Timeline window. Move it to the right until the tooltip that appears reads 00:00:02:07, *but don't release the mouse.*

As you continue to hold down the mouse, the following menu appears:

This menu allows you to choose from three possible options:

▶ Composite—This option edits the new object on top of any other object in the current layer. If the new object contains transparent areas, the objects already in the Timeline will still be visible.

▶ Insert—This option inserts your footage at the selected frame. Any footage already in the layer will be split at that point and pushed down the Timeline until after the footage you're inserting.

▶ Overwrite—This option inserts the new object and replaces any footage already existing in the Timeline. Sections of existing footage overlapping with the new clip are deleted.

14 Choose Composite and release the mouse.

The new clip, Quirky, appears in the Timeline without affecting our first clip, NewBeginning.

We need to trim Quirky so that it starts right after the NewBeginning clip finishes.

15 Shift-drag the playhead at the top of the Timeline until it snaps to the end of the NewBeginning clip (frame 00:00:02:11).

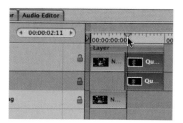

If we set the In point of the Quirky clip here, we'll be covering up the last frame of NewBeginning. We need to move forward one frame.

16 Press the right arrow key to move to frame 00:00:02:12.

17 With the Quirky clip still selected (click it in the Timeline if you need to select it), press I.

This trims Quirky so that it starts at frame 2:12.

18 Move to frame 00:00:05:00 (type *5.00* into the Current Frame field).

This is the first frame after the Quirky clip finishes.

19 From the File Browser, drag **LeftTurnZoom.mov** into the Timeline and release it as soon as it snaps to the playhead (at frame 5:00).

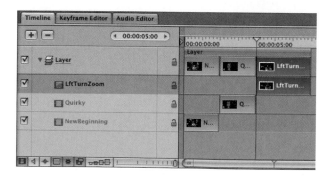

In this case, we didn't pause to allow the Composite/Insert/Overwrite menu to appear. When you just drag and release a new object, Motion defaults to the Composite mode.

It's now time to add the final clip.

20 Move the playhead to 00:00:07:04.

21 From the File Browser, drag **BflyRelease.mov** onto the track labeled Layer in the Timeline (not one of the object tracks beneath it), without releasing the mouse. Snap it to the playhead and wait for the Composite/Insert/Overwrite menu.

NOTE ▶ You must insert the clip over the Layer track, not one of the tracks for the objects contained within the layer. Otherwise, the following Overwrite will not function correctly.

22 Choose Overwrite and release the mouse.

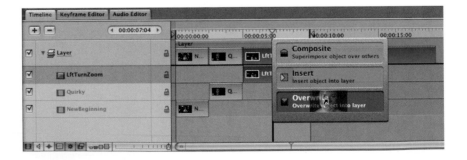

Notice in your Timeline that the LftTurnZoom clip has now been trimmed to end right at the edit point (7:04). That's because it was "over-written" by BFlyRelease.

OK, so we didn't really want to do that. (But it was a great way to demonstrate Overwrite.) We actually want the BFlyRelease clip to fade in over the top of LftTurnZoom.

23 In the Timeline, position your pointer over the right edge of LftTurnZoom.

Your pointer will change into a right-bracket cursor.

24 Click and drag the right edge of the LftTurnZoom clip until it locks to its full length at 00:00:08:17.

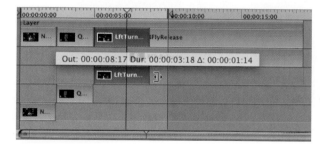

25 Play back the Timeline to take a look.

There's a nice kick drum in the soundtrack at 00:00:07:23, so we'll start fading in BFlyRelease then.

26 Move the playhead to frame 00:00:07:23.

27 Click the BFlyRelease clip in the Timeline to select it.

28 Press I to set the In point of the clip to the current time.

We'll use a behavior to fade the clip in.

29 With BFlyRelease still selected, click the Add Behavior button at the top of the Canvas and choose Basic Motion > Fade In/Fade Out.

30 In the Dashboard (F7), drag the right edge of the left-hand fade triangle until the fade-in is 17 frames long.

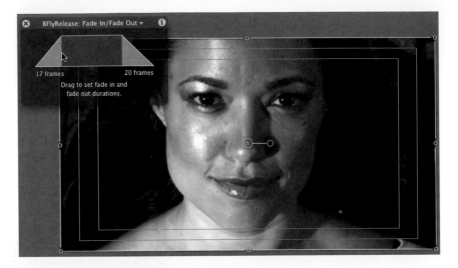

We have 17 frames of overlap between the two clips, so we needed to make sure the fade is complete by the end of the overlap.

No need to worry about the fade-out just yet. We'll deal with that later.

31 Resume playback and take a look.

The main live-action elements have now been edited together.

Bringing On the Butterflies

After all those earlier lessons of turning butterflies into particles, it's time to integrate them into the scene.

> **TIP** ▸ If you've fallen behind, feel free to open the project **B.ClipsAssembled** to catch up.

1 Move to frame 00:00:08:17. Press Cmd-Option-I to set the play range In point.

2   Move to frame 00:00:16:00. Press Cmd-Option-O to set the play range Out point.

This is the new area we're working with, so it's important to set up the play range accordingly.

3   Move to frame 00:00:10:10.

This is where we want the butterflies to emerge.

4   From the File Browser, drag **ButterfliesHD.mov** into the Canvas and release it when it snaps to the center guides.

Chances are, when you released the mouse, you ended up with a black screen. Motion has assumed from the first black frame of the ButterfliesHD movie that it's supposed to be fully opaque. In fact, we want it to be fully transparent (except where the butterflies are, of course). So we need to edit the clip's alpha channel.

5 With the ButterfliesHD clip still selected, press Shift-F.

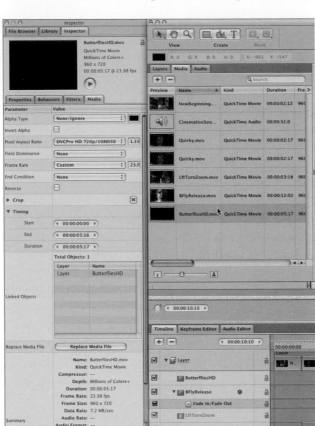

The Media tab of the Inspector is covered in detail in Lesson 7. Right now we're just interested in the Alpha Type pop-up menu, the very first parameter. Motion has incorrectly guessed that we want to ignore the alpha channel (the channel in an image that tells Motion which parts of the image to consider transparent and which parts to consider opaque).

6 Choose Alpha Type > Premultiplied-Black. You should now be able to see the live-action background again.

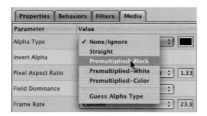

> **TIP** ▶ Don't worry if you have no idea what *premultiplied* means. It's discussed briefly in Lesson 7. If someone ever offers to explain premultiplication to you in more depth, it's worth learning about (as long as the person is well informed). If not, just try the different options until the image looks right. You'll almost always want None/Ignore, Straight, or Premultiplied-Black.

7 Resume playback.

Adding a Lens-Flare Filter

The butterflies are now emerging from the woman's hands on cue, but there's nothing too dramatic about it. Let's add a good old-fashioned lens flare to spice things up.

We want the lens flare to start right when the woman begins opening her hands (frame 10:01).

> **NOTE** ▶ At this point, feel free to set your play range In and Out points to whatever you feel is appropriate for viewing the section of the project you're working on. Remember, Cmd-Option-I sets the play range In point, and Cmd-Option-O sets the Out point.

1 Move to frame 00:00:10:01.

NOTE ▸ If you're still looking at the Media tab of the Inspector, click back over to the Layers tab (or press Cmd-4).

2   In the Layers tab (F5), click BFlyRelease to select it.

3   Click the Add Filter button at the top of the Canvas and choose Stylize > Lens Flare.

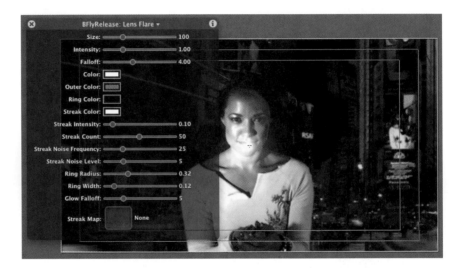

A lens flare is added to the image.

This isn't a horror movie, so we don't need the butterflies to start spewing forth from the woman's mouth.

4   Drag the crosshair at the center of the flare down until it rests in the center of the woman's hands.

NOTE ▸ The astute video students reading this will realize that the woman's hands are half out of Action Safe—a big no-no for something so pivotal to the scene. (It's traditional at this point for the motion graphics artist to blame the director for incorrectly framing the shot. Unfortunately, since the author happens to have shot the footage—albeit in a hurry—he has no one to blame but himself.) The scene should have been shot with room below the hands to ensure that viewers with televisions that crop out lower portions of the image won't miss out on the amazing exploding butterfly extravaganza.

It's now time to animate the flare.

5   Press A to turn on Record Animation mode. (The red Record button should illuminate.)

6   In the Dashboard (F7), drag the Intensity slider to 0.

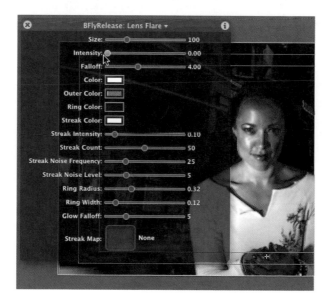

7   Move to frame 00:00:11:15.

8   Set the Intensity slider to 4.0.

9 Set the Size slider to 400.

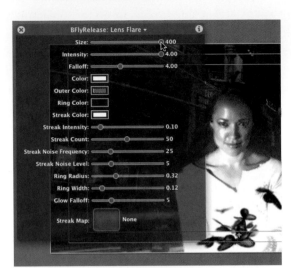

10 Press A to turn off the Record Animation mode.

You now have a nicely animated lens flare to help usher forth the flurry of butterflies.

Adding the Cinematíve Graphics

We need to make a nice transition to the final Cinematíve graphics.

> **TIP** ▶ If you've fallen behind, feel free to open the project **D.LensFlareAdded** to catch up.

1 Move to 00:00:15:00 in the Timeline.

This is where the guitar in the soundtrack begins to slide up, ready for the final "tinkles" as the butterflies explode. It's a perfect place to transition to the graphics.

2 Drag **CinematíveGraphics.mov** out of the File Browser (Cmd-1), and snap it to the center of the Canvas.

Obviously, the graphics completely obscure the butterflies and the woman beneath. This is what's referred to in video-editing terms as a *cut*—playing back the sequence will result in an instant change. The Canvas goes from displaying the woman and the butterflies to displaying the graphics. What we really want is for the graphics to gradually fade in. You could do it with a Fade In/Fade Out behavior, but in this case, keyframing the opacity of the CinematíveGraphics object will offer more control.

3   Turn on the Record Animation mode (press A).

4   In the Properties tab (F1) of the Inspector, drag the Opacity slider to 0%.

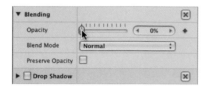

5   Shift-drag the playhead in the Timeline to snap to the end of the ButterfliesHD timing bar (at timecode 00:00:16:02).

NOTE ▶ Be careful not to snap the play range Out point at 00:00:16:00.

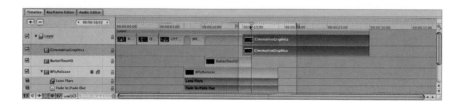

6   Drag the Opacity slider back up to 100%.

If you step back through the Timeline now using the left arrow key, you'll see that the CinematíveGraphics object fades in between the two keyframes we set. Unfortunately, the graphics are fading in over the top of the butterflies as well as over the woman. We want the butterflies to bridge the two scenes, so we don't want them to be obscured by the graphics.

7 In the Layers tab (F5), drag the CinematíveGraphics object down between ButterfliesHD and BFlyRelease. When the position indicator appears, release the mouse.

8 Turn off the Record Animation mode (press A).

The butterflies are now always on top of the CinematíveGraphics object.

Adding the Explutterfly

It's time to add that particle explosion you spent all that time building in Lesson 6.

> **TIP** ▶ If you've fallen behind, feel free to open the project **E.CinemativeGraphicsAdded** to catch up.

1   Shift-drag the playhead in the Timeline to snap to the end of the ButterfliesHD timing bar again (00:00:16:02).

We want a little bit of overlap between the butterflies' being pulled into the top left of the screen and the explosion so that the shock waves appear onscreen immediately after the butterflies disappear. We'll move back five frames.

2   Make sure the Canvas is active, and press the left arrow key five times to step back five frames (to 00:00:15:21).

3   Drag **ExplutterflyHD.mov** from the File Browser (Cmd-1) into the Canvas, and snap it to the center.

If you move forward in the Timeline (say, 00:00:17:18), you should notice a dark ring around the edges of the shock waves.

Dark rings like this around the edges are a clear indication that Motion has incorrectly guessed the alpha type of the object (hey, it's called guessing for a reason).

4   Press Shift-F to jump to the Media tab of the Inspector for
ExplutterflyHD.mov.

5   Set the Alpha Type to Premultiplied-Black.

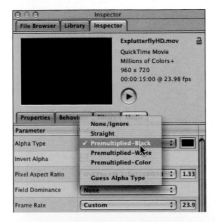

The edges no longer have the dark ringing.

6   Click back to the Layers tab (or press Cmd-4).

You'd like to think the rings are now perfectly composited, but if you
scrub forward through the Timeline, you'll see that they manage to

completely obscure parts of the Cinematíve text at certain points. You don't need to read a company's style guide to know that's a bad thing.

The problem is that in Normal blend mode, the rings are composited over the CinematíveGraphics object, obscuring the text. We'll use a different blend mode to solve the problem.

7   Select ExplutterflyHD in the Layers tab.

8   In the Dashboard (F7), change the Blend Mode to Screen.

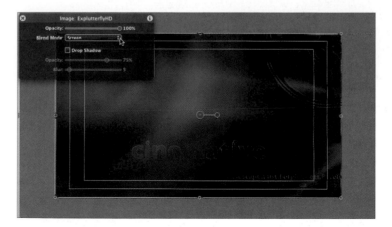

In the Screen blend mode, the rings now blend with the text instead of covering it.

9   Still in the Dashboard, drag the Opacity slider to 60%.

This pulls the ExplutterflyHD object back a bit in the mix, so that it doesn't overpower the rest of the composite.

Adding the Hero

Every movie needs a hero, and this one's no exception. We have a separate QuickTime movie of a solitary butterfly morphing into the Cinematíve logo. It's time to drop it into place.

> **TIP** ▶ If you've fallen behind, feel free to open the project **E.ExplutterflyAdded** to catch up.

1   Move to frame 00:00:16:02 (the end of the ButterfliesHD object).

2   In the File Browser (Cmd-1), drag **BFly2Logo.mov** into the Canvas and snap it to the center.

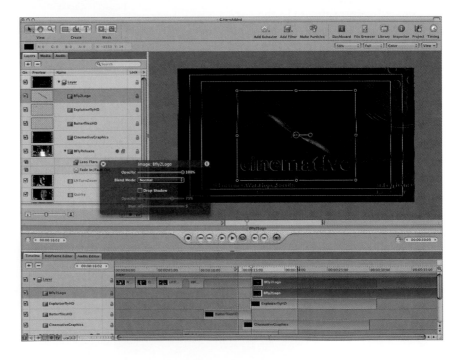

What we want to do is time this butterfly so that he appears to watch wistfully as his comrades explode in a shower of colors. We'll drag the object in the Timeline to achieve that goal.

3   Drag BFly2Logo in the Timeline (F6) until the In point in the tooltip reads 00:00:09:10.

It's a little harder to notice here, but the BFly2Logo object is also suffering from dark edges.

4   With BFly2Logo still selected, press Shift-F to jump to the Media tab of the Inspector.

5   Set the Alpha Type to Premultiplied-Black.

6   Click back to the Layers tab (or press Cmd-4).

All that's left to do is animate the BFly2Logo object so that this butterfly initially appears to fit in with the rest of the flock.

7   Move to frame 00:00:20:00.

We first need to position the logo; at 00:00:20:00 the butterfly has fully morphed into the Cinemative logo, making it easier to align things at this point in the Timeline.

8   Turn on the Record Animation mode (press A) to begin setting keyframes.

9 Drag the BFly2Logo object up the screen (still snapping to the vertical Dynamic Guide) until it's positioned comfortably above the text of the logo.

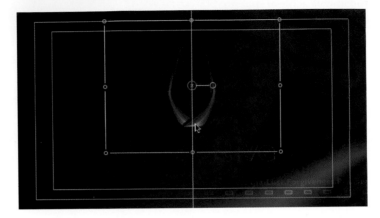

10 Move to frame 00:00:10:10 (the point at which the other butterflies emerge).

11 With the BFly2Logo object still selected, press I.

This trims the start of the BFly2Logo object to the same point in time when the other butterflies emerge.

12 Move the BFly2Logo object down in the Canvas until its anchor point is positioned at the center of the woman's open hands. The anchor point is the circle at the center of the object (with a smaller circle, used to rotate the object, connected to it).

Because we've already keyframed the position of the logo at a later frame, the object will slowly move into position between the keyframes we've automatically set.

13 In the Properties tab (F1) of the Inspector, set the Scale to 10%.

We also need the butterfly to be invisible at this point, just like the other butterflies about to emerge.

14 Still in the Properties tab, set the Opacity slider to 0%.

15 Move forward to frame 00:00:11:00.

16 Drag the Opacity slider to 100%.

The butterfly now fades up, just like all the others.

Finally, we need the butterfly to reach its full scale at about the same time as the other butterflies do.

17 Move to 00:00:16:00.

18 Set the Scale to 100%.

The hero butterfly now scales up to 100% right about the same time as the other butterflies.

Fading Out

We've almost finished our masterpiece. Just one more step: We need to fade out at the end.

> **TIP** ▶ If you've fallen behind, feel free to open the project **G.HeroAdded** to catch up.

1   In the Layers tab (F5), select the main Layer itself.

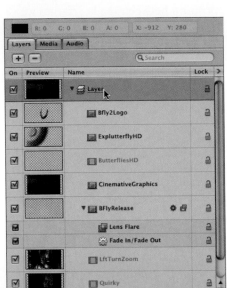

2   Click the Add Behavior button at the top of the Canvas and choose Basic Motion > Fade In/Fade Out.

3   Drag the Fade In triangle to 0 and the Fade Out triangle to 24.

4   Press End to move to the last frame of the project.

5   Press O to set the Out point of the behavior to this frame.

The entire composite now fades out over the last second of the project.

And that's a wrap. Go ahead and render the final version in the codec of your choice.

What You've Learned

▶   Basic Composite, Insert, and Overwrite edits can be performed from the Motion Timeline.

▶   Timecode is a more convenient method for calculating hours, minutes, seconds, and frames than a standard frame count.

▶   It's important to make sure that clips containing alpha channels are correctly interpreted as either straight or premultiplied.

▶   Butterflies travel in flocks.

11

Lesson Files APTS_Motion > Lessons > Lesson11

Time This lesson takes approximately 30 minutes to complete.

Goals Learn about the two audio views in Motion

Perform basic audio edits and waveform envelope animation

Create markers on the fly and using scrubbing techniques

Modify marker properties

Lesson **11**
Audio and Markers

In this lesson we'll take a look at how Motion handles audio. As usual we'll be working on real-world tasks. We'll begin work on an entirely new project: the opening credits for a fictional cop show called *Heist Squad*. (We'll continue to work on *Heist Squad* in Lessons 12 and 13 as well.)

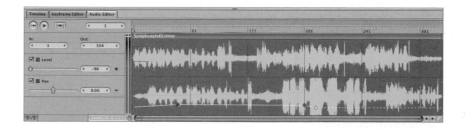

Heist Squad—the Backstory

Heist Squad is about a police department dedicated to tracking down thieves, and the writers of the series are pushing for a tongue-in-cheek '70s vibe, which our opening needs to reflect.

Before we start, take a moment to view the final version of the project to see this style: In the File Browser, navigate to APTS_Motion > Lessons > Lesson11, and double-click **CompleteSequence.mov** to launch the final movie.

To re-create the entire background step-by-step might take an entire book in itself, so in this lesson we'll just re-create the first scene. Lesson 12 addresses keyframing the scene, and Lesson 13 deals with the animated text effects used in the project.

The would-be producer of the show wanted to shoot the series in high definition (HD), but her budget for the pilot wouldn't allow it. Instead, she compromised and created the show in standard definition, but cropped to a wide-screen 16:9 aspect ratio. We'll create our project at 800x450 to give us nice, easy numbers to work with (and square pixels, an added bonus).

Mixing the Soundtrack

Before we start creating the background, we need some audio to cue events to.

1   Press Cmd-O, navigate to APTS_Motion > Lessons > Lesson11, and open **A.HeistSquadStart**.

2   In the File Browser (Cmd-1), navigate to APTS_Motion > Lessons > Lesson11 and drag **HeistTitleTrack.aif** into the Canvas.

3   In the Project pane (F5), click the Audio tab (or press Cmd-6).

4   Begin playback.

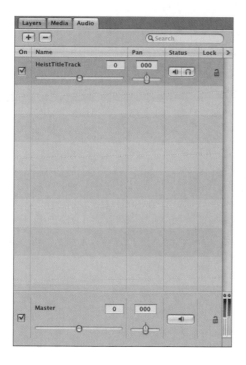

You've just added a soundtrack to your project.

You'll see that the Audio tab in the Project pane lets you make basic changes to the level and pan of an audio track. *Level* is the volume of the track, while *pan* refers to its stereo position—whether the sound is coming more from the left or right side of a pair of stereo speakers, or is evenly balanced.

The Audio tab also offers master level meters, as well as master level and pan controls for adjusting the overall mix of all audio tracks. While Motion is no replacement for a dedicated multitrack audio application such as Apple's Logic, it does provide useful tools for basic audio editing and mixing.

Like the Layers tab, the Audio tab doesn't offer a Timeline interface. For this you'll need to access the Audio Editor.

Working in the Audio Editor

Before starting to work in the Audio Editor, make sure you have a good set of speakers attached to your Macintosh. If you don't, you might want to attach a set of headphones now. This exercise requires that you clearly hear what's playing back in the Timeline. Since the soundtrack is very bass heavy at the opening, it'll be hard to hear on your Mac's built-in speaker.

1   Press F6 to open the Timeline.

2   Click over to the Audio Editor (Cmd-9).

The Audio Editor allows you to see the waveform of the audio you're editing, adjust the level and pan over time, scrub to locate specific events in the audio, and shift the timing of the tracks.

TIP You can also display an audio track's waveform in the Timeline by clicking the Show/Hide Audio button in the lower-left corner.

If you listen to the soundtrack, you'll notice that it has a nice funky beat, but nothing says "police."

3   In the mini-Timeline, move the playhead to frame 1.

NOTE ▶ The playhead in the Audio Editor is independent of the playhead in the main Timeline. Make sure, therefore, that you move the playhead in the mini-Timeline when a step calls for it.

4   In the File Browser (Cmd-1), drag **Crime.wav** into the Canvas.

The Audio Editor now displays the waveform for **Crime.wav**. The editor displays only the waveform for the currently selected audio file.

If you play back the project, you'll instantly realize that the new audio is way too loud and is drowning out the music bed.

5   In the Audio Editor, drag the Level slider down to −21.

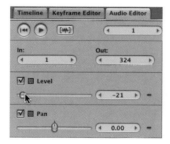

The audio is a little less in your face now, but it really should fade in at the start and fade out right at the horn stab at the end of the preview range. We'll use a curve to control the audio levels.

If you look carefully at the waveform in the Audio Editor, you'll see two dotted lines, often referred to in audio applications as *envelopes.* These lines represent the audio and pan levels of our clip. You may have noticed the bottom line moving as you adjusted the Level slider down to –21.

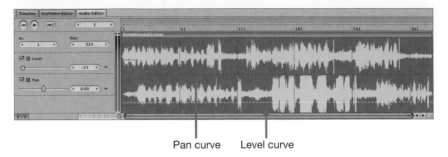

Pan curve   Level curve

6   In the frame ruler at the top of the Audio Editor, drag the playhead to frame 48.

Notice as you drag the playhead that you can hear the audio you're dragging over. This is known as *audio scrubbing* and is a great way to quickly locate specific events in a soundtrack.

7   Click in the waveform section of the Audio Editor, and then press Option and position the pointer over the Level curve (the lower of the two dotted lines).

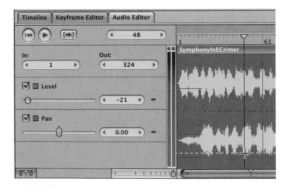

With the Option key pressed, your pointer turns into a crosshair as it hovers over the Level curve.

8 Option-click to create a keyframe.

A small diamond appears where you clicked, indicating that a keyframe has been added to the Level curve.

9 Option-click again on the Level curve somewhere to the left of the keyframe you just created.

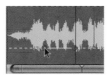

It doesn't matter exactly where you click; you're about to reposition the new keyframe, anyway.

10 Drag the new keyframe down and to the left as far as it will go.

Now you've moved the keyframe to frame 1 (the farthest to the left) and set the audio level to its lowest possible setting, –96.

NOTE ▶ In Motion, as in many other audio applications, an audio Level setting of 0 means that the clip will play back at its original volume. So don't be confused into thinking that a value of 0 turns off the audio—it's actually the normal volume level. An audio Level setting of –96 means that the clip has been made 96 dB (decibels) quieter than the original volume, effectively muting it.

11 Click the Play button at the base of the Canvas to play back the clip (and its audio) in the Timeline.

Much better. Now let's take care of the fade-out at the end.

NOTE ▶ When the Audio Editor is active (that is, you've been working in it), pressing the spacebar will begin playing back the audio in the editor, not in the Timeline. That's why you needed to click the Play button at the base of the Canvas to resume playback of the clip in the project Timeline.

12 In the Audio Editor, drag the playhead to frame 181.

13 Click in the waveform section of the Audio Editor, and then Option-click the Level curve to add a keyframe.

14 Move to frame 193.

15 Option-click the Level curve.

16 Shift-drag the new keyframe (the one at frame 193) down to the bottom of the Audio Editor.

By pressing Shift, you constrain the modification of the keyframe to the vertical axis only (assuming that's the direction in which you move the mouse immediately after pressing Shift). This means you can adjust the value of the keyframe without accidentally changing the frame on which it occurs.

17 Click the Play button at the base of the Canvas to play back the audio in the Timeline.

Crime now fades out just before the big horn stab.

The Level and Pan curves in the Audio Editor actually have all the same functionality as regular curves in the Keyframe Editor. We're going to learn all about the Keyframe Editor in the next lesson; you can apply what you learn to the curves here.

Adding Markers

In motion graphics as in life, timing is everything. Every element in your composite needs to hit its mark at just the right time in order to sell the piece. This is especially true of projects with rhythm-heavy soundtracks like this one. To make it easier to line up events in the Timeline with what's happening in the soundtrack, we'll add some markers at strategic locations. Let's take a look at a couple of different strategies for adding markers.

Marking on the Fly

The easiest way to quickly add markers to your project is to mark them on the fly—in real time as you listen to the audio playing back. (This requires a good sense of rhythm, so if you were the kid who was always given the kazoo in music class instead of the triangle, you may want to use the method described in the next exercise, "Marking While Scrubbing.")

The first marker we want to set is the start of the second bar of music, which happens around frame 49 (OK, it actually happens *at* frame 49, but that would be giving away its location, so pretend you didn't read that).

If you're musically illiterate, don't worry: The start of the second bar just means the place where the bass guitar melody begins to repeat itself.

> **TIP** ▶ If you've fallen behind, feel free to open the project
> **B.AddingMarkers** to catch up.

1   Click the Timeline tab (Cmd-7).

2   Resume playback.

3   Listen to the sequence loop a couple of times. When you're satisfied that you know exactly where the second bar starts, press Shift-M when it comes around to set a marker.

NOTE ▶ There are two types of markers: *project markers* and *object markers.* Project markers can be seen in the Timeline regardless of which object is selected. Object markers are visible only on the selected object. We'll be using project markers for *Heist Squad.* To create object markers, press M instead of Shift-M.

If you look at the Timeline, you'll see a small green marker that looks like an upside-down Monopoly house just above the ruler. This is a project marker.

4   Shift-drag the playhead toward the marker. The playhead will snap to the position of the marker.

Pressing Shift while you drag allows you to snap exactly to the frame at which a marker is set.

You may also have noticed that as you held down the Shift key and dragged, a thin vertical hairline appeared in the mini-Timeline at the frame where the marker was located. This allows you to see the positions of markers even when the Timeline is hidden.

5   Press the spacebar to resume playback.

You should hear the bass riff (the main repeated melody that the bass guitar is playing) play out right from the first note. If it sounds clipped or starts too late, you must have misjudged the position of the marker. You can press Cmd-Z to undo and try step 3 again, or give up and use the marking-while-scrubbing method described in the following exercise. And yes, if your marker landed at frame 49, you got it right on the money.

Marking While Scrubbing

Marking on the fly is a fast way to knock out markers, but if you're having more of a Seattle grunge day than a Motown one, it might be more frustrating than useful. Here's a more scientific method that doesn't require quite so much rhythmic dexterity.

1   Press Option, and then click and drag in the mini-Timeline.

As you drag, you'll hear a very small loop of audio play, starting at the frame you're on.

You may find that the Crime track makes it hard to clearly make out the rhythm in the music. Let's deactivate it for now.

2   In the Audio tab (Cmd-6 if it's not already open), uncheck the On box next to Crime.

We'll turn it back on again when we're done.

3   Pressing Option again, click and drag in the mini-Timeline around frame 49.

You should notice that frame 49 is where bass guitar sound is strongest; at frame 48 there's too much "air" preceding it, and at frame 50 the start of the bass is clipped.

4   At frame 49, press Shift-M to create a marker.

Customizing Markers

Once you've created a marker using one of the methods in the preceding two exercises, you might want to distinguish it from other markers.

> **TIP** ▶ If you've fallen behind, feel free to open the project **C.CustomizingMarkers** to catch up.

1   In the Timeline, double-click the marker (the upside-down Monopoly house) at frame 49.

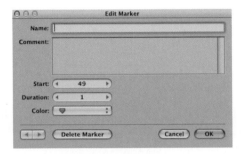

The Edit Marker dialog that appears allows you to name your marker, add comments, change its position in the Timeline, modify its duration, and change its color.

2   Name the marker *2nd Bar*.

3   Click OK to close the Edit Marker dialog.

The name 2nd Bar now appears to the right of the marker in the Timeline.

There are three other markers to add before we continue.

4   Move to frame 181 and press Shift-M to add a marker.

5   Double-click the marker to open the Edit Marker dialog.

6 Name it *Bass Slide* and change its color to something other than green.

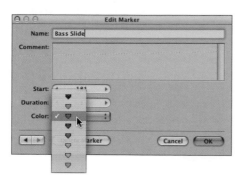

7 Create another marker at frame 193, call it *Horn Stab*, and change its color.

8 In the Audio tab (Cmd-6 if it's not open) reactivate Crime.

By using markers judiciously, you can quickly time events to the action in the soundtrack. In the next lesson we'll create keyframed events at each of these markers to help our animation groove with the music.

What You've Learned

▶ Motion provides two views for modifying and monitoring audio: the Audio tab in the Project pane and the Audio Editor.

▶ Audio-clip levels and pan can be automated in the Audio Editor.

▶ Project markers can be used to set reference points for specific events in an audio soundtrack.

▶ The name, color, position, and duration of markers can be edited in the Edit Marker dialog.

Keyboard Shortcuts

Shift-M	adds a project marker
M	adds an object marker

12

Lesson Files APTS_Motion > Lessons > Lesson12

Bonus Files APTS_Motion > Lessons > Lesson12 > GoingFurther

Time This lesson takes approximately 90 minutes to complete.

Goals Understand the concept of keyframes in motion graphics

Record animation during real-time previewing

Learn about different types of keyframe interpolation

Work with animated layer masks

Lesson 12
Keyframing

Keyframing is the process of creating "snapshots" of where you want an object to be onscreen—and how you want it to look—at specific moments in time. When you create several of these snapshots, Motion figures out where the object should be in between these times.

As mentioned back in Lesson 1, the concept of keyframes comes from the world of traditional cartoon (cel) animation. In traditional animation, a senior artist draws stills of the primary poses that a cartoon character will assume during a given scene. It's then the job of another artist or group of artists to draw the in-between frames from one pose to the next, to create a final animated sequence. The poses drawn by the senior artist are the *key frames* of the animation.

With Motion, you take the role of the senior animator creating the key poses, while Motion draws the images in between. Let's say we want a ball to start at the top of the screen at frame 1 and move to the bottom of the screen by frame 20. We make two keyframes: one at frame 1 with the ball positioned at the top, and another at frame 20 with the ball positioned at the bottom. Then, when we move the Timeline to frame 10, Motion will calculate where the ball needs to be at that point in time if it's to reach the bottom of the screen by frame 20. We don't need to create a keyframe at frame 10; Motion automatically calculates the position of the ball based on the keyframes we created at frames 1 and 20.

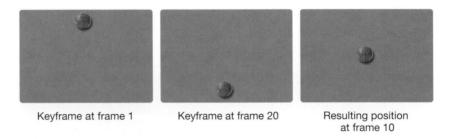

Keyframe at frame 1   Keyframe at frame 20   Resulting position
                                                            at frame 10

Keyframes obviously save a lot of time. Instead of having to position an object in different locations at every single frame, you only have to do it at specific points in the Timeline. The example we used here was the position of a ball, but keyframes can be used to change an object's rotation over time, the intensity of a blur, or even an object's color.

Animating the Blueprint

In Lesson 11 you laid down some markers. Now it's time to start building the first scene of the title sequence, syncing to the soundtrack using those markers. You may want to periodically take a look at the QuickTime movie **CompleteSequence.mov**, located in the APTS_Motion > Lessons > Lesson11 folder, to see how the final piece will look.

The first element of the scene is an architectural blueprint—presumably being examined by a nefarious group of thieves in preparation for a big heist. It's been created in a nice, large format so that we can pan it around the Canvas.

> **TIP** ▶ We're not working with text until Lesson 13, so the Safe Zone overlays aren't as important here. If they're turned on and you'd like to deactivate them, you can do so from the View menu in the upper-right corner of the Canvas.

1   Press Cmd-Option-W to close any open projects. Press Cmd-O and open APTS_Motion > Lessons > Lesson12 > **A.Start**.

2   In the File Browser (Cmd-1), navigate to APTS_Motion > Lessons > Lesson12, and drag **FloorPlan.jpg** into the Canvas, positioning it so that its upper-left corner sits just outside the upper-left corner of the Canvas. Zoom in or out using Cmd-+ or Cmd--, and press the spacebar and drag to pan the Canvas to the center of the screen if necessary.

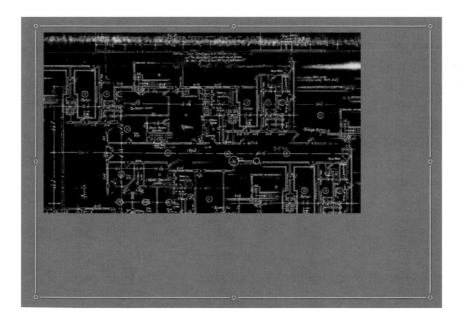

Since the object is larger than the Canvas, you'll see the bounding box extending beyond the Canvas, and only the part of the floor plan that's inside the Canvas will be visible.

3   Choose Mark > Recording Options.

So far you've created keyframes by turning on Record Animation (either by clicking the Record button at the bottom of the Canvas or by pressing A) and dragging sliders. Because Record Animation was turned on, a keyframe was set for the slider you adjusted.

When we did this, we made sure that playback was stopped. A keyframe was set for the specific frame at which the playhead was parked. But what would have happened if Motion had still been playing through the play range as you adjusted the sliders? One of four things, depending on what you've chosen in the Recording Options dialog.

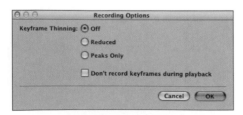

Keyframe Thinning decides how often Motion will set a keyframe. If Keyframe Thinning is set to Off, Motion will create a keyframe at every single frame as you drag a slider or move an object. That's usually undesirable, since it results in fairly shaky, staccato motion. That's fine if you're going for the *Blair Witch Project* look, but most likely you'll want to settle on one of the three other available options.

If Reduced thinning mode is selected, Motion will attempt to articulate the changes you make over time using as few keyframes as possible. This usually results in smoother transitions from one value to the next. So if your hands are a little shaky from your morning coffee binge, you'll probably need to use this mode.

If Peaks Only thinning mode is selected, Motion will record keyframes *only* at the extremes of your actions. So if you're moving a slider back and forth, Motion will create keyframes only at the points where you change direction and start moving the slider back the other way. This is a much more drastic thinning than the Reduced thinning mode.

Finally, if you want to safeguard against accidentally setting a whole truckload of keyframes by mistake while you're experimenting, you can check the "Don't record keyframes during playback" box. When this box is checked, you'll still be able to use Record Animation mode to set keyframes at specific frames (as we've done up till now), but if your Timeline is playing back, no keyframes will be set as you make adjustments.

Regardless of which mode you choose, Record Animation will always create keyframes if you adjust something with playback paused.

4   Make sure that Keyframe Thinning is set to Off and click OK.

5   Press Home to jump back to frame 1.

6   Click the Record button (or press A), and turn *off* the Loop Playback button to the right of the Play button.

Up to this point, Motion has always looped playback of the play range. But we're trying to record animation while playing back, and when the playhead loops back to frame 1, we might record over earlier keyframes by mistake. That's why we just turned off the looping.

Now we're going to animate the background so that it moves up, then down and to the left, up again, and then down and to the right over the course of the play range, as shown in the following figure:

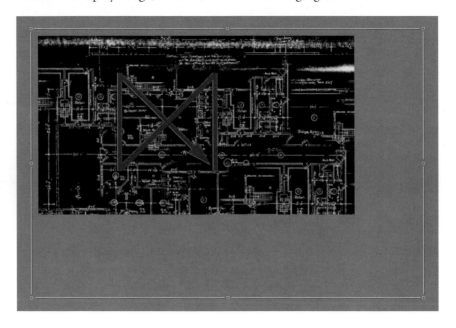

7   Click and hold down the mouse button over FloorPlan in the Canvas.

8   Press the spacebar to begin playback, and drag FloorPlan according to the arrow in the preceding figure, all before the playhead reaches the end of the play range.

> **TIP ▶** You may want to deactivate snapping by pressing N before you begin.

Chances are things didn't go so well. Even if you were extremely fastidious, you probably ended up with something that resembles the following figure:

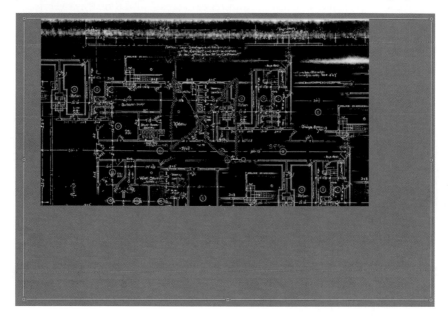

That weird collection of hollow diamonds in the Canvas is an overlay of all the keyframes Motion created as you dragged. It created a keyframe for every frame in the Timeline.

9 Move the playhead back to frame 1 (Home) and resume playback.

Most likely you're looking at very shaky, stilted movement as Motion plays back the sequence. That's fine if the movement is supposed to represent something fiendishly unpredictable, but we're trying to achieve a smooth, natural motion.

10 Press Cmd-Z to undo the creation of the keyframes. (If things went horribly wrong, you can close the project and open **B.FloorPlanAdded**. Make sure that the Record Animation button is turned on.)

11 Choose Mark > Recording Options.

12 Change the Keyframe Thinning setting to Peaks Only and click OK.

13 Make sure you're at frame 1, and repeat steps 7 and 8 of this exercise.

If you worked really hard at it, you may have ended up with a keyframe overlay something like the one in the following figure. (It only took me eight tries and seven undos.)

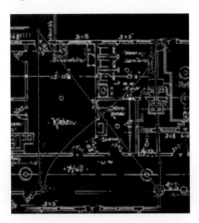

Notice how few keyframes there are. The keyframes are the hollow diamonds; the little notches you see are positions Motion has calculated for the frames in between keyframes.

If you play back the sequence again, you should notice that the motion is much smoother.

Smoother, but not perfect. Now that we've played with the tool set, let's get a bit more precise about the values.

TIP Once you've created a peaks-only curve, you can go into the Keyframe Editor to delete any stray keyframes that were created by your shaky mouse movements.

14 Press Cmd-Z to undo the creation of the keyframes.

15 Choose Mark > Recording Options, and change the Keyframe Thinning setting back to its default of Off.

Setting the Keys Manually

We're about to explore the Keyframe Editor, but first let's set precise values for FloorPlan's movement by using Record Animation mode with the playback halted.

> **TIP** If you've fallen behind, feel free to open the project **B.FloorPlanAdded** to catch up.

1   If the Loop Playback button 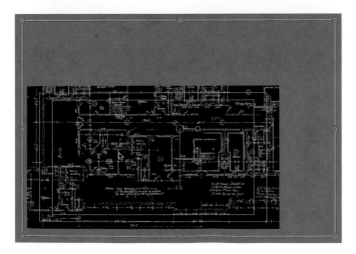 is still off, click it to reactivate it.

    Let's turn on the safe zones to make sure all the movement we're about to choreograph takes place inside the Action Safe area.

2   Choose View > Overlays > Safe Zones.

3   Move to frame 1 and make sure the Record button is on (press A if it isn't).

4   Drag the FloorPlan object in the Canvas and position it so that its upper-left corncr sits just outside the upper-left corner of the Canvas.

    Even though it should already be in position, we need to jiggle the layer to force Motion to generate a keyframe.

5   Move the playhead to frame 60 and drag FloorPlan up so that its lower-left corner sits just outside the lower-left corner of the Canvas.

6 Move the playhead to frame 120, and drag FloorPlan down and to the left so that its upper-right corner sits just outside the upper-right corner of the Canvas.

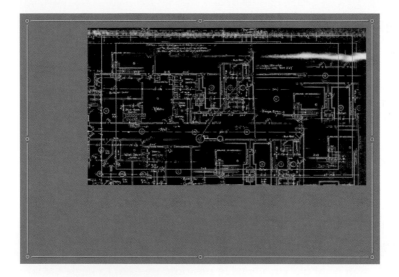

7 Move to frame 180, and drag FloorPlan up so that its lower-right corner sits just outside the lower-right corner of the Canvas.

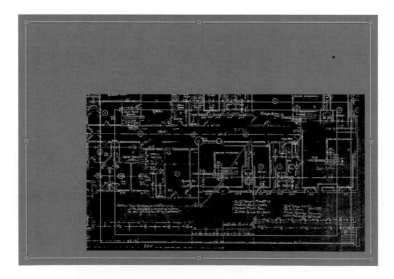

8   Finally, move to frame 240 and drag FloorPlan down and to the right so that its upper-left corner returns to the position just outside the upper-left corner of the Canvas.

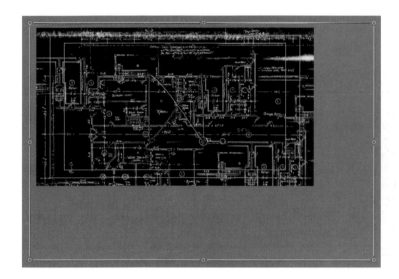

We've created the same basic animation as before, but this time using only four keyframes.

9   Turn off the Record button (or press A) to exit Record Animation mode.

10   Press Home to go back to frame 1, and then resume playback.

The direction of the animation seems OK, but the turns at the corners are too abrupt. To fix them we'll use the Keyframe Editor.

Working in the Keyframe Editor

The Keyframe Editor is where you finesse the paths set up by your keyframes. Even though we've set specific keyframes for our FloorPlan object, Motion can calculate the position of the object in between these frames in different ways. It's the paths between the keyframes that interest us right now.

TIP If you've fallen behind, feel free to open the project **C.WorkingInKeyframeEditor** to catch up.

1 Press F6 to reveal the Timeline if it's hidden.

2 Click over to the Keyframe Editor (Cmd-8).

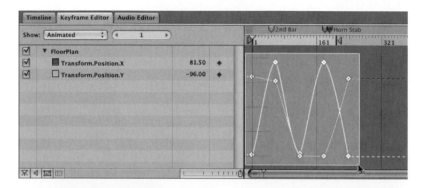

You'll see two entries in the Keyframe Editor: Transform.Position.X and Transform.Position.Y. These refer to the horizontal and vertical positions of the FloorPlan object.

A lot of people get confused when they first encounter a keyframe graph. In the Keyframe Editor everything is plotted in relation to time. The value of a keyframe is its vertical position in the graph; the frame at which the keyframe is set is its horizontal position. So when the FloorPlan object moves to the right of the Canvas, the graph of its X (horizontal) position in the Keyframe Editor actually moves upward. That is, when an object is at the right side of the Canvas, the value of Position.X is greater than if the object were on the left side, so the curve in the Keyframe Editor increases. It takes a little while to get your head around this, but once you do, it makes perfect sense.

3 Uncheck the box to the left of Transform.Position.X to deactivate it.

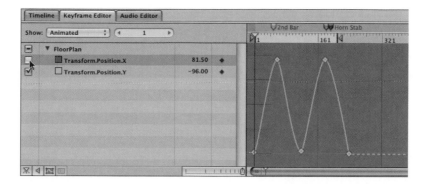

The Keyframe Editor can get very crowded when you're looking at lots of parameters. Hiding the ones you're not editing can help save you from moving the wrong keyframe by mistake.

4   Click the keyframe closest to the 2nd Bar marker to select it. The keyframe turns white to indicate that it's selected.

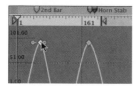

Notice the Bezier handles to the left and right of the keyframe. These behave in exactly the same way as the Bezier shapes we learned about in Lesson 9, "Keying."

5   Right- or Ctrl-click the selected keyframe, and position the pointer over Interpolation in the pop-up menu.

You'll see that there are six types of interpolations. *Interpolation* refers to the way Motion calculates the path between each keyframe. The six types of interpolation are as follows:

▶ Constant—Keyframes set to Constant hold the same value all the way to the next keyframe, where the value instantly changes. Think lightbulb: Now it's on, now it's off.

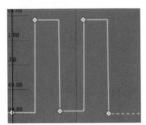

▶ Linear—Keyframes set to Linear move in a straight line from one keyframe to the next. Think of a car on a freeway with cruise control turned on: It moves smoothly without slowing down or speeding up. (Unfortunately, the analogy breaks down for freeways in Los Angeles.) When the direction of the curve changes at a keyframe (as in the following figure), the change is instant—there is no deceleration or acceleration through the change of direction.

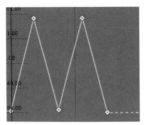

▶ Bezier (pronounced "bez-ee-ay")—Keyframes set to Bezier allow you to control how the curve enters and leaves the keyframe using the Bezier handles. This is great for customizing Ease In and Ease Out motions (see the last two types of interpolation).

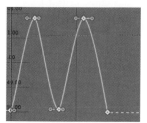

▶ Continuous—Keyframes set to Continuous allow for a smooth transition of the curve coming in and leaving the keyframe. Think ocean waves undulating up and down. Continuous keyframes are very useful for making graceful changes to the direction of the curve.

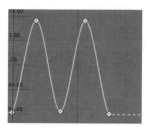

NOTE ▶ In Adobe After Effects, the Continuous keyframe type is called Easy Ease.

▶ Ease In—Keyframes set to Ease In cause the curve to gradually taper off (slow down) as they enter and sharply dip as they leave. Think of a car coming to a smooth stop at a red light and then accelerating sharply as the light turns green.

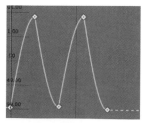

▶ Ease Out—Keyframes set to Ease Out cause the curve to enter sharply but gradually taper off as they leave. They're the opposite of Ease In. Think of that car slamming on the brakes to stop at the red light and then accelerating gently as the light turns green.

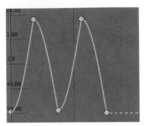

Every keyframe can have its own interpolation; one keyframe might be Bezier, while its neighbors might be set to Linear.

We want to create a smooth, graceful motion as FloorPlan moves in the background. To achieve this, we'll set all the keyframes to Continuous.

6   Click away from the contextual menu to cancel out of it.

7   Reactivate Transform.Position.X by checking the box to the left of its label.

8   Marquee-drag through all the keyframes of both parameters. All the keyframes should turn white, indicating that they're selected.

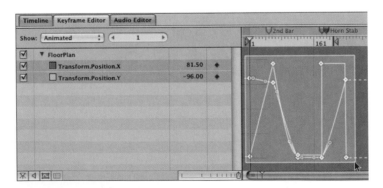

9   Right- or Ctrl-click one of the keyframes (it doesn't matter which, since they're all selected), and choose Interpolation > Continuous from the contextual menu.

Both curves should now have gentle slopes from point to point.

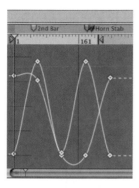

10 Return to frame 1 and resume playback.

11 Turn off Record Animation mode (press A).

12 Close the Keyframe Editor (F6).

The FloorPlan object should now move and change direction very smoothly.

NOTE ▶ If you find the edge of FloorPlan coming inside the Canvas, you may need to go back and adjust the position at one or more of our keyframe points—frames 1, 60, 120, 180, and 240.

Stylizing the FloorPlan Object

In any good heist movie the bad guys go high-tech. Their floor plans don't just sit there—they glow. We'll add a little pizzazz to ours using a filter called Bloom.

TIP ▶ If you've fallen behind, feel free to open the project **D.ReadyToStylize** to catch up.

1   Make sure that FloorPlan is selected by clicking it in the Layers tab or in the Canvas.

2   Click the Add Filter button at the top of the Canvas and choose Glow > Bloom.

3   In the Dashboard (F7), set the Amount to 4, Brightness to 100, and Threshold to 53.

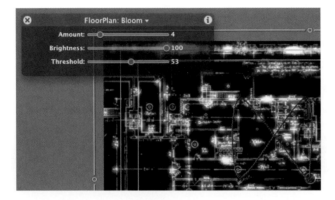

FloorPlan is nicely "bloomed up." Now let's throw in some animation.

4   In the Filters tab (F3) of the Inspector, right- or Ctrl-click the Brightness label and choose Oscillate from the pop-up menu.

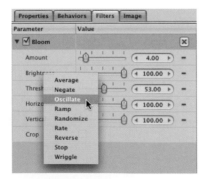

Oscillate will allow us to animate the bloom effect so that it pulses up and down.

5   In the Oscillate parameters, set the Phase to 5, Amplitude to 50, and Speed to 30.

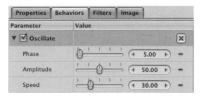

6   Resume playback. You should now see an oscillating glow.

FloorPlan needs to fade in from black and fade out at the end of the scene. We'll use a Fade In/Fade Out behavior to do that, but first we need to set the Out point of our object so that the behavior lines up exactly with the correct position when applied (remember, behaviors last for the duration of the object to which they're applied). We want the FloorPlan object to disappear by frame 205.

7   Select the FloorPlan object again (*not* the Bloom filter or the Oscillate parameter) by selecting it in the Layers tab or pressing D until the Dashboard cycles back to the FloorPlan properties.

8   Stop playback and then move to frame 205.

9   Press O to set the Out point.

10   Click the Add Behavior button at the top of the Canvas and choose Basic Motion > Fade In/Fade Out.

11   In the Dashboard, set the In Fade to 48 and the Out Fade to 11.

FloorPlan now fades in and out on cue.

Masking Off the Canvas

An old motion graphics trick for making things disappear is to stick something black over them. It's not an elaborate technique, but you'd be surprised how often it comes in handy.

> **TIP** ▸ If you've fallen behind, feel free to open the project
> **E.ReadyToMask** to catch up.

1 Make sure you're at frame 1.

2 Select the Rectangle Shape tool at the upper left of the Canvas.

So far you've only used the Rectangle Mask tool. The Rectangle Shape tool is identical, except that it creates a new, distinct object in the Layers tab as opposed to a mask attached to an existing object.

3 Verify that snapping is turned on by choosing View and confirming that there's a check mark next to Snap.

4 Marquee-drag to draw a rectangle, beginning outside the lower-left corner of the Canvas, so that it completely covers the entire bottom half of the Canvas. Don't worry about getting the top edge of the shape exactly centered just yet.

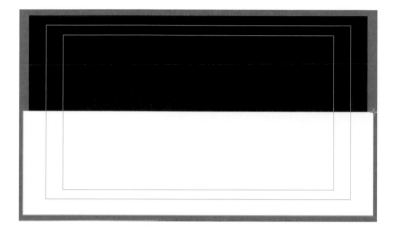

5 Switch back to the Select/Transform tool by pressing Shift-S.

6 Drag the top edge of the shape up or down until it snaps to the center alignment guide.

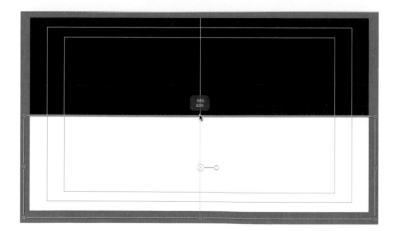

The alignment guides work only with the Select/Transform tool, which is why we switched to it.

The shape is white; we need to make it black.

7   In the Shape tab of the Inspector (F4), change the Fill Color to black.

We want this black shape to initially obscure the lower half of FloorPlan and then fade out at the second bar of the soundtrack. We could use a Fade In/Fade Out behavior for this, but for timing fades precisely, it's usually better to keyframe the Opacity property of an object.

8   Move to frame 32.

9   In the Properties tab of the Inspector (F1), click and hold the Animation menu button to the right of Opacity's numeric entry box.

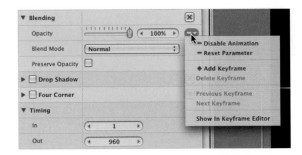

The Animation menu lets you add and delete keyframes, move between keyframes in the Timeline, load keyframes into the Keyframe Editor, disable keyframed animation, and reset the parameter, removing any keyframes or parameter behaviors that had been applied to it.

10   Choose Add Keyframe.

Notice that the button is now a solid diamond. This indicates that the Opacity parameter now has keyframes applied to it.

11 Move to frame 72.

Notice that the diamond is hollow at this frame. This tells you that the parameter has keyframes applied to it but that there isn't a keyframe at the current frame (in our case, frame 72).

We want to apply another keyframe here, but right- or Ctrl-clicking and selecting Add Keyframe from the Animation menu is a little tedious. We'll use a hot key to speed up the process.

12 Option-click the diamond.

The diamond becomes solid, indicating that you've created a keyframe at the current frame.

NOTE ▸ It's essential that you create a keyframe *before* modifying the value of the slider. If you adjust the slider before you add a keyframe, you'll actually be adjusting *all keyframes for that parameter* up or down by the amount you move the slider.

13 Drag the Opacity slider to 0, making the rectangle invisible.

14 Resume playback.

The shape now fades away to reveal the FloorPlan object, but it does so a little too early. It would be nice if it waited until the beginning of the second bar of music before it fades. (Didn't we create a marker in the previous lesson for the second bar of the soundtrack? Coincidence? I think not.)

15 Click the Animation menu button for Opacity and choose Show in Keyframe Editor.

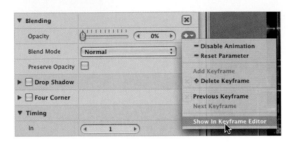

Magically, mystically, mysteriously, Motion opens the Keyframe Editor (if you'd previously closed it), and the Opacity parameter with its keyframes is automatically loaded there, ready to edit. This is a great feature, and it saves you a lot of time searching through dozens of parameters for just the one you want to edit.

16 Marquee-drag through both keyframes in the Keyframe Editor.

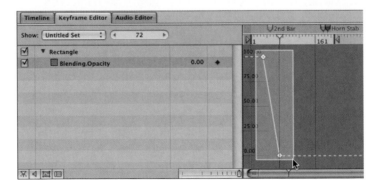

17 In the lower-left corner of the Keyframe Editor, activate snapping (the Snapping button appears shaded when snapping is active).

Snapping in the Keyframe Editor is different from snapping in the Canvas, and it is *not* activated or deactivated via the hot key N.

18 Click and hold the mouse over the first keyframe (the one you created at frame 32). While holding down the mouse button, press Shift to constrain the keyframes to horizontal movement only (we want to move their positions in time, not change their values), and then drag them to the right until the first keyframe snaps to the 2nd Bar marker.

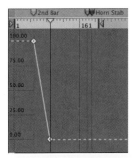

You might find this a little tricky to coordinate at first. That's OK. There's always that Undo command (Cmd-Z) if things go awry and you need to try again.

19 Resume playback.

The black rectangle should now begin fading out right after the start of the second bar of music.

20 In the Layers tab (F5), rename the Rectangle object *LowerHalfHider*.

It's essential to give useful names to your objects. Rectangle may sound like a fine name right now, but later in the project when you're trying to figure out which shape does what, the name Rectangle 48 won't sound so cute.

Adding Circle Strings

Now for a little digital "interference" to help add some kinetic energy to the background.

> **TIP** ▶ If you've fallen behind, feel free to open the project **F.FloorPlanMasked** to catch up.

1 Make sure you're at frame 1.

2 From the File Browser (Cmd-1), drag **CircleStrings.mov** into the center of the Canvas.

3 Option-drag either the left or right side of CircleStrings' bounding box until the CircleStrings movie snaps to the edges of the Canvas.

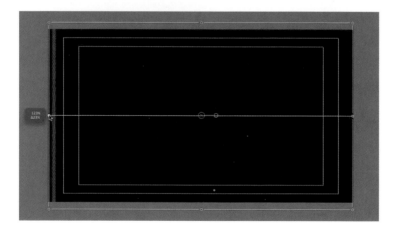

Pressing Option while you dragged caused the CircleStrings object to scale from its center so that both sides resized equally.

4 In the Dashboard (F7), set the Opacity to 50% and the Blend Mode to Color Dodge.

5 Resume playback.

The strings now dance across the screen, interacting with the background, courtesy of the Color Dodge blend mode.

▶ **Keeping Sync at Full Frame Playback**

If Motion is unable to play back audio and video at the full frame rate, it will skip frames of the video in order to keep sync with the audio. This can cause a problem with Motion's caching.

When you first add new footage to the Timeline, Motion takes the frames of your footage from the hard drive and caches them into system RAM. If Motion is skipping frames to try to keep audio synced, the skipped frames won't get cached the first time around. In fact, it may take several loops through the play range before all the frames of the new footage are cached.

The solution is to temporarily mute the audio while caching new footage. To do this, go to the Audio tab of the Project pane (Cmd-6) and uncheck the On box for Master at the lower left of the tab. When the footage has finished caching, check it again.

Adding the Rising Gun

Our fancy floor plan is all well and good, but what's really going to grab the viewer in the opening scene is the image of a firearm being raised into view, with softly focused police lights in the background. This will play in nicely with the half-screen format we're using, since most of the action is occurring in the top half of the image. Let's add this clip to the scene now.

> **TIP** ▶ If you've fallen behind, feel free to open the project **G.CircleStringsAdded** to catch up.

1   Make sure you're at frame 1.

2   Drag **GunRaise.mov** from the File Browser into the center of the Canvas.

3   Move to frame 135 so that the gun is clearly visible.

4   Drag the layer up, and then press Shift while continuing to drag (to constrain the movement to the vertical direction only) until the gun is framed within the top half of the Canvas.

We now want to mask off part of the image so that it's visible only in the top half of the screen.

5   Select the Rectangle Mask tool (*not* the Rectangle Tool in the Create toolbar), and drag a mask around the top half of the Canvas.

6   Adjust the bottom edge until it snaps to the center guide.

7   Adjust the sides of the mask until they snap to the edges of the Canvas. (If snapping is turned off, press N to toggle it back on.)

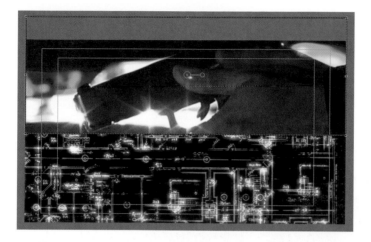

The clip is now masked off so that we see only the top half of the footage. Now it's time to animate the mask. The idea is to have the gun wipe in from the left. We'll do this just by animating the mask, as opposed to moving the entire object.

8 Move back to frame 1.

9 In the Layers tab (F5), make sure the Rectangle Mask is still selected. In the Properties tab (F1) of the Inspector, set the X position (the left numeric entry box for the Position parameter) to 850.

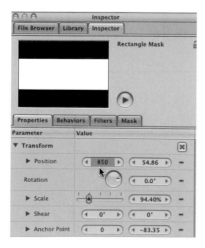

The mask has now been pushed off to the right of the Canvas, thus hiding the GunRaise image.

10 Click the Animation menu button for Position, and choose Add Keyframe.

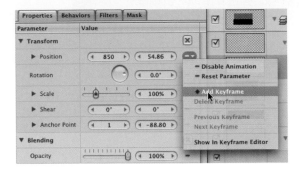

NOTE ▶ Because there are two parameters to key here, Option-clicking will not create a keyframe.

11 Jump to frame 49.

12 Add another keyframe for Position via the Animation menu, and then set the X value to 0.

13 Resume playback.

The mask now slides into place, but it should really ease in more gently.

14 Click the Animation menu button again for Position and choose Show In
Keyframe Editor.

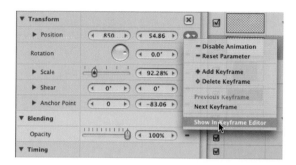

If your Keyframe Editor was closed, it will automatically pop open, with
the curves for your mask's position automatically loaded. (You may see
other curves, such as the LowerHalfHider shape's Opacity, listed here as
well—don't worry about that right now.)

While we're here, let's take a quick look at two other features of the
Keyframe Editor.

15 Click and hold the Show pop-up menu.

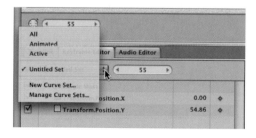

You'll see a list of options. In Motion you can create customized sets of
curves for quick access simply by dragging parameters from the Inspector
into a curve set. For example, if you're continually adjusting the blur and
color of an object at the same time, you might want to create a curve set
with just these two parameters in it.

16 Choose Animated.

When Animated is selected, only the parameters in the currently selected object that already have keyframes will appear.

Notice that the Keyframe Editor also has a keyframe diamond to the right of each parameter's label. Clicking the diamond will bring up an Animation menu similar to the one found in the Inspector.

17   Click and hold the Animation menu button for Transform.Position.X.

The Animation menu that pops up is similar to the one found in the Inspector, but it has a few extra features. Here you can choose how Motion repeats the pattern laid out by your keyframes before the first keyframe in your curve (Before First Keyframe) and after the final keyframe (After Last Keyframe). You can also "thin" your keyframes using the Reduce Keyframes option. This resamples the number of keyframes you have to create a potentially smoother curve.

NOTE ▶ For more information on using keyframe sets, adjusting before and after methods, and thinning keyframes, see the Motion user guide.

18   Click outside the Animation menu to cancel out of it.

After that brief detour, let's get back to modifying the mask's motion.

19 In the parameter list to the left of the Keyframe Editor, uncheck
Transform.Position.Y to hide it.

Notice the slider at the base of the list of parameters. This is the Zoom
Time View slider, and you can use it to zoom in on your keyframes. Also
notice the scroll bar at the bottom of the keyframe graph. You can use this
to pan around the Timeline in the Keyframe Editor.

20 Drag the Zoom Time View slider to the left to zoom into the keyframes.

21 Drag the scroll bar at the base of the Keyframe Editor all the way to the
left to make sure you can see the keyframe at frame 1.

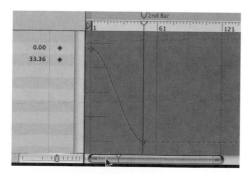

22 Marquee-drag through both keyframes.

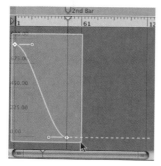

23 Right- or Ctrl-click one of the keyframes, and choose Interpolation > Ease In.

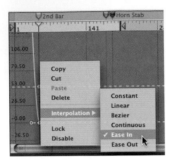

24 Resume playback.

The mask should now gracefully slow to a halt.

To finish, let's soften the edge of the mask and have it become solid right when it comes to a stop. This type of *feathering* creates a soft blur at the mask's edge.

25 Stop playback and move to frame 1.

26 Make sure the Rectangle Mask is still selected. In the Mask tab of the Inspector (F4), Option-click the Animation menu button for Feather to add a keyframe.

27 Set the Feather value to 50.

28 Move to frame 49.

29 Option-click the Animation menu button for Feather to add another keyframe, and then set the Feather value back to 0.

30 To perfectly match the animation of the mask's movement, load the Feather parameter into the Keyframe Editor and set its frame 49 keyframe to an Ease In according to steps 14, 22, and 23.

The feather occurs vertically as well as horizontally, which doesn't work with the way we've split the screen in two. Let's just use the LowerHalfHider to hide the vertical feather.

31 In the Layers tab (F5), drag the GunRaise object below LowerHalfHider to reorder it.

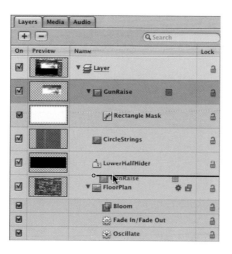

Because the GunRaise object is now below LowerHalfHider, LowerHalf-Hider covers up the vertical part of the feather.

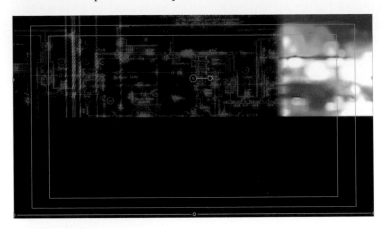

Blurring the GunRaise Object

To finish off the GunRaise object, let's blur the image as it rolls in, resolving it to a crisp, clear image when it comes to a halt.

> **TIP** ▶ If you've fallen behind, feel free to open the project **H.BlurringTheGunRaise** to catch up.

1   Make sure that GunRaise is selected in the Layers tab, click the Add Filter button at the top of the Canvas, and choose Blur > Gaussian Blur.

> **NOTE** ▶ Do not select GunRaise's Rectangle Mask, or the blur will be applied to the mask instead of to the object.

2   Move to frame 1.

3   In the Filters tab (F3) of the Inspector, Option-click the Animation menu button for Amount to add a keyframe. Then set the Amount to 50 and Vertical to 0, and check the Crop box.

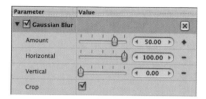

Because you've set the Vertical value to 0, the blur will only occur horizontally. Checking the Crop box means that Motion will only calculate the blur inside the borders of the object so that it doesn't spill out over the rest of the screen. Since we want to contain the blur within the top half of the screen, this is a good thing, and it means that Motion needs to do less work, giving us better playback.

> **TIP**▸ Whenever you apply a blur to an object and you don't need the blur to spread outside the borders of the object, check the Crop box in the blur's parameters. This will reduce the amount of overhead that the calculation of the blur causes in the system.

4   At frame 49, Option-click to set another keyframe for Amount, and then drag its value to 0.

5   In the Keyframe Editor (make sure the Show menu is still set to Animated), set the keyframes for the Gaussian Blur's Amount to Ease In, using the method described in the previous exercise.

We now have a nice, soft blur resolving to a crisp image by frame 49.

Adding Crazy Squares

We're almost there. To wrap up, we'll first add an element to break up the crispness of the border between the top and bottom halves of the screen.

> **TIP**▸ If you've fallen behind, feel free to open the project **I.SquareCrazy** to catch up.

1   Make sure you're at frame 1.

2   From the File Browser (Cmd-1), drag **CrazySquares.mov** into the center of the Canvas.

Let's start with CrazySquares offscreen, and then have it fly in from the left.

3   In the Properties tab (F1) of the Inspector, set the horizontal position to –850, the Scale to 70%, and the Blend Mode to Screen.

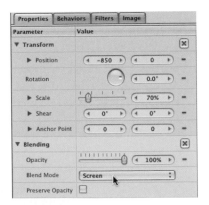

By setting the horizontal position to –850, we've effectively pushed the squares off to the left of the Canvas, ready to be brought on.

4   Click the Add Behavior button at the top of the Canvas and choose Basic Motion > Throw.

5   In the Behaviors tab (F2), set the Increment type to Ramp to Final Value.

6   Click the disclosure triangle to the left of Throw Distance.

7   Set the X distance to 850.

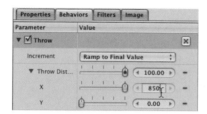

The Throw will now bring the CrazySquares back to the center of the Canvas, but we need to make sure the squares hit their mark at frame 49, when all the other elements are assembled.

8   With the Throw still selected, move to frame 49 and press O to set an Out point. CrazySquares is now fully onscreen by frame 49.

Adding the Final Scene Transition

At the very end of this scene, we want the screen to fade to white during the bass slide in the soundtrack (the one we created a marker for in Lesson 11).

> **TIP**   If you've fallen behind, feel free to open the project **J.FinalTransition** to catch up.

1   Jump to the Bass Slider marker in the Timeline (frame 181).

Remember, you can press Cmd-Option with the left or right arrow keys to jump between markers. Alternatively, Shift-drag in the Timeline or mini-Timeline to snap to the markers.

2   In the Layers tab, select the GunRaise object; click the Add Filter button at the top of the Canvas and choose Glow > Light Rays.

Light Rays is one of those groovy filters that make anything look good, kind of like pitch correction for actors switching to music careers.

Notice that there's a small crosshair right at the center of the object. That's the center of the Light Rays effect. We want to animate the effect as if it's coming from the tip of the gun.

3   Drag the Light Rays crosshair until its center point sits over the tip of the gun. The values –255, 50 will work for the Center parameter, found in the Filters tab (F3) of the Inspector.

4   In the Filters tab, Option-click the Animation menu buttons for the Light Rays' Amount, Glow, and Expansion parameters to set keyframes for all three parameters.

5   Set Amount, Glow, and Expansion all to 0.

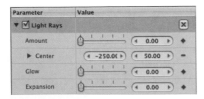

6   Jump to the Horn Stab marker (frame 193). Option-click the Animation menu button to create keyframes for Amount, Glow, and Expansion.

7   Set the Amount to 200, Glow to 8, and Expansion to 1.

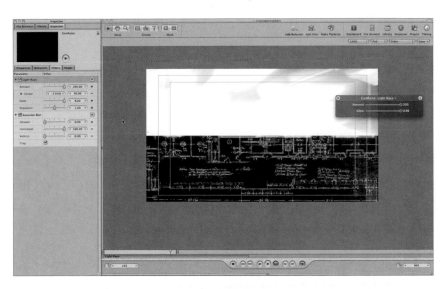

Everything's done, except that we're only "whiting out" half the screen. Let's animate GunRaise's mask to cover the whole screen.

TIP To catch up to this point, open **K.LightRaysAdded**.

8   In the Layers tab (F5), select the Rectangle Mask attached to the GunRaise object.

9   Activate Record Animation mode (press A).

We need to jiggle the bottom edge of the mask to create a keyframe at its current position in the center of the Canvas, so we'll change the shape of the mask and then set it back again to force a keyframe.

10 Navigate to the Bass Slide marker (frame 181), and move the lower edge of the mask downward. Release the mouse and then drag up again until the edge snaps back to the center of the screen, creating a keyframe for that position.

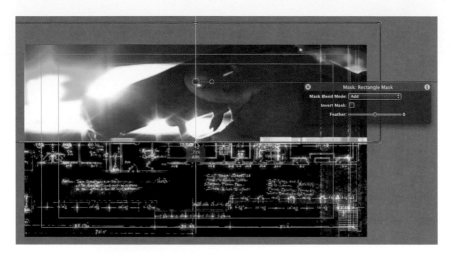

11 Navigate to the Horn Stab marker (frame 193).

12 Drag the lower edge of the mask down to cover the entire Canvas.

13 Turn off Record Animation mode (press A).

And that's a wrap. Render out a QuickTime movie or create a RAM Preview to take a look.

The opening scene's complete. In the next lesson we'll create the title animation to sit on top of our background.

Going Further

It really would take almost a whole book to cover in detail the steps for creating the entire background for this mock title sequence. If you're interested in going further with what you've been learning, you may want to take a stab at it yourself. If so, the additional content used to create the rest of the title sequence can be found in APTS_Motion > Lessons > Lesson12 > GoingFurther.

What You've Learned

▶ Keyframing is the concept of setting up the position and properties of objects at certain frames and allowing the computer to calculate the frames in between.

▶ Record Animation mode can create keyframes as you adjust parameters in real time.

▶ Keyframe thinning can be used to limit the number of keyframes generated in Record Animation mode.

▶ The Keyframe Editor lets you fine-tune the position, value, and interpolation of keyframes.

▶ Interpolation modes can be used to create different kinds of motion between keyframes in a curve.

▶ The Animation menu provides options to modify keyframes, reset a parameter, and quickly load a parameter into the Keyframe Editor for adjustment.

13

Lesson Files   APTS_Motion > Lessons > Lesson13

Time   This lesson takes approximately 2 hours to complete.

Goals   Animate text using keyframes

Get an overview of the primary text parameters

Animate text on a path

Work with motion blur

Create a preset

Work with Motion's customizable text behaviors

Creating Text Effects

Text is at the heart of motion graphics design. Text can be used to communicate the core message of a project, or it can be purely a decorative background element. Whatever the purpose, Motion's text engine allows you to create unbelievably complex text effects with very little effort.

In this lesson we'll take a look at how to create text effects, and in the process we'll also discover the power of user presets.

Building a Frenetic Text Effect

Before we get started, let's take a look at what we're trying to achieve.

1   In the File Browser, navigate to the folder APTS_Motion > Lessons > Lesson13.

2   Double-click **HeistSquad.mov** to launch its preview QuickTime movie.

3   Play through the first 10 seconds of the movie.

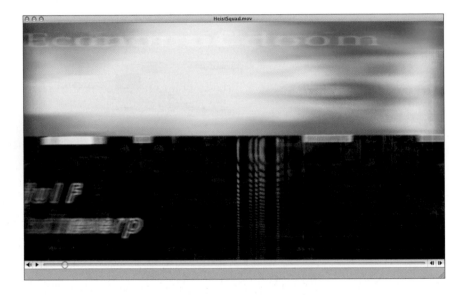

As you watch the movie, you'll see that the first two sets of titles fly in from the left, buzz frenetically, and then zoom off again. We're going to create that effect using behaviors and keyframes. What's even cooler is that once we've created it, we'll save it as a preset so that we can reuse it.

4   Click the red Close button at the top-left corner of the preview QuickTime window to close it.

First we'll create the text.

5   Press Cmd-Option-W to close any projects you may have open.

6   Press Cmd-O to open a new project. Navigate to the folder APTS_Motion > Lessons > Lesson13 and open the file **A.Start**.

7   Make sure your safe zones (the blue lines indicating where action and titles will safely be seen on any TV set) are active. If not, choose View > Safe Zones from the menu at the top-right corner of the Canvas to activate them.

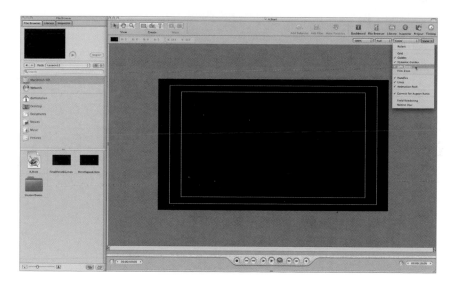

8 Select the Text tool (press T), and click in the lower left of the Canvas inside the Title Safe area—the inner of the two blue safe-zone rectangles.

It doesn't matter exactly where you click; just try to click somewhere close to the location indicated in the preceding figure.

9 Type *Fluffy Dice Studios* on one line, press the Return key (*not* the Enter key on the numeric keypad—that will pull you out of text entry mode), and then type *presents*. If the text went beyond the Title Safe area as you typed, drag it back into Title Safe.

10 Press the Esc key (or the Enter key on the numeric keypad) to exit text entry mode.

11 In the Dashboard (F7), click the disclosure triangle next to the font-name selection box to reveal the pop-up list of fonts.

12 Click and drag your pointer down over the names of the fonts (position it on the names of the fonts themselves, not the scroll bar to the right) and watch as Motion dynamically updates the appearance of your text in the Canvas.

This is a really cool feature in Motion, and it even works while you're playing back other animated elements in real time in the Canvas.

13 Set the font name to Helvetica and the style to Bold.

I know, I know, it's a very boring font choice. Cheer up, though—we'll make up for it by giving it some serious kinetic attitude.

NOTE ▸ In the sample movie the text was centered. Here, for simplicity's sake, we'll leave it as left aligned.

Working with Text Parameters

Before we move on, let's take a quick tour through all the parameters that can be adjusted in the Text tab of the Inspector.

1 Open the Text tab of the Inspector by pressing F4, and click the Format button.

The Text Inspector consists of three panes: Format, Style, and Layout. The Format pane contains properties that determine the size and shape of the text. Here are some of the main parameters:

▸ Font Type—Allows you to choose between system fonts and LiveFonts, Apple's animated font format.

TIP ▸ LiveFonts come from an application called LiveType, which is bundled with Apple's Final Cut Pro application. Motion ships with ten new LiveFonts, but LiveFonts already installed on your system will automatically show up in Motion ready to be used.

▸ Collection—Allows you to narrow your font search to a certain group of font types.

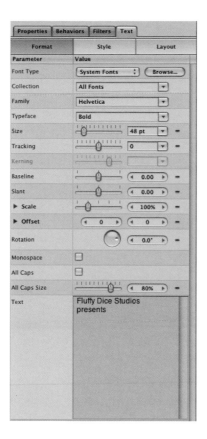

▶ Family—Names the specific font.

▶ Typeface—Identifies the style of the font, such as bold or italic. Fonts will vary in terms of which and how many typefaces are supported.

▶ Size—The point size of the font.

▶ Tracking—The spacing between each of the letters.

▶ Slant—The "tilt" of the letters.

▶ Rotation—The rotation of each of the letters. Each letter will individually rotate around its base.

▶ Text—This entry box, at the bottom of the Format pane, allows you to enter a string of text. Even if the text you're typing disappears off the edge of the Canvas, you can still see what you're typing here.

2   Click the Style button.

The Style pane offers options for the color and shading of the text. The important options here are the following:

▶ Face—This is the fill of the text. By default, the face is all that's active, so you see solid text.

▶ Outline—A border around the text. It's off by default, but you can create some really nice text effects by varying the Outline and Face settings. In fact, we'll be taking advantage of this later in this lesson.

▶ Glow—Creates a glow in the color of your choice around the text.

▶ Drop Shadow—Adds a drop shadow to the text, which is very important for separating text from its background.

3 Click the Layout button.

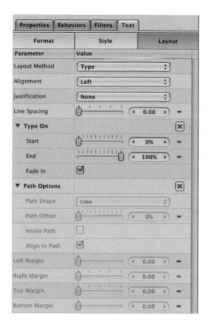

The Layout pane contains all the information about how the type is positioned. Its options include the following:

▶ Layout Method—Allows you to choose among three types of layouts: Type, which creates single lines of text that can stream off forever to the right side of the screen; Paragraph, which creates a bounding box that forces the text to wrap around once it reaches the edge of the box; and Path, which allows you to draw a path along which the text will travel. Path is great for having text travel in an arc across your composite, for example.

▶ Alignment—There are three alignment types: Left, in which the text starts flush with the left border and extends to the right; Center, in which the text spreads out left and right so that the center of the text is always where you first clicked to start typing; and Right, in which the text starts flush with the right border and extends out to the left.

▶ Justification—Determines whether the lines of text end evenly at both left and right margins.

▶ Line Spacing—The distance from one line of text to the next.

▶ Type On—A quick way to animate the letters of your text so that they appear to type onto the screen.

TIP To quickly set up the Type On effect, throw a Ramp parameter behavior on the End parameter. Set the Ramp Start to 0 and End to 100, and then adjust the In and Out points of the Ramp in the Timeline.

▶ Path Options—Determine how text follows a path when the Layout Method has been set to Path.

Now that you have an overview of the Text Inspector, let's take a look at some animation methods.

Animating Text on a Path

Placing text along a path can be a little confusing at first, so even though we're not going to use a path for our current example, let's take a quick detour here and experiment.

TIP If you've fallen behind, feel free to open the project **B.TextCreated** to catch up.

1 Make sure you have the Layout pane open in the Text Inspector (F4).

2 Change the Layout Method to Path.

As soon as you do so, the Path Options at the bottom of the Inspector become available.

3   In the Path Options section, change the Path Shape to Loop.

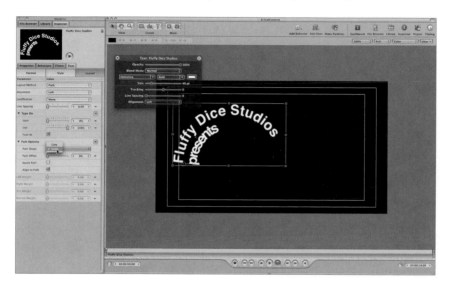

As you do, the text becomes curved in the Canvas. You can create any shape path you want, but because curved text is a common effect, Motion offers curved text as a preset. This is great, because creating perfect arcs from scratch with Bezier points sometimes requires a degree in advanced trigonometry and the fine motor skills of a brain surgeon.

4   Set the Path Shape back to Line.

We're just here to play around right now, so a straight path will work fine. Now here comes the important part, so follow carefully.

5   Select the Text tool (T).

6   Click the text in the Canvas to enter edit text mode.

NOTE ▶ You *must* be in edit mode in order to see the motion path of the text in the Canvas.

What you'll now see in your Canvas is a straight line with three points. This is your motion path. The text will start from the point on the left, travel through to the point in the middle, and finish at the point on the right.

Notice that you also have the insertion point on the screen (the flashing vertical line). You have to be careful when moving the path points that you click exactly on the points; otherwise, Motion will think you're trying to move the position of the insertion point.

7   Click and drag the middle of the three points (the hollow circles) upward to bend the path.

Notice that you have Bezier handles on the point. These work just like Bezier handles everywhere else in Motion.

Three points creates a simple Motion path, but to do something like having text follow the contours of a sports coupe for that Mercedes-Benz commercial you're working on (it's OK to dream), you'll need more.

8   Hover your mouse halfway between the middle point and the end point of the path. Making sure your pointer is exactly over the path, Option-click to add a new point.

You'll know your pointer is in the right place to add a point when it turns into a little pen nib with a plus sign next to it.

9   Drag the new point down to create a path that would make San Francisco's Lombard Street jealous.

10   Press the Esc key to exit text entry mode.

11   Press the spacebar to begin playback.

You'll be disappointed to discover that nothing happens. That's because text follows the motion path based on the Path Offset parameter in the Text Inspector.

12   Halt playback.

13   Drag the Path Offset slider to the right, and watch the result in the Canvas.

As you drag the slider, the text moves along the path.

NOTE ▶ Depending on the speed of your processor, you may experience a delay when working with text on a path. Calculating the positions and orientation of the letters on the path takes quite a bit of brainpower for your shiny little Macintosh.

The quickest, easiest way to turn this into an animation is to use our old friend the Ramp parameter behavior.

14 Set the Path Offset back to 0.

15 Right- or Ctrl-click the Path Offset label and choose Ramp.

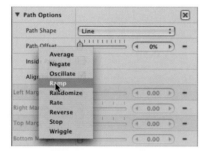

16 In the Behaviors tab of the Inspector (you should automatically be taken there when you choose Ramp—if you've tabbed away, press F2), set the End Value to 100%.

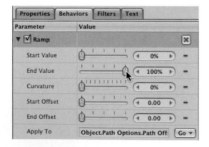

17 Resume playback.

Your text will now glide (or crawl, depending on the speed of your CPU) along the path.

Change the Ramp's In and Out points in the Timeline to experiment. You might also want to toggle off and on Align to Path back in the Layout pane of the Text Inspector (F4) to see what happens.

18 In the Text Inspector (F4), set the Layout Method back to Type.

19 In the Behaviors Inspector (F2), select the Ramp behavior and press Delete to blow it away.

The party's over. Let's get back to the task at hand.

Animating the Tracking and Slant

We want to create the illusion that our text is flying in from the left of the screen, with the later letters overtaking the earlier ones. Adjusting the tracking is a great way to do this. It adjusts the spacing between the letters. To add a little extra comedic feel, we'll *slant* the letters to add the impression that the letters are truly accelerating.

You'll start by animating only the tracking and slant. The position will be animated last so that it's easier to see what's happening with the tracking and slant.

> **TIP** ▶ If you've fallen behind, feel free to open the project **B.TextCreated** to catch up.

1 Make sure you're at frame 1 (press Home).

2 Make sure the text is still selected, and press F4 to jump to the Text tab of the Inspector.

3 Activate Record Animation mode (press A).

4 In the Text Inspector, click the Format button.

5   Drag the Tracking slider to the left, watching the effect in the Canvas.

As you drag the slider, the letters fly back to the left. Hey, that would make a pretty cool animation …

Unfortunately, the slider only goes to −100, which isn't quite enough for this gig, so we'll type in a number instead of using the slider.

6   Click in the numeric entry box next to the Tracking slider and type *−160*.

7   Drag the Slant slider all the way to the right (to a value of 60).

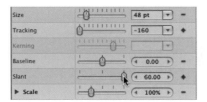

Notice the solid diamonds to the right of each entry box, indicating that keyframes have been set. They were set because we activated Record Animation mode. (Did you forget to turn it on? If so, you'll need to turn it on and then Option-click the Animation menu button—the small horizontal bar—of both parameters to set a keyframe.)

It's time to move on. We'll speed through the rest of the settings for Tracking and Slant. In the next steps, move the playhead to the designated frame and adjust the values as stated.

8   At frame 19, set Tracking to 0 and Slant to 0.

9   At frame 23, set Tracking to 10 and Slant to −10.

10 At frame 31, set Tracking to 0 and Slant to 0.

We haven't set a preview range yet, so let's do that now.

11 Move the playhead to frame 70 and press Cmd-Option-O to set the play range Out point.

12 Resume playback.

The text now zooms in from the left, appears to overshoot a little, and then comes back to its original position. None too awe-inspiring just yet, and it has that stilted feel of an accountant trying to sing the blues at a karaoke bar. That's because we haven't interpolated the keyframes to give a little acceleration where it's needed.

13 In the Text Inspector, click the Animation menu button (the diamond) for Tracking and choose Show In Keyframe Editor.

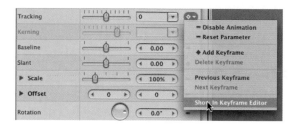

14 Back in the Text Inspector, click the Animation menu button for Slant and again choose Show In Keyframe Editor.

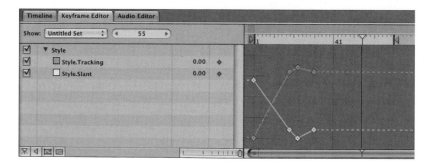

Slant quietly joins Tracking in the Keyframe Editor.

15 Drag-select through the keyframes for both parameters at frame 19 (that's the second pair of keyframes appearing in the Curve Editor).

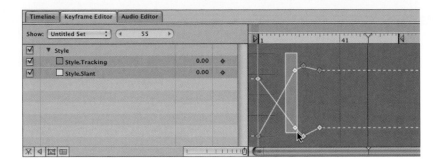

16 Right- or Ctrl-click one of the newly selected keyframes, and choose Interpolation > Ease Out.

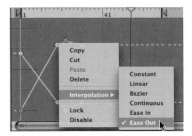

The change might seem subtle, but these keyframes will now ease out, creating a graceful acceleration in the animation.

17 Drag-select the next pair of keyframes (at frame 23).

18 Right- or Ctrl-click one of the newly selected keyframes, and choose Interpolation > Continuous.

19 Drag-select through the last pair of keyframes (at frame 31).

20 Right- or Ctrl-click to set the interpolation to Ease In.

TIP ▶ If you're finding the Keyframe Editor too cramped, you can always pull the drawer handle (the thin line between the Timing pane and the Canvas) up to expand its size. If you set the Keyframe Editor to auto-scale (the magnifying glass button in the top-right corner of the editor), it will automatically resize the curves for you. You can also drag the Keyframe Editor tab out of the Timing pane to turn it into a floating window, and then drag it onto another monitor—but remember that using a second monitor will affect your real-time performance.

21 Press Cmd-R to render a RAM preview of the play range. When finished, resume playback to watch the result.

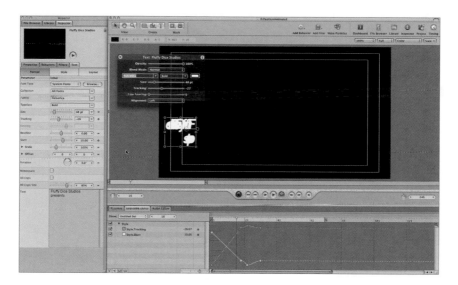

The text should now appear to be coming from the left, trying to slow down, overshooting a little, and finally coming to rest in the correct location.

Animating the Position

The whole animation is a little unsatisfying because the *F* in *Fluffy Dice* never moves; the other characters all fly by it. That's because we haven't animated the position yet. It was much easier to adjust the tracking before we animated the position; if we had animated the position first, the text would have been offscreen while we were trying to adjust the tracking, and we wouldn't have been able to see what was going on.

TIP ▶ If you've fallen behind, feel free to open the project **C.TrackingAndSlantSet** to catch up.

1   Make sure that Record Animation mode is still active, and move to frame 1 (the Home key).

2   In the Properties tab of the Inspector (F1), drag left in the horizontal Position numeric entry box (the X position) until the *F* in *Fluffy* is well off the Canvas (about −520).

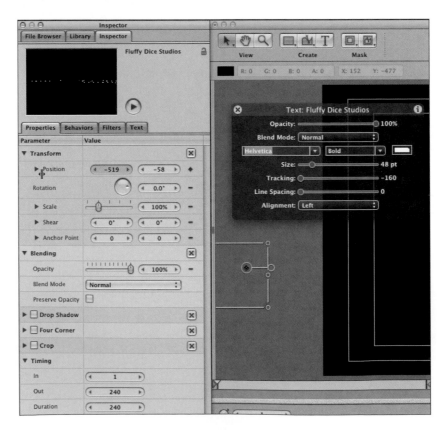

3   Move to frame 23 and adjust Position again so that the text is where you want it to finally come to a rest in the Canvas (let's use –300).

4   Move to frame 58 and jiggle the Position value—move it away from –300, release the mouse, and then set it back to –300. This forces Record Animation to set a keyframe.

Now that the text has spent some time sitting onscreen, we need to get it out of there. We'll animate the position to send it off to the right.

5   Move to frame 68. Adjust the horizontal Position value until the text is completely offscreen to the right (a value of 450 will work).

6   Resume playback.

The text is animated, but it doesn't quite look right. That's because we haven't adjusted the interpolation of the Position keyframes to match the Tracking and Slant.

7   In the Properties Inspector, click the Animation menu button to the right of Position, and choose Show In Keyframe Editor.

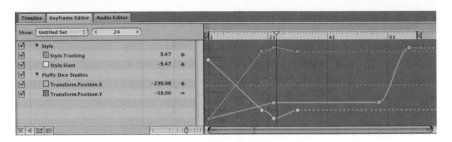

The Position parameters for Fluffy Dice Studios are added to the Keyframe Editor.

Transform.Position.X (the horizontal position) is the only parameter we want to adjust right now, so let's hide the other curves so that we don't accidentally move one of their points by mistake.

8   Uncheck the boxes to the left of Style.Tracking, Style.Slant, and Transform.Position.Y.

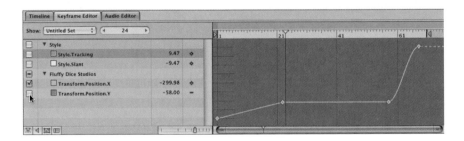

Transform.Position.X is now the only visible curve.

9   Click the first keyframe (at frame 1) to select it.

10 Right- or Ctrl-click, and choose Interpolation > Continuous.

11 Select the second keyframe (at frame 23), and set its interpolation to Ease In.

12 Select the third keyframe (at frame 58), and set its interpolation to Ease Out.

13 Select the final keyframe (at frame 68), and set its interpolation to Linear.

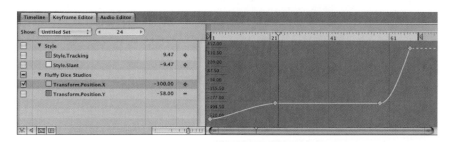

14 Render another RAM preview (Cmd-R).

We're almost there; we just need to adjust the slant to help send the text off in haste.

15 Move to frame 58.

16 In the Format pane of the Text Inspector (F4), Option-click the Slant Animation menu button to set a keyframe of 0.

17 Move to frame 68 and set Slant all the way to 60.

18 Turn Record Animation off (press A).

19 Render a RAM preview.

The text now leans its way offscreen.

Applying Motion Blur

In the real world, when a camera films a moving object, the movement creates motion blur. Motion blur is the result of an object's refusing to stay still while a camera tries to capture a single moment in time.

A film camera needs to hold each frame of film in its gate for a certain amount of time to get enough light onto that frame to correctly expose the image. If an object is moving while the gate is held open, it will appear smeared in the final developed frame.

Until now we've been dealing with crisp animation; each frame is a perfect snapshot of a single moment in time. To add a bit of style, we'll activate motion blur.

1 From the View menu in the top-right corner of the Canvas, choose Motion Blur.

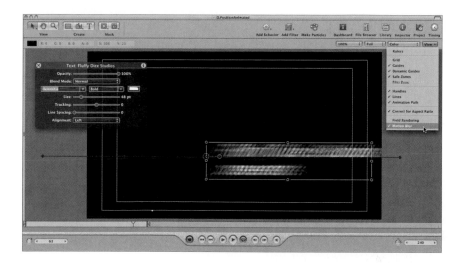

If you're looking at a frame where the text is moving (try moving the playhead to frame 18, for example), you'll notice an odd stepping effect, in which the text seems to be ghosted horizontally. To simulate motion blur, Motion renders out "in-between" positions for the text and then blends them together with the actual position of the text at a specific frame. Even though it looks a little odd in the still frame, it's quite nice played back in real time.

Unfortunately, you won't get real-time design performance with motion blur turned on. That's because Motion effectively renders many frames at once to create the effect. We can see the results with a RAM preview, though.

2   Create a RAM preview of the Timeline (Cmd-R).

3   Resume playback.

As I said, once the text is moving, the effect is quite nice. The motion of the text appears much smoother than when we had it turned off.

4   Press Cmd-J to open the Project Properties dialog.

5   Click the Render Settings tab.

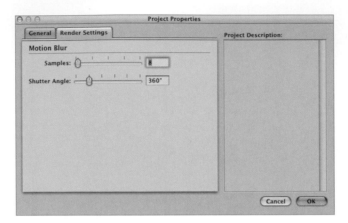

This pane offers global settings for motion blur. The Samples parameter determines how many in-between frames Motion renders to blend with the original.

6   Set Samples to 20, and click OK to close the Project Properties dialog. You may need to move the playhead to force the Canvas to update.

The number of samples dramatically increases, and so does our render time. A value of 8 is sufficient for most situations.

7   Open the Project Properties dialog (Cmd-J) again, and set Samples back to 8.

The other parameter, Shutter Angle, simulates different lengths of time during which a film camera's shutter might stay open on a single frame.

The visual effect in the Canvas is that a higher value stretches out the blur, while a lower value makes it tighter.

8 Set the Shutter Angle to 720° and close the dialog.

The blur now stretches out much more horizontally.

9 Open the Project Properties dialog again, and set the Shutter Angle back to 360°.

TIP ▶ The standard shutter angle of a film camera is 180°, so to simulate a real camera, the Shutter Angle should be set to 180°. However, motion graphics is all about style, not realism. In fact, more often we're interested in exaggerating reality than in accurately simulating it. That's why the default motion blur in Motion is 360°—it gives an exaggerated blur that looks pretty cool.

10 Go back to the View menu, and uncheck Motion Blur to turn it off.

We need all the real-time preview speed we can get right now, so it's best to deactivate the motion blur while working.

TIP ▶ Since motion blur prevents real-time playback, you want to activate it only during strategic RAM previews and when rendering your movie to the hard drive. When rendering your final movie, you can override the project's motion blur setting and choose a different state—either on or off.

Adding Personality to the Text

Our text is moving across the Canvas quite happily now, but it doesn't have a lot of attitude. We want angry text. We want the kind of text that's been driving around in traffic for three hours trying to travel two blocks with the radio stuck on a station playing Latvian piano-accordion rap fusion. Our text should be buzzing. We should be feeling lucky that text doesn't pack heat when it travels.

We'll achieve this by making the text jiggle and blur. We'll animate the scale and apply a slight blur to give a sense that the text is bristling with energy. And to lower the risk of carpal tunnel syndrome from excessive keyframing, we'll use behaviors to do it.

TIP If you've fallen behind, feel free to open the project **D.PositionAnimated** to catch up.

1 Make sure that Record Animation mode is off.

2 In the Properties tab of the Inspector (F1), set the Scale to 98%.

3 Right- or Ctrl-click the Scale label and choose Randomize.

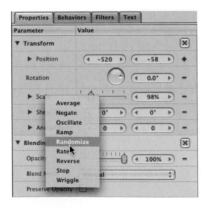

4   In the Behaviors tab of the Inspector, set the Amount to 3% and check the Link box.

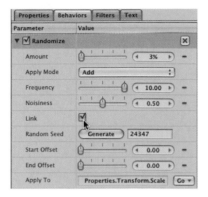

The Randomize behavior generates random values for the parameter in the same way as the Random Motion behavior gave our butterfly particles a mind of their own in Lesson 5. Randomize will add up to 3% to the total scale of the text. That's why we set the Scale down to 98% initially—to give a little bit of headroom.

The Link option, when checked, scales the horizontal and vertical by the exact same amount. Otherwise, the horizontal scale would be randomly different in its relationship to the vertical scale, creating a squash-and-stretch effect that we don't want here.

5   Click the Add Filter button at the top of the Canvas and choose Blurs > Gaussian Blur.

6   In the Filters tab of the Inspector (F3), set the Gaussian Blur's Amount to 0.

7   Right- or Ctrl-click the Amount label and apply another Randomize parameter.

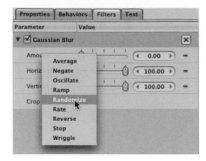

We've now added a second Randomize behavior. Be careful here; we're about to change the Randomize behavior affecting the blur, so make sure you adjust the correct one—they look identical.

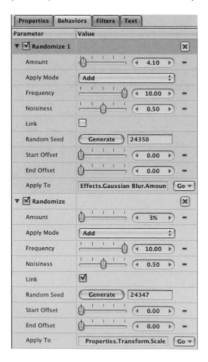

8   In the Behaviors Inspector, identify the Randomize parameter that has Effects.Gaussian Blur.Amount in its Apply To box. It should be Randomize 1.

9   Set the Amount to 2.

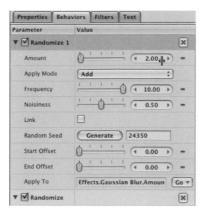

10   Render a RAM preview (Cmd-R).

Your text should now be buzzing frenetically. Let's ice the cake by animating the face opacity of the text.

Right now our text is solid. That's because the only portion of the text that's visible is the face. We also have the option of turning on an outline around the edges of the text. We'll do just that and then animate the face, or fill, of the text to create a nice little effect.

11   Go to the Style pane of the Text Inspector (F4).

12   Check the Outline box.

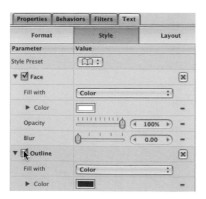

If you look carefully, you'll see that your text now has a red outline. We actually want the outline to be white, just like the face (the center fill).

13 Click the white Color swatch in the Face section of the Style pane, and drag the swatch down onto the red Color swatch in the Outline section.

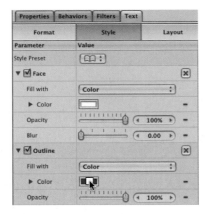

The outline takes the color of the fill (white).

Now that we have the outline set to white, let's animate the opacity of the face (the inside of the text).

14 Move to frame 1.

15 Turn on Record Animation mode (press A).

16 Drag the Face Opacity slider to 0.

Be careful—you're supposed to be animating the face opacity, not the outline opacity.

17 Move to frame 19. Option-click the Animation menu button for Face Opacity to set another keyframe of 0.

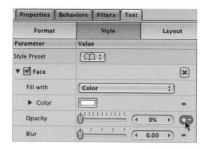

We're now seeing only the outline of the text.

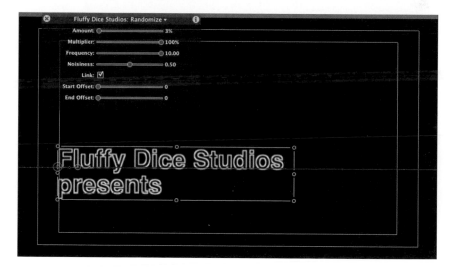

18 Move to frame 31, and set the Face Opacity to 90%.

19 Move to frame 44, and Option-click the Animation menu button to create another keyframe of 90%.

This fills in the text, but because it's not 100% opaque, it leaves a little differentiation between the face and the outline.

20 Move to frame 58, and drag the Opacity slider back to 0.

21 Turn off Record Animation mode.

22 Render a RAM preview.

The text now starts out "hollow," fills in while it's standing still, and then empties and takes off. Congratulations—you're done.

Creating a Preset

As you've no doubt come to realize, quite a bit of work can go into creating text animations. So what happens when you need five instances of text in your project to do the same move? We could keyframe it all over again, but that's real work. And let's face it—you found your way into the whole computer graphics thing so that you wouldn't have to get a real job.

Motion comes to the rescue with some amazing functionality. Simply by dragging and dropping, you can turn anything into a preset (called a *favorite*)—and I mean *anything*: text, particles, clusters of behaviors, even entire composites. Let's take a look.

> **TIP** ▶ If you've fallen behind, feel free to open the project **E.ReadyToPreset** to catch up.

1 Open up the Layers tab (F5).

The first step in creating a preset is to make sure that everything you want included in the preset is contained under one roof. That is, everything should live inside a master layer. (If not, just select all the objects and/or layers, and choose Object > Group to group them all into a new master layer.)

In the case of our text, there's only one object, so it's already contained within a master layer.

2   Double-click the label for Layer (the main layer containing the text object) and rename it *Frenetic Text*.

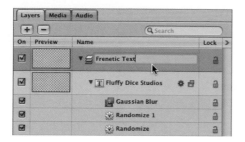

The second step is to give the master layer the name you want for your preset, but first ...

3   Save a copy of your project.

If you realize later that you need to change something, it's always good to have the original version available.

4   Move to frame 31.

Fluffy Dice Studios presents is a little too specific for a preset. Before you create a preset, it's worth turning things like this into more generic placeholders.

5   Select the Fluffy Dice Studios object in the Layers tab, and then double-click it in the Canvas.

This jumps you back to text edit mode.

6   Type *Insert Text* on the first line and *Here* on the second line, and then press the Esc key to exit text edit mode.

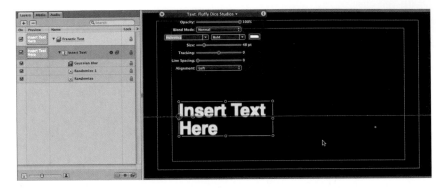

It's now time to create the preset.

7   Open the Library (Cmd-2).

8   Drag the Frenetic Text layer out of the Layers tab and drop it onto the Favorites Menu folder.

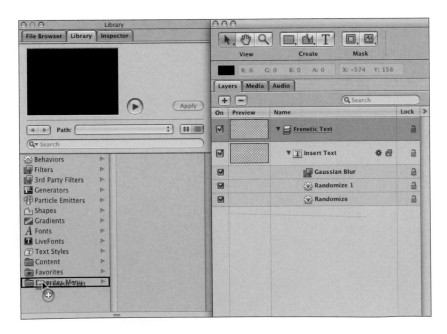

Believe it or not, you've just created a preset. Let's try it out.

9   Save and close your project.

10 In the File Browser, open **G.Background**.

This is the compilation of the background for our TV opener without text.

11 Move to frame 39.

This is where we want the first title to make its entrance.

12 From the Favorites menu choose Frenetic Text.

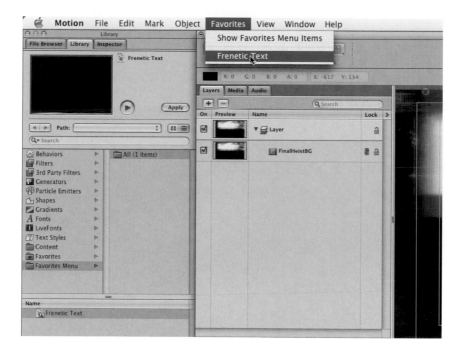

I thought you'd like that. Any preset dropped in the Favorites Menu folder automatically shows up in the Favorites menu at the top of the screen.

13 Move to frame 82 so that you can clearly see the text.

14 Select the Insert Text copy layer in the Layers tab, and then double-click the text in the Canvas and change it to *Fluffy Dice Studios presents*. Press Esc to exit text edit mode.

First title accomplished.

15 Move to frame 113.

16 Choose Favorites > Frenetic Text.

Another instance of Frenetic Text is added to your comp.

17 Move to frame 156 and repeat step 14, this time typing *a Scoppettuolo original series*.

Congratulations—you've just created two title animations out of a single preset. You may want to center the text vertically to clean up. When you're done, render out a QuickTime movie and take a look.

TIP ▶ Create folders inside your Favorites Menu folder to organize your presets into different categories.

Applying Text Behaviors

Fine-tuning a text animation like the one we just created can take some time, but Motion ships with dozens of text behaviors that make animating text almost criminally simple.

1 Save whatever you're working on and close all open projects (Cmd-Option-W).

2 Create a new project (Cmd-N) with the preset NTSC Broadcast SD.

3 Set the play range to preview the first 120 frames by moving the playhead to frame 120 and pressing Cmd-Option-O.

4 Move the playhead back to frame 1. Select the Text tool and type *Text on a Budget*. Press Esc to exit text entry mode.

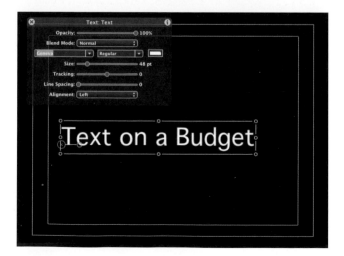

5   In the Dashboard (F7), choose your favorite font (I've gone with Gill Sans Ultrabold because it's got the kind of name that marketing people dream about).

6   Resume playback.

So we've got text in our Timeline and it's playing back, but we need a way to bring it to the screen.

7   Click the Add Behavior button at the top of the Canvas and choose Text Glow > Sci Fi Glow.

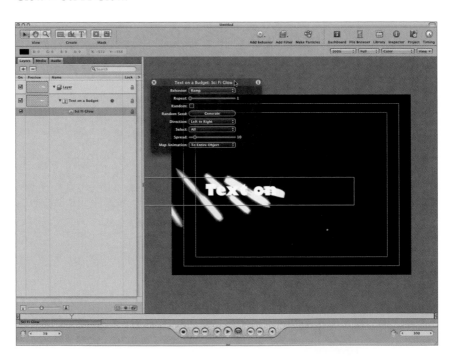

It's as simple as that. No keyframing, no messy behaviors. Just one click and your text turns into glowing flying saucers landing in your Canvas. (It might take one time through the play range to cache before you get the real-time playback.)

Motion comes with a truckload of these preset behaviors. In fact, if you look at the behaviors list, the majority of them are for text.

You can even go into the Behaviors tab of the Inspector (F2) and tweak the values.

8   Delete the Sci Fi Glow behavior, and play with some of the other presets.

Really, go on and play a while. The book will still be here when you're done.

Working with the Sequence Behaviors

Presets are a lot of fun, but the problem is that the compositor down the street might be using them as well. What if you want to create something uniquely yours? You could animate using keyframes and parameter behaviors the way we did earlier in this chapter, but what if you have only 5 minutes to tweak the look instead of 5 hours?

Enter sequence behaviors. Sequence behaviors are an incredibly powerful way of creating custom text effects very quickly. In fact, most of Motion's text presets are just sequence behaviors tricked out.

1   In the Layers tab, delete any behaviors you applied to your Text on a Budget text object.

2   Resume playback.

3 With the text selected, click the Add Behavior button at the top of the Canvas and choose Text-Basic > Sequence In From Left.

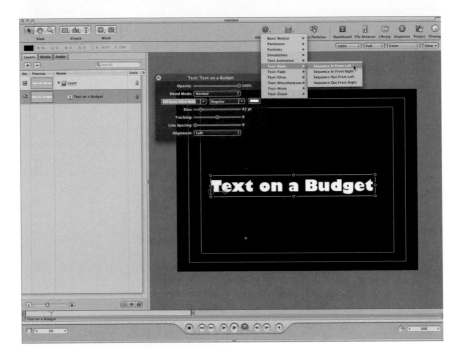

You might be disappointed to see what appears to be a typical cheesy type-on effect. Actually it's not—it's something far cooler.

4 In the Behaviors Inspector (F2), set the Spread to 5.

You should now be seeing a completely different behavior in your text.

Each letter now starts its life tiny and grows up to be full size.

Take a look at the Scale parameter for the Sequence behavior. The Scale slider is set to 0%.

The entire line of text is beginning its life with a scale of 0%—so tiny that it's invisible. Over time, each character grows to being 100% of its original size. This "growing up" happens from left to right.

The Spread parameter we adjusted earlier determines how long it takes each character to grow and, consequently, how much the characters overlap as they grow.

But the great news is that sequence behaviors are not all about scaling. *Anything* we want to change about the text can be changed over time. We can set up some initial conditions for the text, and it'll revert to the original form it held before we applied the behavior. An example should help illustrate.

Let's assume that we have a specific task: We need the text to start big, invisible, and blurry, and then gradually scale down to a crisp, opaque object.

5   In the Behaviors Inspector, click the Add pop-up menu to the right of the Parameter label and choose Face > Blur.

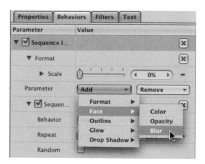

This action adds a blur to the list of parameters that will be affected by the sequence (previously the list only contained Scale).

6 Set the Scale slider to 300% and the Blur slider to 10.

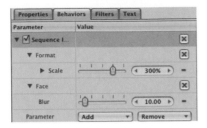

The letters of the text now start at 300% of their normal size and with a blur of 10%, and over time they revert back to their original size with a blur of 0.

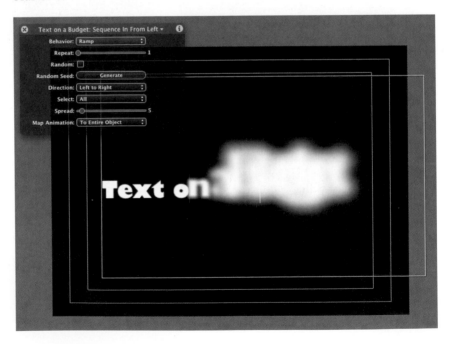

Are you starting to get it? Let's try another.

7   Again from the Parameter Add menu, choose Face > Opacity.

8   Set the Opacity to 0.

The text now starts invisible and then becomes visible as the line of text sequences in from the left.

Why stop there?

9   Choose Add > Format > Tracking.

10   Set the Tracking to –100.

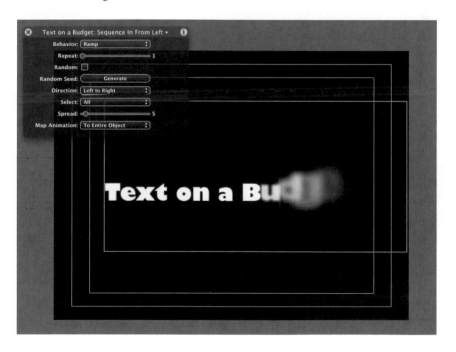

The text now appears to wrap around from the left.

Because of the real-time preview feedback in Motion, it's easy to quickly get great results simply by experimenting with the parameters. Try rotating the characters as they come in, or changing their color. Or try adjusting the spread again, or experimenting with some of the other settings.

There are behaviors for sequencing in and out from the left, or in and out from the right. There are also straight sequence behaviors that ripple through text from one side to the other without taking the text offscreen or bringing it in. With the Sequence behavior's Select parameter, you can group the animation so that it affects characters (the only way we've looked at so far), entire words, entire lines of text, or the whole block of text all at once.

Going Further with Text

The entire background for the *Heist Squad* opener is included in the movie **FinalHeistBG.mov**. In this lesson we've just looked at the first couple of titles. To experiment with text effects, go ahead and try to add the other titles into the project.

Feel free to experiment with all the weird and wonderful permutations and combinations that the sequence behaviors offer. And remember, if you strike gold during your experimentation, you can always turn it into a preset by throwing it into the Favorites Menu folder.

What You've Learned

▶ Parameters in three separate panes of the Text Inspector can be keyframed to create sophisticated text animations.

▶ Text can be animated on a path using the Path layout method, and by animating the Path Offset.

▶ Motion blur is global in Motion and activated from the View menu.

▶ Any part of a Motion project can be converted into a preset by dragging it into the Favorites Menu folder in the Library.

▶ Motion's sequence behaviors can be used to quickly generate custom text animations without keyframing.

14

Lesson Files APTS_Motion > Lessons > Lesson14

Time This lesson takes approximately 45 minutes to complete.

Goals Learn about the integration between Motion, Final Cut Pro, and DVD Studio Pro

Import a lower-third title created in Motion into Final Cut Pro

Import a motion graphics background created in Motion into DVD Studio Pro

Integrating Apple Pro Applications

The integration of Motion with Apple's Final Cut Pro and DVD Studio Pro may not be its most glamorous feature, but it *is* one of the most powerful. The tight integration between these applications allows a workflow between editing and DVD authoring that's hard to match with any other system. By taking advantage of this integration, video editors can add Motion elements right into the Timeline and dynamically update them without ever leaving the edit. DVD authors can build sophisticated motion menus and update them instantly without the need to re-render.

Creating a Lower Third for Final Cut Pro

To explore the integration between Motion and Final Cut Pro, let's look at a typical graphic requirement in video editing—the lower third. The term *lower third* refers to a title graphic laid over video, usually labeling a place or person onscreen. Lower thirds feature heavily in news broadcasts and in documentaries. They are called lower thirds because they occupy the lower third of the screen.

In this exercise we have an image of San Francisco's Golden Gate Bridge in the Final Cut Pro Timeline. For some reason, it's important that the audience know it's the Golden Gate Bridge and not some generic bridge somewhere else in the world. We want to take the footage into Motion, create a graphic title overlay, and then layer the graphic over the footage back in Final Cut Pro.

> **NOTE ▶** The following exercises assume that you have Final Cut Pro HD 4.5 or later installed on the same system you're using for Motion, and that you have a basic working knowledge of Final Cut Pro. They also assume that you're using the NTSC version of Final Cut Pro. If you live in the PAL universe, you can temporarily set Final Cut Pro to NTSC DV (in the Easy Setup menu) so that you can follow along with this tutorial.

Exporting from Final Cut Pro

Let's start by exporting the Final Cut Pro Timeline into Motion.

1   Launch Final Cut Pro HD.

2   Choose File > Open, navigate to APTS_Motion > Lessons > Lesson14, and open the project **MotionExport**.

In the Final Cut Pro Timeline you'll see that we've created a simple test scene. You'll notice two small clips sitting above the main clip. These clips serve no design function, except perhaps to show you what *not* to do. (Anyone who thinks video clips spinning inside other video clips is cool needs to hear this: Wham! split up. The '80s are over. Move on.) They've been included only to demonstrate Final Cut Pro–to–Motion export capabilities.

3   Double-click the **Golden Gate SD.mov** clip in the V1 video track of the Timeline.

4 In the Viewer (the left of the two video display windows), click the Motion tab.

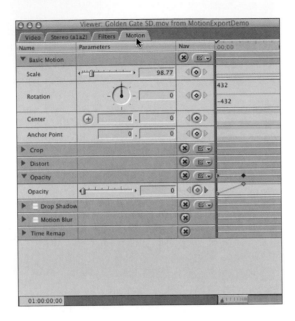

You'll notice that there are keyframes in the Opacity section. They are there to fade the clip in from black over the first few frames of the Timeline.

5 Make sure you're at frame 1 in the Timeline (if not, press the Home key).

6 Press Option-P to preview the Timeline.

You'll see we have a few things happening. First, the main clip fades in. Second, another small clip of the bridge fades in spinning and then fades out again. Third, while that clip is spinning, a third clip with a bad case of drop shadow fades in, scales down, and then fades out.

7   Double-click the two smaller clips in the Timeline, and look at their parameters in the Motion tab.

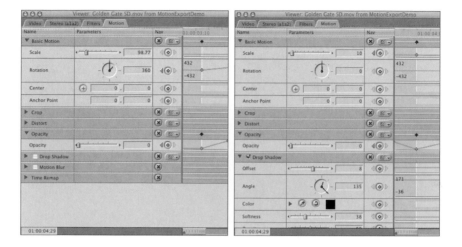

You'll see that for the first of the two smaller clips, the Rotation and Opacity parameters have been keyframed. For the second smaller clip, the Scale and Opacity have been animated, and the Drop Shadow has been activated and set.

What we'll discover shortly is that any keyframes or modified settings in the Motion tab of Final Cut Pro will be exported to Motion. The only exceptions to this rule are time remapping and motion blur; in Motion, time cannot be remapped in the main interface, and Motion Blur is a global setting.

It's just as important to know what *isn't* exported. Most significantly, transitions are not exported. The export to Motion is what's sometimes referred to as a *cuts-only* export. If you want to bring a cross dissolve from Final Cut Pro into Motion, you have to keyframe the opacity of one clip and fade it up over another (instead of using a cross-dissolve transition).

Let's go ahead and export the Timeline to Motion.

8   Click in the Timeline, and then press Cmd-A to select all of the elements.

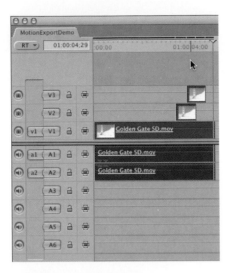

9   Choose File > Export > Export to "Motion" Project.

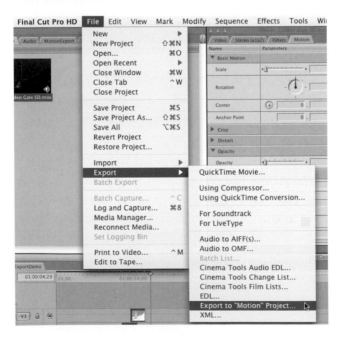

The Motion Export dialog appears.

There are two options when exporting: Launch "Motion" and Embed "Motion" Content. If the Launch "Motion" box is checked (which it is by default), then Motion will automatically open once you click the Save button.

If the Embed "Motion" Content box is checked, then Final Cut Pro will delete the footage you've selected in the Timeline and replace it with a reference to the Motion project you're creating.

If you're roughing out your composite in Final Cut Pro but plan to fine-tune it in Motion, go ahead and opt to embed Motion content. It means that Final Cut Pro will transfer your Timeline (or at least the part you selected) into Motion and leave a single clip in the Final Cut Pro Timeline where the content used to be. This single clip is a reference to the Motion project that now contains your content.

NOTE ▶ Video clips appearing in the Timeline in Motion and Final Cut Pro are only references to real media stored on the hard drive. At no time during this process is the media's location changing on the drive. Rather, the *references* to the clips are being moved from Final Cut Pro to Motion.

Another time you'll use the embed-content option is when you want to apply a Motion effect to a single clip in your Timeline. Maybe you want to apply a Light Rays filter to a clip of an alien abduction. (Light rays are involved in seven out of every ten alien abductions in the state of New Mexico alone.) You would simply select the clip and export with the embed-content option, and the clip would then be automatically replaced in the Timeline with a reference to the Motion project. The Motion project would contain one clip, to which you'd apply the Light Rays filter.

In our case, we want to create a lower-third graphic to be used in Final Cut Pro. So we want to leave the footage of the Golden Gate Bridge in the Final Cut Pro Timeline to preserve the option of making changes to the edit later.

10 Uncheck the Embed "Motion" Content box.

11 Navigate to APTS_Motion > Lessons > Lesson14 > StudentSaves.

12 Name the file *MotionExportDemo* and click Save.

Creating the Lower Third in Motion

Because we left Launch "Motion" selected in the previous exercise, the Motion splash screen should display, and then Motion will open with the new project. We can now create the lower third.

1 Press F6 to open the Timing pane.

2 Turn on the Show/Hide Keyframes button in the lower-left corner of the Timeline.

This will display a diamond under the timing bar of an object at any frames containing keyframes for that object.

3 Press the spacebar to begin playback.

Notice that the three clips from the Final Cut Pro Timeline are now stacked in identical formation in the Motion Timeline. As anticipated, the Opacity, Rotation, and Scale keyframes are intact.

In the interest of saving time, we'll import a previously created lower third. Feel free, of course, to create your own.

4   Halt playback, move to frame 1 (Home), and click the Layers tab (F5).

5   In the File Browser (Cmd-1), navigate to APTS_Motion > Lessons > Lesson14. Select **LowerThird,** and click the Import button in the Preview area.

A new layer is created, and the **LowerThird** Motion project is imported into this layer.

NOTE ▸ Importing one Motion project into another Motion project, as we've just done, is a one-way street. The objects and layers of the imported project are simply copied and pasted into the open project. The original project is unaffected. If you make changes to the original project later, they will not be updated in the project into which it was previously imported.

6   Resume playback.

You should now see a lower third consisting of the Flow 2 particle preset and the text "Golden Gate Bridge, San Francisco." It's time to bring the lower third back into Final Cut Pro. If we were to bring it in as is, we'd also be bringing in the footage of the bridge with it. Since we already have the footage of the bridge inside Final Cut Pro, let's turn it *off* in the Motion project.

7   In the Layers tab, uncheck the boxes for Layer 1, Layer 2, and Layer 3.

These clips were useful as a reference while we created the lower third, but we can turn them off now to make sure that only the lower third is imported back into Final Cut Pro.

We also want to make sure that audio is not imported back into Final Cut Pro.

8   In the Audio tab (Cmd-6), uncheck the On box for **Short Mix.aif**.

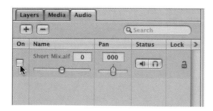

9   Save the project (Cmd-S) and quit Motion.

Importing Motion Clips into Final Cut Pro

Let's bring the Motion clip back into Final Cut Pro.

1 In Final Cut Pro, choose File > Import > Files.

2 Navigate to APTS_Motion > Lessons > Lesson14 > StudentSaves > **MotionExportDemo.motn**, and click Choose.

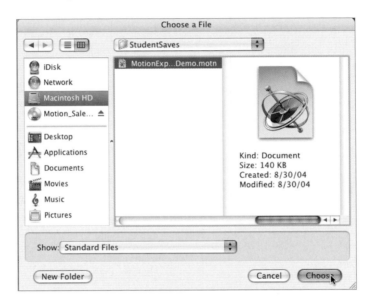

3 Click over to the MotionExport project tab in the Browser.

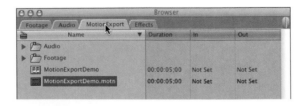

You should find a clip in the MotionExport project tab called **Motion-ExportDemo.motn**. The .motn filename extension tells you it's a Motion project file.

4   Drag **MotionExportDemo.motn** from the MotionExport project tab into
the top left of the Final Cut Pro Timeline, creating a new video layer and
inserting the clip at frame 1.

5   Move to frame 1 (Home), and press Option-P to preview the Timeline.

You should see the lower-third form just as you did in Motion. We have
imported a reference to the Motion project into Final Cut Pro.

What if you decide you want to change the lower third? Maybe you want
to add a glow to the text. With the seamless integration between Motion
and Final Cut Pro, you can do this without any need to reimport footage.

6   In the Final Cut Pro Timeline, right- or Ctrl-click **MotionExport-Demo.motn**, and choose Open in Editor from the pop-up menu.

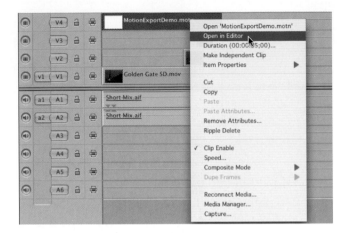

Motion launches again, opening your project, **MotionExportDemo.motn**.

7   In the Layers tab (F5), select the Golden Gate text object.

8   In the Style pane of the Text Inspector (F4), activate Glow (check the box).

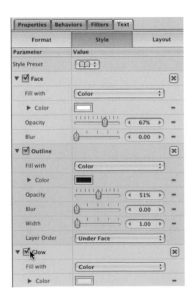

9   Save the project (Cmd-S).

10   Press Cmd-Tab to switch back to Final Cut Pro.

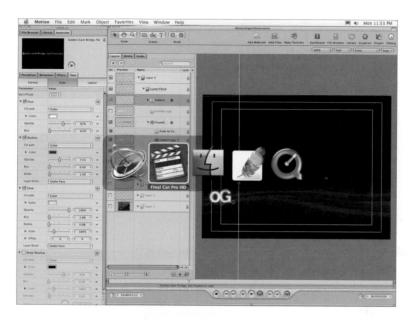

Your lower-third text should now appear with a glow in Final Cut Pro.

You can keep both Final Cut Pro and Motion open at the same time, and if you make and save any changes in Motion, they will be automatically updated in Final Cut Pro.

▶ Using Final Cut Pro's Video Scopes

An incredibly useful by-product of the integration between Motion and Final Cut Pro is that it gives Motion projects access to Final Cut Pro's Video Scopes. By referencing a Motion project inside Final Cut Pro, you can preview broadcast-safe color information in the scopes. You can then apply a global color corrector to the referenced Motion project to adjust levels until everything is within broadcast-legal values.

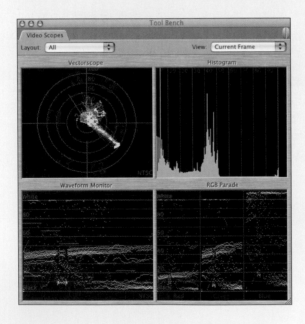

Creating a DVD Motion Menu

Motion menus for DVDs have quickly become a staple of the modern motion graphics design firm. They provide the perfect playground for techniques that might appear too garish elsewhere. Motion and DVD Studio Pro make a killer combination for creating motion menus.

Normally, motion menus are rendered out as QuickTime movies and then brought into the authoring application to be used as a menu background. The problem with this workflow is that if you need to make a change to, say, animated text in your menu, you typically have to re-render the movie in the motion graphics package and then reimport it into the authoring package.

With Motion and DVD Studio Pro, however, you can import a Motion project file into DVD Studio Pro. Then, if you need to make changes, simply update the Motion project and your menu background will automatically update in DVD Studio Pro. It's a simple solution to a traditionally painful workflow.

> **NOTE ▶** The following exercises assume that you have DVD Studio Pro 3.0 or later installed on the same system you're using for Motion, and that you have a basic working knowledge of DVD Studio Pro. They also assume that you're using the NTSC version of DVD Studio Pro. If you live in the PAL universe, you can temporarily set DVD Studio Pro to NTSC (in the Encoding section of the Preferences pane) so that you can follow along with the tutorial. In order to follow the exercises, set your DVD Studio Pro configuration to Basic (choose Window > Configurations > Basic or press F1).

Importing Photoshop Files

We'll create our motion menu using an Adobe Photoshop file as the starting point.

1   Launch Motion. If you have any other projects open, press Cmd-Option-W to close them.

2   Press Cmd-N to create a new project. Choose NTSC DV from the Preset menu in the Select Project Preset dialog.

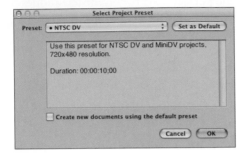

TIP ▸ NTSC DV is the best choice for NTSC DVD development. This is because NTSC MPEG2 streams are 720x480 pixels, which is also the resolution of NTSC DV (as opposed to D1 video, which is 720x486). If you're fortunate enough to live in the PAL world, you can use the PAL Broadcast SD preset for your motion menu creation.

3   In the File Browser (Cmd-1), navigate to APTS_Motion > Lessons > Lesson14.

4   Open the Layers tab (F5).

Be sure to read through the next step before performing it.

5   Drag **HiSpy.psd** into the Layers tab *but don't release the mouse button.*

By pausing with the mouse button pressed down, you bring up the drop menu. As you can see, when importing a Photoshop document, you're given several options. First, you can choose to import merged layers. This means the Photoshop file will come in as a single element, with all of the layers it contains collapsed into single object in the Layers tab. This is the default behavior when you drag and drop a Photoshop document into your project without pausing to wait for the drop menu to appear.

Second, you can choose to import all layers. This brings in all of the layers of the Photoshop document and creates separate objects in your Motion project for each layer.

Finally, you can choose to import a specific layer in the Photoshop document. The individual layers of the document appear in a list below the Import All Layers option.

6   Choose Import All Layers from the drop menu.

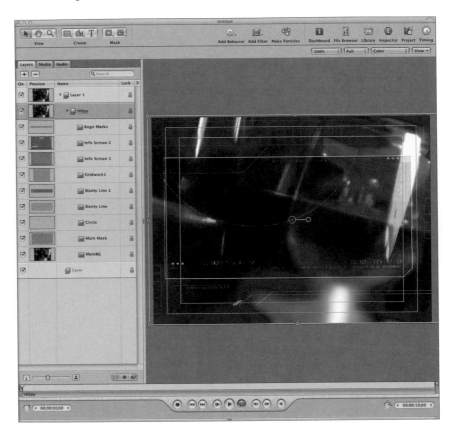

Each layer of the Photoshop document is imported as a separate object.

Viewing Opacity and Blend Modes

By clicking each object and looking at the Dashboard, you can see the Opacity and Blend Mode settings for each object. Sometimes, however, you'll want to quickly compare the opacity and blend modes for several objects at the same time. This is where a couple of options in the Layers tab come in handy.

1   Click the right-pointing arrow (called the Show Columns button) in the top-right corner of the Layers tab, just to the right of the Lock column title.

2   Choose Opacity from the pop-up menu.

3   Click the Show Columns button again, and choose Blend from the pop-up menu.

4 Expand the Layers tab to display the Opacity and Blend Mode columns by dragging its drawer handle (the thin line separating the Project pane from the Canvas) to the right.

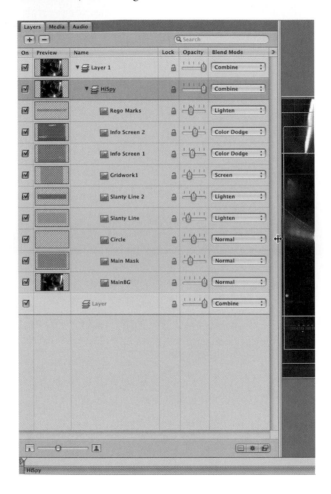

Being able to view the Opacity and Blend Mode settings for each object is very handy for making quick changes to your comp.

5   When you're finished, deselect the Opacity and Blend Mode options in the Show Columns menu, and return the Layers tab to a normal size by dragging its drawer handle to the left as necessary.

> **TIP** You can also import vector artwork—such as drawings created in Adobe Illustrator and Macromedia FreeHand—into Motion. Motion will perform what's called a *continuous rasterize* of the artwork, preserving anti-aliased edges even at extreme zooms. To import vector artwork, it must be saved as a single-layer Adobe PDF document. Motion does not support direct import of Illustrator or EPS documents.

Applying an Image Mask

Since we're here to learn about integration with DVD Studio Pro, let's jump ahead to a version of the project that's already "wired up."

1   Close any open projects (Cmd-Option-W).

2   Press Cmd-O, navigate to APTS_Motion > Lessons > Lesson14, and open **A.MotionMenu**.

3   Press the spacebar to begin playback.

The project has been set up with some nice animated elements. However, the main background image just pops onto the screen at frame 25. We want to create a transition effect to bring it onscreen, and we'll use an object image mask to achieve this.

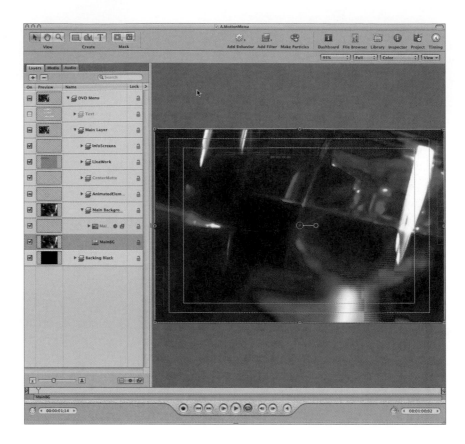

4   In the File Browser, double-click **TransitionMatte.mov** and play it in the QuickTime preview window that pops up.

You'll see a transition movie that consists of simple box particles. If you'd like to look at the Motion project used to create this clip, it can be found in APTS_Motion > Lessons > Lesson14 > ExtraContent, and is named **TransitionCreator**.

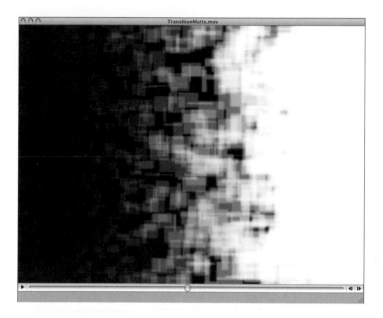

5   Close the QuickTime preview window.

6   In the Layers tab, make sure that MainBG is selected (*not* the layer it belongs to, Main Background).

7   Choose Object > Add Image Mask.

A new mask object is added directly under the MainBG object.

8   Open the Image Mask tab (F4) of the Inspector.

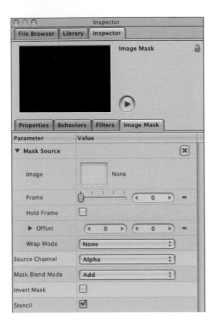

An image mask is just like a shape mask, but it uses image data instead of one of Motion's shapes to define the mask. *Anything* in Motion can be used as an image mask—a QuickTime movie, a still, a particle system, or even a layer containing multiple objects.

9   Move to frame 25 in the Timeline (type *25* into the Current Frame field box in the lower left of the Canvas).

10   Drag **TransitionMatte.mov** from the File Browser into the Layers tab and onto the dividing line between Image Mask (the image mask you just

added to MainBG) and the Backing Black layer. Release the mouse button
when the position indicator lines up with the MainBG object's label (*not*
the Image Mask's label).

NOTE ► There are three positions that the position indicator can take
on the border between Image Mask and Backing Black. Make sure you
choose the one where the hollow circle of the position indicator lines up with
the small picture icon of the MainBG item, as in the following figure.

11 Uncheck the On box for the TransitionMatte object.

We've added the TransitionMatte clip to the Timeline, but we've turned it
off, so it won't appear in the Canvas. We only want to use it as a reference
for the image mask.

12 In the Layers tab, select Image Mask.

13   Open the Image Mask tab (F4) of the Inspector.

14   Drag the ghosted TransitionMatte object from the Layers tab into the rounded square labeled Image in the Inspector, and release the mouse button.

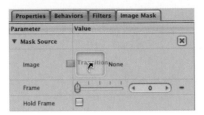

This rounded square is known as an *image well*. You'll see them all over Motion, and they allow you to quickly select a source image for certain masking and effects operations.

15   Still in the Image Mask Inspector, set the Source Channel to Luminance.

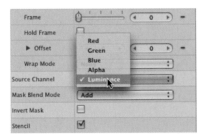

By default, Motion looks at the alpha channel for the information to use for the mask. In this case, the image data is in the normal RGB channels, so we chose to use the luminance image data for the mask instead of the alpha.

16 Move to frame 1, and press the spacebar to resume playback.

The background image now materializes gradually onto the screen from right to left.

Importing Motion Projects into DVD Studio Pro

The final version of the motion menu project is the file **C.FinalMenu**. Let's bring it into DVD Studio Pro. There are several ways to import clips into DVD Studio Pro; we'll use the File > Import method.

1 Close Motion if it's open.

2 Launch DVD Studio Pro.

3 Make sure you're using the Basic configuration by pressing F1.

4 In the Encoding tab of the Preferences pane (DVD Studio Pro > Preferences), make sure the Video Standard is set to NTSC.

If it isn't, you'll need to change it to NTSC, close the existing project, and then choose File > New to create a new NTSC-based project.

5 Make sure you have a new project open, and choose File > Import > Asset.

6 Navigate to APTS_Motion > Lessons > Lesson14, and double-click **C.FinalMenu**.

The **C.FinalMenu** Motion project is imported into your Assets bin. If your Assets bin wasn't already open, it will automatically pop to the front of the screen.

7   Drag **C.FinalMenu.motn** from your Assets tab into your Menu tab, *but don't release the mouse button.*

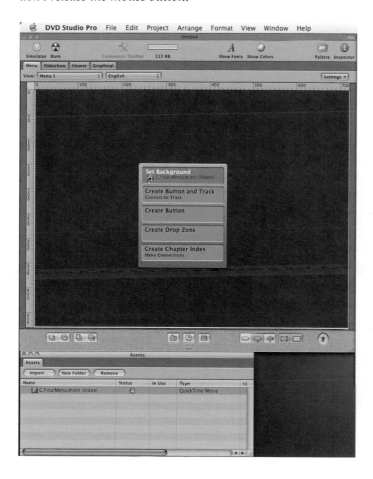

8   Choose Set Background from the drop menu and release the mouse button.

Don't panic if you experience a lengthy pause after releasing the mouse button or if you see the ominous Mac OS X spinning beach ball. Within a few moments, you should be greeted with a nice black screen in your Menu tab viewer.

9 Click the Start/Stop Motion Menu button (otherwise known as "that little walking guy") at the bottom right of the Menu tab viewer to preview the menu.

You should now see an animated—albeit stilted—preview of the Motion project happily integrated as a motion menu background.

From here you can use DVD Studio Pro's shapes to create button over-lays and the like. (There is content in the Lesson 14 > ExtraContent folder that you can use to create additional submenus if you feel adven-turous.)

How do you make changes to the Motion project?

10 Stop the preview by clicking the Start/Stop Motion Menu button.

11 In the Assets tab, right- or Ctrl-click **C.FinalMenu.motn** and choose Open In Editor from the pop-up menu.

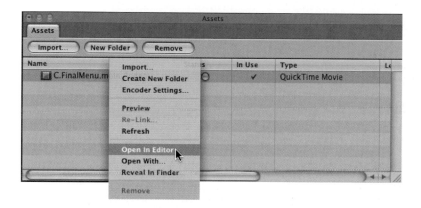

Motion automatically launches with the **C.FinalMenu** project open. In the same way as described for Final Cut Pro, you can modify the project in Motion, save it (Cmd-S), and press Cmd-Tab to switch back to DVD Studio Pro, where the menu will dynamically update, reflecting your changes.

> ▶ **Motion-Shake Integration**
>
> Before we wrap, here's one last tip on integration as it applies to Motion and Apple's Shake. Shake is an incredibly powerful visual-effects compositing system, but it lacks a particle system. Using the same integration we've seen with Final Cut Pro and DVD Studio Pro, you can import a Motion project into Shake and use it as a particle system "plug-in." The only catch is that you'll first need to rename the project file in the Mac OS X Finder from **MyProjectFile.motn** to **MyProjectFile.mov** so that Shake will recognize it as a valid file type.

TIP ▶ You can also use this renaming method to open Motion projects in QuickTime Player.

The integration between Motion, Final Cut Pro, and DVD Studio Pro is a huge boon for smaller studios. On one machine you can edit, finesse, and author DVDs as well as create custom effects for video programs without the need for multiple renders and imports. It may not have the excitement of exploding particle showers, but Motion's integration with the other Pro apps may well become your favorite feature.

What You've Learned

▶ The Final Cut Pro Timeline (or selected sections of it) can be imported into Motion with tracks, position, and motion tab settings preserved.

▶ The Embed "Motion" Content export option can be used to replace sections of the Final Cut Pro Timeline with a reference to a Motion project.

▶ Motion projects can be imported into Final Cut Pro as virtual video clips and will then dynamically update when modifications are made in Motion.

▶ The Open in Editor command is used to edit an instance of a Motion project in the Final Cut Pro Timeline.

▶ Motion can import Photoshop documents as a merged single image; a layer consisting of objects for each Photoshop layer; or as a single, specified layer.

▶ Image masks can be used to mask off an object using any other object in the project as the source of the mask.

▶ Motion projects can be imported into DVD Studio Pro as assets, and they will then dynamically update when modifications are made in Motion.

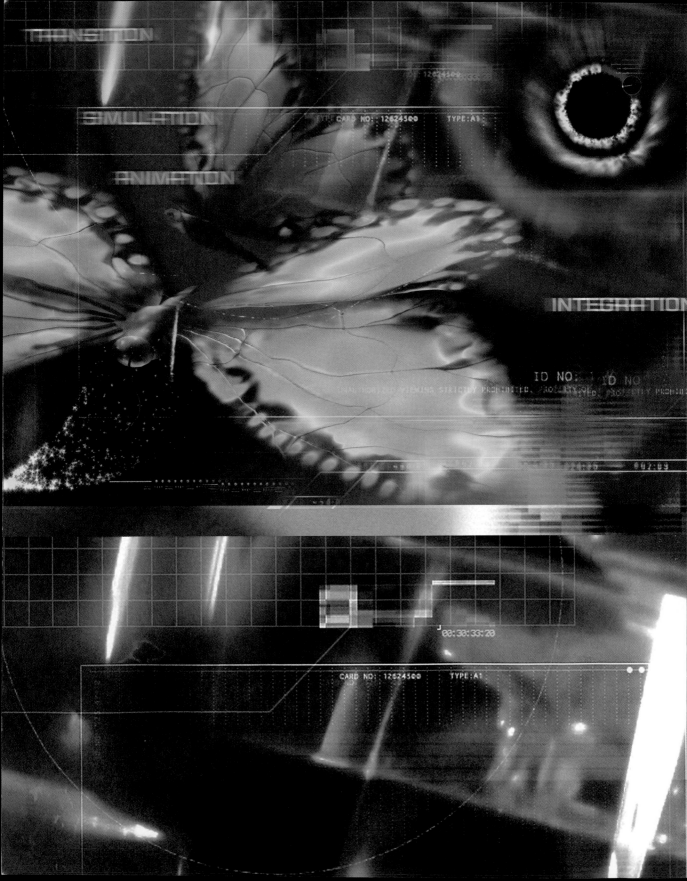

Motion for After Effects Users

Adobe After Effects is a powerful and time-tested platform for motion graphics, and it makes a perfect partner to Motion in a postproduction pipeline. A lot of artists go back a long way with After Effects (as is reflected in the oft-uttered phrase "I've been using it since it was CoSA," heard at user groups worldwide). Thus many people will be looking to transfer their knowledge of After Effects to Motion. If that's you, then this appendix should provide you with a good starting point for transitioning to Motion.

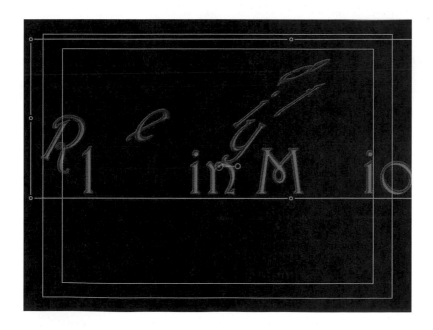

This Book and the Seasoned Veteran

This book has been written with an understanding that many readers will be new to the field of motion graphics, as well as new to Motion itself. However, don't by any means think you should skip earlier exercises in the book and head straight to the "advanced stuff."

The user interface in Motion is so dramatically different from the interface in any software you've been using that every lesson will contain information relevant to you, regardless of your years of experience creating digital motion graphics. You will find that newbie explanations are concise and easy to skim, so they shouldn't bog you down as you read through the lessons to discover the power of Motion's feature set.

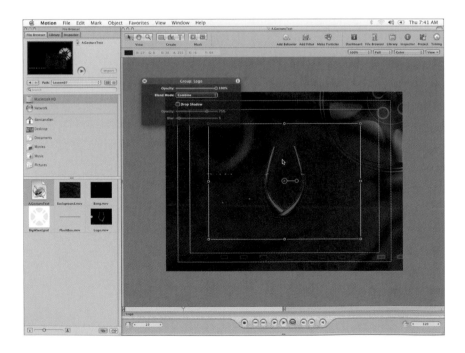

Real-Time Design

The most dramatic difference between Motion and After Effects is the real-time design engine built into Motion. With it, you'll be able to perform many of the tasks you do on a daily basis in After Effects, but without having to render a RAM preview.

A suggested workflow for creating motion graphics with Motion and After Effects is to begin in Motion, playing with various elements and coming up with design concepts for the project you're working on. Once you've figured out how you want things to flow, you can move into After Effects to make use of its extended tool set to create the basic elements for your final comp. As a last step, you can bring these prerendered elements back into Motion for real-time manipulation, color correction, and final tweaks in real time in front of the client.

As you begin to work in Motion, you may find yourself fighting the urge to pause playback while you make changes. You'll discover that the Modify > Render RAM preview > View > Modify cycle is deeply entrenched in your subconscious. As a result, you'll continually be pausing playback while you adjust parameters, for no apparent reason. It's important to fight the urge as much as possible. Once you get a sense of the power of making real-time adjustments, you'll be amazed at how much more productively you can work.

At some point you'll reach the limit of your hardware to play back all the elements in your comp in real time. Then you'll have two options. First, you can solo a particular element of your project (Ctrl-S) to restore real-time performance to it. Motion does this by hiding all other elements and dedicating the processing power to that single soloed item. Unsoloing (Ctrl-S again) will return the other items to the screen.

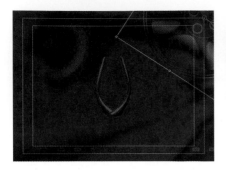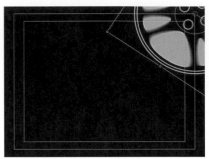

Elements in larger compositions can be soloed to restore real-time performance.

The second option is to render a RAM preview. As in After Effects, you can generate a RAM preview of your play range. The hot key for this is Cmd-R. Even though using this method doesn't give you real-time tweaking (each time you tweak a parameter, you'll need to rerender the RAM preview), you still benefit from Motion's speed. In an informal test, I found that Motion could render scenes up to ten times faster than After Effects because of the way it leverages the graphics card's GPU.

You may find that even when Motion drops below the intended frame rate for your project, the playback speed is still acceptable enough to make design judgments. In such cases you'll render RAM previews infrequently, just to be sure the timing is set as you want it.

Behaviors Before Keyframing

Motion has a fully fledged keyframing system, and you could jump in and start setting keyframes in a workflow similar to that of After Effects. Before you do, though, you should spend some time with Motion's behaviors.

Motion's behaviors are designed to free motion graphics artists from the banality of common tasks. Designers are always making objects fly on and off the screen, fade in and out, and animate along motion paths. Instead of requiring laborious keyframing, Motion's behaviors allow you to perform these tasks with incredible ease.

Take spinning an object, for example. In After Effects, you would set a rotation keyframe at frame 1 and another at, say, frame 200. You'd have to make sure that the keyframes had linear interpolation to keep the spin from speeding up and slowing down.

You'd render a preview. If the spin was too slow, you'd increase the rotation angle at frame 200 and then render another RAM preview. If it was too fast, you'd decrease the rotation angle and preview.

Then what if you decided to have the rotation continue to frame 300? You'd have to divide the angle by 200 and then multiply by 300, and place the new keyframe there.

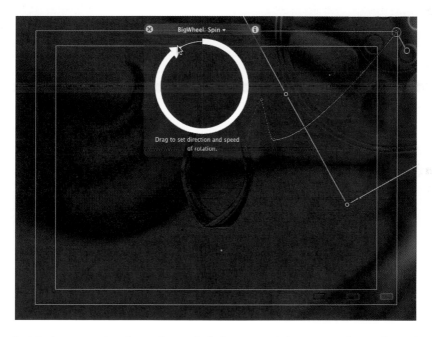

But in Motion, you simply apply a Spin behavior and drag around a circle in the Dashboard (Motion's quick parameter access window), and your object will spin. If you don't like the speed, you can interactively adjust it by dragging around the circle—there's no need to render. If you extend the rotation to frame 300, there's nothing to change; since the Spin behavior is a rate of rotation, it will automatically be correct across the Timeline.

By using behaviors, you can save the heavy-duty keyframing for where it's needed. And if you're a die-hard control freak, you can "bake" the behaviors and turn them into keyframes ready to be tweaked.

As you'll see in the very first lesson, behaviors can be used for simple things like moving an object, but they can also be used to create complex physical simulations that would be nearly impossible using keyframes, and extremely difficult to code in JavaScript.

Be a Stranger to the Timeline

After Effects is based around the all-powerful Timeline; when you're designing in After Effects, you pretty much eat, work, and sleep in the Timeline. Motion also has a Timeline—however, once you go native and start "thinking in Motion," you'll find that you very rarely visit it.

That's because of a very cool feature called the *mini-Timeline*. The mini-Timeline contains a single timing bar for the object you've selected in the Canvas (that is, Motion's viewer). Essentially, it solos the timing information for just the comp element you're working with. That way, there's no need to sort through a list of 30 or 40 layers to find the one you need to adjust. You can set In and Out points and shift clips in time all from the mini-Timeline.

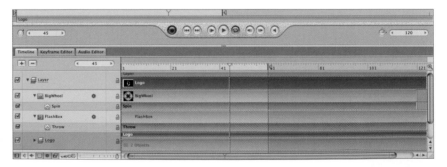

The mini-Timeline (at top) eliminates the need for frequent visits to the Timeline.

The only occasion on which you'll really need to visit the Timeline is when you need to align the timing of one clip with another. To select and reorder your elements, you can use the Layers tab. The Layers tab contains all the information about elements in your comp without the Timeline tagged on, taking up much less space on your screen.

What about keyframes? Unlike After Effects, Motion has a fully dedicated Keyframe Editor, so you have plenty of space to tweak out Bezier curves and the like. If you're worried about getting parameters into the Keyframe Editor to edit, don't be—all you need to do is click a parameter's Animation menu button and Motion will automatically bring that parameter up in the Keyframe Editor, ready to tweak.

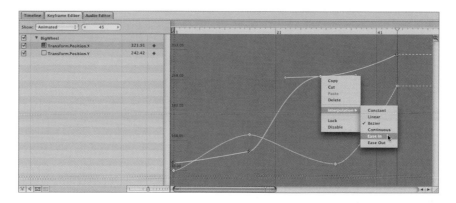

If you need the Timeline as a security blanket at first, that's OK. In fact, you can even click a little button at the bottom left of the Timeline to have all your keyframes appear in it. You'll still need to edit them in the Keyframe Editor, but you'll be able to see and navigate through the keyframes in a fashion similar to that in After Effects.

While we're talking keyframes, Motion has a global auto-keyframing system instead of the per-parameter auto-keyframe system used in After Effects. That means when Record Animation mode is on (Motion's term for auto-keyframe), moving *any* parameter will generate a keyframe.

The Record button (far left) turns on automatic keyframing for any adjusted parameter.

The other missing piece of the Timeline puzzle is access to parameters. In After Effects you expand the transform parameters or effect parameters of a layer to access their controls. In Motion you have the Inspector.

The Inspector contains four tabs: the Properties tab (hot key F1), the Behaviors tab (F2), the Filters tab (F3), and the object tab (F4). These tabs contain all the parameters you would usually adjust in the Timeline in After Effects. The transform parameters will be found in the Properties tab in Motion. Like the mini-Timeline, the Inspector will show the parameters only for the object currently selected in the Canvas. (The last of the four tabs, the object tab, changes its name depending on what type of object is selected.)

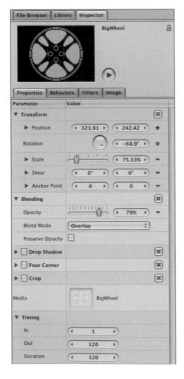

Just to reiterate: Once you start working with the Layers tab in Motion, you really won't need to make regular visits to the Timeline. So try out the workflow before you jump back to your Timeline-hugging ways.

Everything Has a Timing Bar

In After Effects, if you want to deactivate a filter on a layer for a certain part of the Timeline, you need to either set all its parameters to 0, or split the layer in two and delete the filter from one of the split segments.

In Motion, *everything* has a bar in the Timeline. So if you want a filter to affect an object only from, say, frames 1 to 12, all you need to do is set the *filter's* In point to frame 1 and its Out point to frame 12. You can do the same for behaviors. This makes it very easy to apply multiple behaviors to affect an object at different points in time.

Be aware of this while you're working. If you don't keep it in mind, you might think you're trimming the Out point of a piece of footage and then discover that you've trimmed the Out point only for a filter or behavior attached to the object.

Motion Nomenclature

If you're used to certain nomenclature in After Effects, you may be in for a surprise when you start working in Motion. Terms you might recognize, such as *layers,* have slightly different meanings, and sometimes Motion uses a wholly different word to identify a familiar concept.

The following sections clarify the meanings of some key terms in Motion.

Layers, Objects, and Comps

One item that will undoubtedly stump a few After Effects users is the naming convention for elements in a project. Here's the skinny:

▶   What After Effects calls a *layer,* Motion calls an *object.*

▶   What After Effects calls a *comp* (or *composition*), Motion calls a *layer.*

So you combine several objects (such as QuickTime movies, stills, and so on) and gather them in a layer. Layers can be nested inside other layers. When you initially create a project, there's a default layer into which all the objects are assembled.

To "precompose" several objects, you select them and choose Object > Group (Cmd-Shift-G). This will take the selected objects and place them in a new layer.

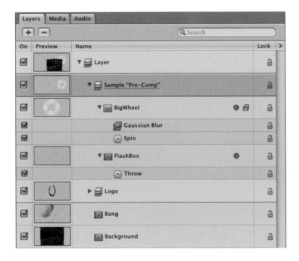

To summarize, a *layer* in Motion refers specifically to the container (or *comp* in After Effects–speak) that holds one or more objects.

Play Range vs. Work Area

In After Effects, the *work area* defines that portion of your Timeline currently being edited. When you render a RAM preview, it's the work area that gets cached.

In Motion, the *play range* is essentially the same concept, with the exception, of course, that the play range defines the area that Motion previews for you in real time.

One important distinction in the way the two applications work occurs in the render settings. By default, After Effects renders only the work area unless the user specifies otherwise. In Motion, the settings default to rendering the entire length of the project unless the user checks a box to specify that only the play range is to be rendered.

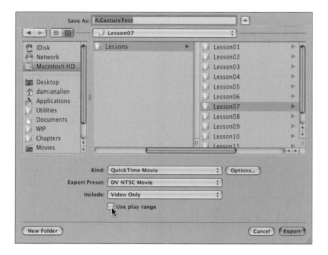

Transfer/Blend Modes

After Effects refers to the various methods of overlaying elements of a composite as *transfer* modes. Motion follows the Adobe Photoshop convention of calling them *blend* modes.

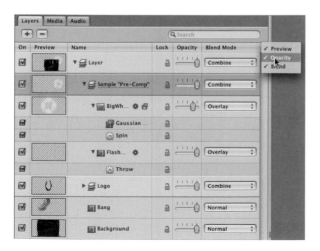

Blend mode and opacity settings are available in the Dashboard or the Properties tab of the Inspector for each object as it's selected. You can, however, view them for all objects and layers at the same time by selecting those view options in the Layers tab.

Types of Interpolation

When keyframing, Motion offers the same interpolation methods for keyframes as After Effects, although the names are a little different. Linear, Bezier, Ease In, and Ease Out all correspond to the same functions, but the two other names in Motion correspond to After Effects interpolations as follows:

▶   Constant = Hold

▶   Continuous = Easy Ease

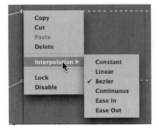

JavaScript vs. Parameter Behaviors

There is no scripting in Motion. In a room full of motion graphics designers, this statement would no doubt elicit sniffles from a handful of people and silent celebration from the rest.

Artists are notoriously intimidated by scripting, even the efficient JavaScript available in After Effects via the pick whip. However, in place of scripting, Apple has developed a very clean way of creating sophisticated animations without the user's having to learn a lick of code. It is called *parameter behaviors,* and they can be applied to individual parameters within an object, its behaviors, or its filters.

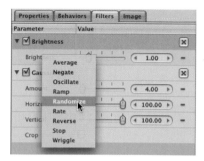

For example, if you wanted an object to flicker on the screen, you could apply a Brightness filter to the object and then apply a Randomize parameter behavior to the brightness level (simply by right- or Ctrl-clicking the label for the Brightness slider). Alternately, if you wanted it to pulse in a steady rhythm, you could apply an Oscillate parameter behavior. You can instantly get a meaningful result and, with a few easy tweaks, dial in the exact setting you need.

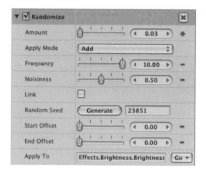

Certainly some things can be scripted in After Effects that would be impossible with parameter behaviors, but it's amazing how far you can take your animation simply by tweaking parameter behaviors.

Particle Systems

Motion has incredibly intuitive real-time particle systems. In conjunction with behaviors, particle systems can create just about any 2D particle effect you're after. Each particle can inherit behaviors to cause it to randomly move on an individual motion path, scale up or down, accelerate via gravity, swarm around a specific object, or even be repelled by an object.

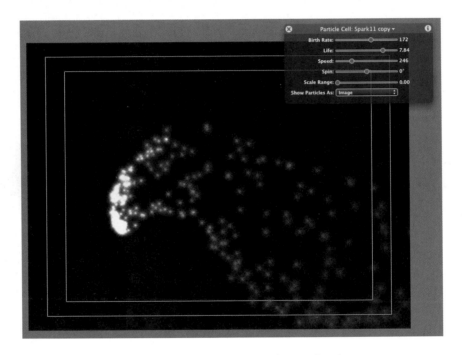

Motion ships with a host of presets, but the interface makes it very easy to develop custom effects for specific applications. In addition, *anything* in Motion can become a particle—a QuickTime movie, a still, shapes, text, or even a nested layer of elements.

Text in Motion

Motion has a comprehensive text feature set, with three tabs full of tweakable parameters in the user interface. It ships with dozens of text preset effects, which can be previewed in real time.

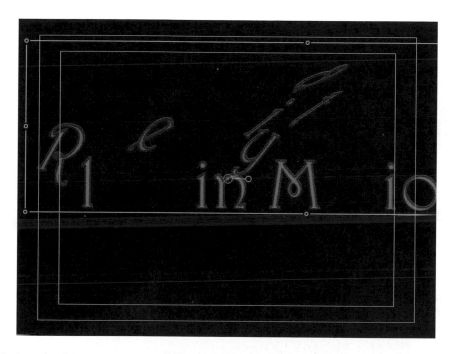

Motion also has text sequence effects, similar to the text animators available in After Effects. With Motion's real-time preview capabilities, these sequence behaviors become far more intuitive to set up and manipulate.

Motion Coordinate System and Dynamic Guides

In After Effects, the positions of objects in the comp are measured from the top-left corner of the viewer. So if a composition were 640x480 pixels, an object at its center would have position values of 320, 240 (half the width and half the height).

In Motion, the coordinate system originates from the center of the screen. So if an object were dead center in the Canvas, its position values would be 0, 0. If you moved it 20 pixels to the left, its value would be –20, 0. Move it 20 pixels to the right, and its value would be 20, 0, and so on.

This may seem a little odd at first, but it's actually incredibly useful. How many times have you had to divide an unusual comp resolution in half horizontally and vertically, just to determine the center position for an object? With Motion, whenever you set its position to 0, 0, it's automatically centered (at least, its anchor point is).

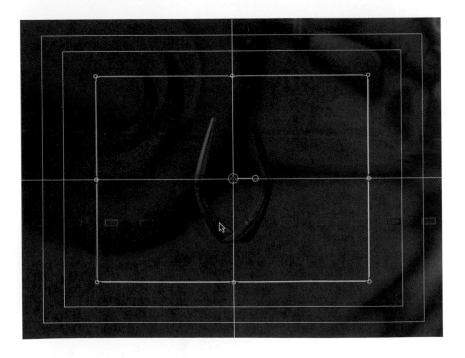

In addition to this coordinate system, Motion offers *Dynamic Guides.* These are yellow guides that appear as you drag objects in the Canvas. They allow you to snap objects to the center or edges of the Canvas, or to automatically align them horizontally or vertically with other objects already onscreen. This in itself is a significant time-saver.

The Dashboard

The Dashboard doesn't really have an After Effects equivalent. The closest equivalent is the floating effects window used in After Effects to edit effects parameters. In Motion, the Dashboard provides easy access to the most important controls. This allows users to quickly make changes to fundamental aspects of objects, filters, and behaviors without having to dig through dozens of parameters.

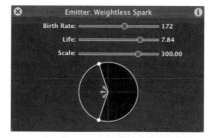

After Effects–Compatible Plug-ins

Many of your favorite After Effects plug-ins will work with Motion; all you need to do is point Motion's preferences to their installed location on your hard disk. Be aware that when using third-party filters, you may not get the real-time performance you experience with Motion-native plug-ins, since they're not optimized to take advantage of your graphics card's GPU.

More Feature Crossover

There are other ways in which the features and capabilities of Motion overlap with those of After Effects. Here are just a few.

Interpret Footage

In After Effects, Ctrl- or right-clicking a video clip in a project window gives you access to its interpret footage settings. In Motion, selecting an object in the Layers tab and pressing Shift-F will jump you straight to the Media tab of the Inspector, where things like alpha interpretation, field order, and frame rate can be adjusted.

Motion Blur

In After Effects, motion blur is enabled or disabled for individual layers. In Motion, motion blur is a global setting applied to all moving objects and activated via the View menu at the top right of the Canvas.

Settings for the quality and intensity of the motion blur can be adjusted in the Render Settings tab of the Project Properties window (the keyboard shortcut for opening the Project Properties is Cmd-J). The Project Properties window in Motion is similar to Composition Settings in After Effects.

Color Values

In Motion, RGB color values are usually listed in the range 0 to 1 instead of 0 to 255. To convert from After Effects' values of 0 to 255, simply divide by 255.

Masking

Motion offers four main masking tools: Rectangle, Circle, Bezier, and B-Spline. Each object can have multiple masks that can combine by adding, subtracting, or intersecting.

Motion also provides image masks, added via the Object menu. These are the equivalent of using a Track Matte in After Effects.

Markers

You can create markers while audio is playing back by pressing Shift-M. This is similar to pressing the asterisk key on the numeric keypad during playback in After Effects.

Conclusion

This has been just a brief summary of the crossover between Motion and After Effects. Take the time to explore the interface, and try to learn the "Motion way" before trying to make Motion behave like After Effects. You'll find yourself becoming far more productive as you begin using behaviors, the Dashboard, and the mini-Timeline.

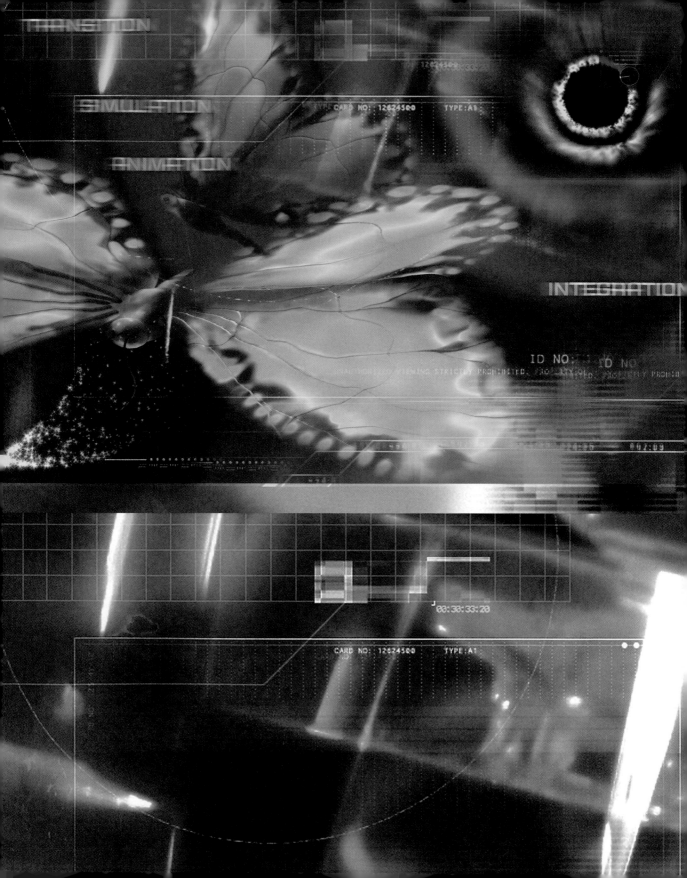

Appendix **B**

Round-Trip Production

Since the introduction of Final Cut Pro in 1999, Apple's portfolio of content creation software has expanded to include a dozen professional applications that aid the entire production process, including editing, graphics and effects, music and audio, and delivery tools.

Just as there is an unending stream of new video formats, the tools and techniques in postproduction continue to evolve to meet the demands and budgetary requirements of today's sophisticated producers and viewers. Fortunately, there are a few typical production workflows that stand out as standard operating practices.

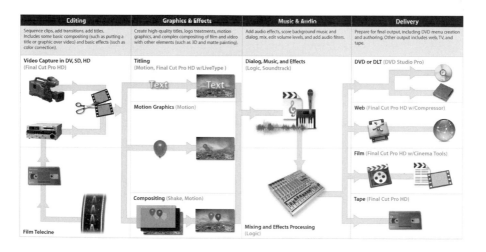

At different stages in the process, these workflows may involve audio (dialog, music, and sound effects), video (whether originated from film or some video format, including high definition), and other elements (text, 2D graphics, and 3D objects and characters). The professional production workflow is the art and science of blending together these separate elements into a single project, hopefully one that is as technically sound to the engineer as it is captivating to the audience.

Content Creation Workflows with Apple's Professional Applications

In this appendix, we'll examine how professionals can leverage the latest generation of Apple applications in a *round-trip production* environment—an environment where media and project files can move seamlessly between the different stages of the creative process, and where changes made at one stage, with one application, are automatically reflected in the other stages, in other applications.

For an individual in a home or project studio, this may involve working with multiple applications on the same computer. For the independent artist collaborating with a larger studio, this may include the transfer of media and projects on FireWire drives or a via a wide area network. And for a multi-seat, full-service production facility, this may involve a collective of artists, editors, and engineers accessing terabytes of data on a fiber channel storage area network.

Apple's professional applications have been designed to work in all of these scenarios and are helping to drive the industry in a new direction—one where reasonably priced "off-the-shelf" software can be used effectively to create award-winning content. Just ask the dozens of Academy and Emmy award–winning editors who now cut their films and TV shows on Final Cut Pro, or any one of the hundreds of musical artists whose Grammy award–winning songs were composed on Logic. But enough about them already—let's look at how you can use these tools to create masterpieces of your own.

Editing

After the director shouts "Cut!" the editing process begins. Editing involves logging the best takes, capturing them to the hard drive of the workstation, and trimming and sequencing them in a timeline. Increasingly, this process is taking place on location, with portable systems, during production. Checking for timing, continuity, and performance on location provides an opportunity to get it right before the actors have departed for their trailers.

Apple's wildly popular video-editing application, **Final Cut Pro**, is ideally suited to run on the current generation of PowerBook laptop computers, making effective use of the laptops' FireWire ports to capture a variety of native digital video formats to the hard disk, including DV, DVCAM, DVCPRO, DVCPRO 50, and DVCPRO HD.

While it's entirely possible to complete a DV or offline film project on a Power-Book, higher-resolution formats (SD and HD) require the performance of a dedicated workstation to finish (online) the content. Editing in these formats is best suited to a Power Mac G5, where Final Cut Pro can take full advantage of the desktop's dual processors. Digital video is captured either via FireWire or, for high-bandwidth formats like uncompressed HD, through a PCI-X card installed in the chassis.

> **NOTE ▶** For projects shot on film, Final Cut Pro includes **Cinema Tools**, a relational database that keeps track of the original film negative feet, frames, and audio timecode throughout the entire editorial process. Cinema Tools works in tandem with Final Cut Pro to ensure that every frame of film is properly accounted for during editing.

Today's generation of video producers are comfortable with both the horizontal and vertical nature of the editorial process. In addition to performing cuts and transitions between shots and applying filters and color corrections to clips, they know how to make effective use of multiple video tracks. This routinely involves superimposed titles, split screens, and picture-in-picture effects. It can even involve compositing techniques including travel mattes, blend modes, and keying for blue- and greenscreen effects. Final Cut Pro supports all of these operations.

The latest version of Final Cut Pro includes an architecture called **RT Extreme**, which leverages the power of the host PowerPC processor, the operating system, and the graphics processing unit to calculate transitions and filter effects in real time. This design philosophy—to provide the full creative palette of effects in real time—is at the heart of round-trip production.

Round-trip production also lets you create, import, and revise parts of your project in separate applications, with updates in one application automatically reflected in the others. Apple has leveraged XML (Extensible Markup Language) to make all media metadata and project information accessible to Apple and third-party applications to facilitate this automatic updating process.

Several parts of the production workflow require tools well beyond your basic cut and splice. Those parts include audio (music, dialog, sound effects) and motion graphics (text, illustrations, animations).

Effects and Graphics

Final Cut Pro includes some fairly sophisticated titling tools within the application itself, including the ability to create extruded 3D titles, but **LiveType** (included with the purchase of Final Cut Pro) takes animated titling to another level entirely. The Media Browser of LiveType includes both titling tools and titling content. The content includes LiveFonts, 32-bit animated fonts that dance and draw themselves onscreen. In addition, LiveType includes a massive library of animated textures (atmospheres, liquids, moving canvases) and objects that range from sparkly Particle Effects to organic flames and interstellar explosions. One of the most popular features of LiveType is the ability to apply prebaked animated effects (fades, glows, zooms, caricatures) to otherwise lifeless system fonts.

Motion is to LiveType what the jet engine is to air travel. With it, you can take your titles and graphics much further in less time. Like LiveType, Motion includes a library full of compelling content, including some of the LiveFonts and text animations that come with LiveType, but that's where the similarities end. Motion makes full use of Quartz Extreme (the revolutionary composited windowing system in Apple's operating system, Mac OS X) and Apple's ultra-high-bandwidth hardware architecture to provide a level of real-time performance that needs to be seen to be appreciated. Video clips are played back directly from SDRAM (the computer's internal memory). Text, particles, and filter effects are loaded into the VRAM (video memory) of today's state-of-the-art graphics cards. Finally, natural physical simulations or screen behaviors like wind and gravity are applied to objects and particles and calculated in real time by the CPUs—dual processors in all current Power Macs. In LiveType, text animations and other motion graphics need to be rendered into RAM to be previewed, whereas in Motion all effects can be viewed and manipulated in real time.

Shake is the preeminent application for visual-effects compositing, a highly specialized craft used to create special effects that, when seamlessly composited, are impossible to distinguish from reality. The primary objective of visual-effects compositing is to take dozens, often hundreds, of separate elements—matte paintings, computer-generated 3D models and animated characters, live action photography (whether filmed on location or against a green- or bluescreen), and particles—and weave them all into a series of photorealistic images. Media files are often exported and imported between Final Cut Pro and Shake, a process that has been accelerated with the addition of new QuickTime codecs (compression-decompression algorithms) in Shake 3.5. In addition to QuickTime, Shake supports a variety of file formats that are commonly used by visual-effects artists, including those for animation (IFF, RLA) and film (Cineon, DPX)—over 20 formats in total.

Let's return to titles, motion graphics, and round-trip production integration. In LiveType, Final Cut Pro projects simply appear as a movie background. Text is superimposed over the video, enhanced (with color, outlines, drop shadows, and so on), positioned, and animated when appropriate. Objects, like simple particle effects, and filters, like blurs and glows, may be added to further enhance the animated titles. With **Exposé**, which instantly tiles all open windows, the LiveType document can be dragged from its menu bar directly into the Timeline of Final Cut Pro, where it's superimposed over the original video track. There's no longer a need to first render the titles as a movie from LiveType before importing them into the editing environment. Best of all, with round-trip production it's possible to launch the LiveType application directly from within the Final Cut Pro

Timeline, should it be necessary to make any last-minute changes. Once the changes are made in LiveType, a simple save of the project is all that's required to automatically update the title in Final Cut Pro. XML is used communicate the revisions between the two applications. No need to render out a new title from LiveType, no need to copy and paste files between applications; a simple save automatically updates the information from one app to another.

The interoperability between Final Cut Pro and Motion works in exactly the same manner. In addition, it's possible to export the Final Cut Pro project directly into Motion with all editing, scaling, cropping, positioning, and keyframe information for all layers retained during the exchange. Graphic designs can be roughed out in Final Cut Pro and fine-tuned in Motion. Some of the most impressive technologies found in Motion are its advanced particle engine and natural physical simulations, both of which are often used in tandem to create stunning designs. Motion also accepts Adobe Photoshop files and imports them with the separate layers intact or merged into one. Photoshop users, even those who have never worked with video, can easily convert their 2D designs and images into visually stunning animated motion graphics.

Once the motion graphic design work is completed in Motion, the project file can be imported directly into Final Cut Pro. Round-trip production functions exactly the same with Motion as with LiveType. When a save command is executed, all project revisions in Motion are automatically communicated directly to Final Cut Pro. To the user, the media in the Timeline goes offline for a moment and then returns reflecting the updates.

In addition to the content creation workflow that defines the look of your video, Apple's professional applications provide an incredible level of interoperability between music and audio as it relates to the visuals. We'll examine this aspect of round-trip production in the next section of this appendix.

Music and Audio

A great music score can enhance an otherwise lackluster film or video. Conversely, dialog that is inaudible or distorted can ruin an otherwise well-edited scene. When background audio levels and room acoustic dynamics vary dramatically from shot to shot, viewers unconsciously sense that something is wrong, and their ability to remain connected to the message, story, or characters diminishes exponentially. Well-produced music and audio can't salvage inherently poor footage, but poorly produced music and audio can ruin an otherwise completely enjoyable sequence. Fortunately, Apple's portfolio of professional applications includes some very powerful tools for music composition and audio editing, sweetening, and mixing.

Let's first examine music for music's sake.

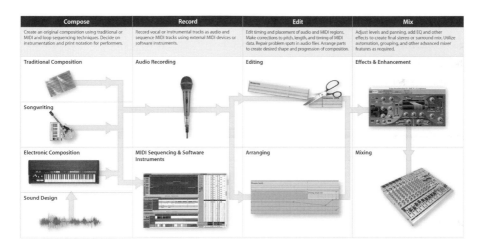

Apple's primary applications for music composition on the computer are GarageBand, Logic Express, and Logic Pro.

GarageBand is an incredibly intuitive application ideally suited for musicians who are composing on a computer for the first time. Songs composed in GarageBand can be exported directly to an iTunes playlist in a single step. These same songs can also be used as music beds for videos in iMovie, Final Cut Express, or Final Cut Pro, or to enhance menus in iDVD or DVD Studio Pro. Because GarageBand does not provide a way to synchronize sound to picture, the job of scoring music to picture is best suited to Logic and Soundtrack, both of which we'll review here.

The production workflow for music consists of four discrete processes that tend to fold back on themselves over and over until either the artist/producer is satisfied with the final song, or the production deadline has elapsed—hopefully the former before the latter. The workflow includes composition, recording, editing, and mixing. Composition can begin with musical notation as supported in Logic, but often it's part of the recording process, roughing out the melody or beat with Logic's built-in MIDI (Musical Instrument Digital Interface) sequencing and software instruments, considered by many to be among the finest ever developed.

Logic Pro includes a collection of vintage instruments that provide near-perfect emulations of classic instruments like the Hammond B3 organ, software synthesizers that can re-create classic analog textures, and a full-featured stereo sampler that provides the songwriter with access to a myriad of sounds from the countless number of sample libraries currently available—from esoteric collections of obscure world instruments to elaborate orchestral libraries. In addition to sound design and electronic composition with MIDI instruments, such as keyboards, Logic is used to record vocals or other real instruments directly to the tracks of each song. Like a multitrack tape recorder, Logic can record multiple audio inputs (vocals, drums, guitars) in real time, whereas GarageBand can only record one input at a time.

Editing involves trimming, timing, and placement of the audio and MIDI tracks in the song. Logic also provides the ability to repair spots in recorded audio files, as well as tools to correct the pitch, length, and timing of MIDI.

The final step in the songwriter's workflow is mixing, and it allows the composer to enhance or "sweeten" the acoustics of each track with a selection of digital signal processing plug-ins including EQ, dynamic compressors, and reverb. The **Space Designer** reverb plug-in that comes with Logic Pro is based on state-of-the-art convolution technology that actually models the physical characteristics of a room so that the exact acoustics of that room (or any room that's been modeled) can be applied to one or more tracks of audio at any time during the mix. During mixing the producer will adjust individual track levels and pan positions in relation to one another (for example, "cowbell louder and to the left side of the stereo image"). This often involves mixing in a surround sound environment to support the increasingly popular multichannel playback capabilities of DVD and high-definition television.

It's important to note that more and more musicians are finding Logic perfectly suited for live performance as well. Mac OS X includes a number of features that have been specifically designed to please musicians and audio engineers. Chief among them is Core Audio, which essentially removes any cap on the number of audio tracks that the computer can support. Core Audio also supports high-definition audio sampling rates and bit rates up to 96 kHz and beyond. For live performance, Core Audio provides the lowest levels of audio latency in the industry. Latency can best be described as the time it takes to move audio from the input (recording) stage through digital signal processing (DSP) and back out again to be monitored. Any significant delays, and it's like hearing yourself talk to yourself, talk to yourself…you get the idea. Mac OS X now provides levels of audio latency well below 1 millisecond in duration, which has helped Apple to retain its dominant position as the preferred platform for live venues. Musical artists can perform in perfect sync with Logic—vocals enhanced with DSP and all tracks mixed in real time on to the waiting ears of the audience.

Soundtrack is a music composition application developed by Apple for musicians and non-musicians alike. Included in Soundtrack is a massive library of over 4,000 audio samples (loops) of sound effects and musical instruments—everything from the aforementioned cowbell to Motown's finest drum riffs. Apple calls these samples Apple Loops because they offer far more functionality than your standard audio samples. Soundtrack takes advantage of the Velocity Engine of Apple's PowerPC processors by providing the unique ability to preview new loops while simultaneously auditioning other tracks in the timeline. The unparalleled power of this feature becomes evident when you realize that loops are originally sampled (recorded to hard disk) in any number of keys and tempos. To help keep your tracks in tune, Soundtrack can restrict the selection of Apple loops to only those that will work best with other tracks already in the song—within two semitones of the project key. While it's still possible to combine instruments into something that sounds like it was just dragged in by the cat, Soundtrack provides the necessary tools and technologies to help keep you from going down that path.

Round-trip production between Final Cut Pro and Soundtrack is accomplished primarily through the use of Scoring Markers. The markers are positioned in the Timeline of Final Cut Pro as a reference between the music score and the visual activity (such as a crescendo at a car crash). When a sequence is exported from Final Cut Pro, the scoring markers appear in the timeline of Soundtrack alongside the QuickTime movie—construction cones on the highway to musical bliss. Apple Loops can be positioned to coincide or snap directly to the markers, but that's not all. Soundtrack allows you to effectively re-time musical cues to the scoring markers by simply dragging the marks to new positions in the timeline to match any additional trim edits made in Final Cut Pro.

Round-trip production between the visual applications in Apple's portfolio and Logic is accomplished primarily through the use of the QuickTime media format. Video movies are exported from Final Cut Pro and Motion and are imported into Logic, where they appear in the audio Timeline as video thumbnails. Perfect sync between picture and sound is maintained via timecode—that dependable timepiece under the hood of QuickTime assets, to keep track of hours, minutes, seconds, and frames. Music is exported from Logic either as discrete tracks or stems (groups of discrete tracks), or as a final mix (stereo or surround) and is imported into Final Cut Pro, where it can be mixed further with location audio and other tracks, like sound effects, replacement dialog, or background ambience.

Producers who recognize the importance of a well-engineered audio mix often ask to be a part of the creative review process—enter DVD, the first mass distribution format to dramatically raise the bar on audio quality, with support for Dolby Digital, DTS, even uncompressed PCM audio, with sample rates up to 92 kHz and dynamic range up to 24 bits in length.

Delivery

Finished audio and video programs are distributed to their audience in a variety of formats, some no bigger than a postage stamp (as viewed on the latest generation of 3GPP mobile phones) and some that span screen projection dimensions bigger than the side of a barn (IMAX theaters).

Apple's production applications are completely scalable—designed to support the creation of content in these formats and every resolution in between. In some workflows, **Compressor**, included with Final Cut Pro, Motion, and DVD Studio Pro, is used to encode the completed project into a small form factor more suitable for mass distribution. In other workflows, **Cinema Tools** acts as the intermediary, forwarding a list of instructions to another application or person that uses the information as a roadmap. Quite often, the finished project is simply printed to videotape. In the case of visual-effects shots and other digital intermediate formats, the high-resolution frames are recorded directly to film via what is essentially a high-resolution printer, referred to as a *film recorder*.

Final Cut Pro has revolutionized the world of broadcast news journalism. Hundreds upon hundreds of reporters take to the streets each day armed with camcorders and PowerBooks. Final Cut Pro was the first generation of nonlinear digital editing applications to embrace the mobile tape formats for DV, DVCAM, and DVCPRO. Video that is acquired in these formats is captured with Final Cut Pro via FireWire. The 21st century video journalist is fully capable of editing in the field—shuttling to find the best takes to edit them together into a finished news story. In news, the first to air the story wins, which is why journalists can no longer wait for the van to make it back to the studio before they can edit their content.

MPEG-4 and MPEG-2 are common file formats used to transfer and transmit news stories from the field back to the news bureau. Video journalists, especially those with tight deadlines and bigger capital expenditure budgets, often transmit edited stories directly to the studio via mobile satellite phone systems. Video journalists, especially those with a bit more lead time between deadlines, modest cap ex budgets, and a hankering for double-tall lattes, will often waltz into the nearest Starbucks, connect to the bureau via AirPort Extreme (Wi-Fi), and transfer their finished stories via FTP, while patiently waiting for their next assignment.

Another popular content distribution format is DVD. Since the launch of DVD in 1997, the format has become a favorite of consumers, surpassing VHS tapes in both rentals and sales for a number of obvious reasons. DVDs provide superior image and audio quality. DVDs are digital, and since the laser-reading mechanism never actually comes in contact with the physical disc, the quality does not degrade even after thousands of viewings. DVDs are multilingual, with support for up to nine different audio mixes and 32 different subtitle tracks synchronized to the same video content. Most important, DVDs are both interactive and non-linear. A few clicks of the remote and you have instant random access to any segment within the program. With all these attributes going for it, DVD makes an ideal distribution format for all forms of video content—feature films, television series, concert films, training videos, product promotions, and client show reels.

iDVD is Apple's consumer DVD authoring application that comes bundled with every Apple computer. Many Final Cut Pro users may consider iDVD to be more than sufficient for their authoring requirements. It's important to know that Apple's DVD Studio Pro application is to iDVD what Final Cut Pro is to iMovie. While it's true that iMovie is a powerful and intuitive consumer video-editing application, there isn't a competent Final Cut Pro editor alive that would trade down to iMovie, because Final Cut Pro offers a level of creative control well beyond anything the iLife application has been designed to deliver.

Likewise, **DVD Studio Pro** provides a level of creative control that goes well beyond the beautiful themes of iDVD. The real-time menu design capabilities of DVD Studio Pro provide the ability to change…well, everything: buttons, shapes behind buttons, movies in buttons, text, motion menu backgrounds, audio beds behind menus, and much more. More important, DVD Studio Pro is engineered to work with still and motion menu templates that have been created by the user.

Audio mixes created in Logic and Soundtrack can be encoded (faster than real time) in **A.Pack**, the Dolby Digital encoding application that is included with DVD Studio Pro. All manner of Dolby mixes, from stereo to 5.1 surround, are supported. For musicians and audio engineers, DVD Studio Pro's Timeline can support multiple audio mixes, which means they can author audio-only DVDs that producers can use to audition different versions of the mix (stereo, surround, music without vocals for karaoke, and so on). Buttons and menus can be created directly within DVD Studio Pro, which has integrated menu design tools to greatly simplify the authoring process.

Round-trip production in DVD Studio Pro perfectly complements still menus created in Photoshop. In DVD Studio Pro, it's possible to select a menu and open-in-editor directly into Photoshop, with all layers intact. You can make any revisions you like within Photoshop, and saving the file communicates the revision update directly back to DVD Studio Pro.

Motion should be considered the ultimate DVD motion menu design application. In the menu-creation workflow, video elements from the originating program are imported into Motion, where filter effects and motion paths are added to convert them into vibrant video montages. Text for buttons, like "play all" and "chapter selection," can be created and animated directly within Motion. For added effect, particles from Motion's built-in particle engine can be incorporated into menu designs. Exporting menus from Motion for use in DVD Studio Pro is as simple as saving the project to the user's Movies folder.

Round-trip production is tightly integrated between Motion and DVD Studio Pro. From the authoring asset bin of DVD Studio Pro it's possible to open-in-editor, launching the application for direct access to those elements originally crafted in Motion. Any changes made to motion menus in Motion are automatically updated to DVD Studio Pro upon saving. This kind of revisionist functionality is perfectly suited to the design of DVD menus, many of which are recycled from project to project—different movies and slideshows in the same overall DVD menu theme.

Workgroup Collaboration

As stated at the introduction to this appendix, round-trip production can range from a single user working with multiple applications on the same computer, all the way up to a large group of editors and engineers accessing vast amounts of data in a shared storage environment. Any facility with two or more artists creating content under the same roof is perfect for workgroup collaboration of this sort because productivity increases exponentially when multiple users can access the very same media. No time wasted copying files; less chance of errors from revision-naming conventions. Investments in hardware can be recouped sooner when the storage is centralized, simply because the storage can be dynamically allocated wherever it is needed most.

A *storage area network*, or *SAN*, is designed for exactly this type of collaboration. A SAN is a network whose primary function is to link multiple storage systems to multiple desktop workstations. Typical SANs today operate on 2-gigabit-per-second fiber channel cabling connected through one or more multi-port fiber channel switches. One of the best features of a properly designed SAN is that the storage volume can be scaled dynamically as the production workload increases, without users' ever having to take the network offline or reboot administrative systems. **Xsan** is in this class. It is what's referred to as an enterprise-class (that is, large-facilities-that-can't-afford-the-slightest-bit-of-downtime), high-performance SAN file system. It runs on Mac OS X and is compatible with systems running on a selection of qualified non-Apple SAN client seats.

Like the best enterprise-class SANs, Xsan includes a *metadata controller* that acts like a network traffic cop. Whenever any user on the network wants to read or write to a file, the user's computer asks the SAN traffic cop for permission to proceed. Xsan's metadata controller software includes a "failover" provision, which means that these traffic cop duties are automatically handed over to another computer in the event the first controller should fail for whatever reason. The whole point of built-in protections like failover and multi-pathing (where a second cable is used if the first is cut) is to ensure that the network is operational and the media and project files on the SAN volumes are available to all users all the time.

Storage area networks offer the promise of tremendous increases in creativity and productivity not unlike those of the networked office environment where multiple users have simultaneous access to the Internet and printers. Apple's pro apps, and the level of round-trip production they provide, are ideally suited for use in a centralized storage, collaborative workgroup environment supported by Xsan.

Summary

Professional production involves a number of creative disciplines, including capture and editing of digital video; design of complex motion graphics and photorealistic visual effects; composition of well-crafted music scores; and editing, sweetening, and mixing all the audio tracks, including dialog and sound effects. Depending on the intended audience, finished projects are either printed directly to videotape, recorded to motion picture film, or compressed for distribution via FTP, satellite transmission, or some other streaming-media format. Thanks to the proliferation of DVD, the creative process doesn't end when songs, videos, or films are mastered. Instead, elements from programs are used to create compelling, interactive DVD menus, the majority of which now include motion graphics and seamless motion menu–to–motion menu transitions.

Apple's round-trip production paradigm heralds a new era in content creation workflows. In the same way that you can save spreadsheets in Microsoft Excel and have them automatically update in Microsoft Word, designers can now save their motion graphics in Motion and have them update automatically in Final Cut Pro and DVD Studio Pro. Xsan's storage area network brings all these apps together in a collaborative workgroup environment. The accompanying increase in productivity is incalculable, with benefits that go well beyond financial measures. The quality of design improves dramatically, simply because there's more time to experiment; more time to try the best filter, behavior, text animation, or particle effect; more time to try various cuts and transitions; more time to create custom DVD menu transitions and designs. And because Apple's system architecture takes full advantage of the stability of Unix and the increased performance of 64-bit processors, powerful graphics cards, and fast SDRAM, new combinations of effects, transitions, filters, behaviors, and particles can be previewed in real time.

Real-time performance and round-trip production, on a single system or in a collaborative workgroup—that's how the creative work *flows* between Apple's professional applications.

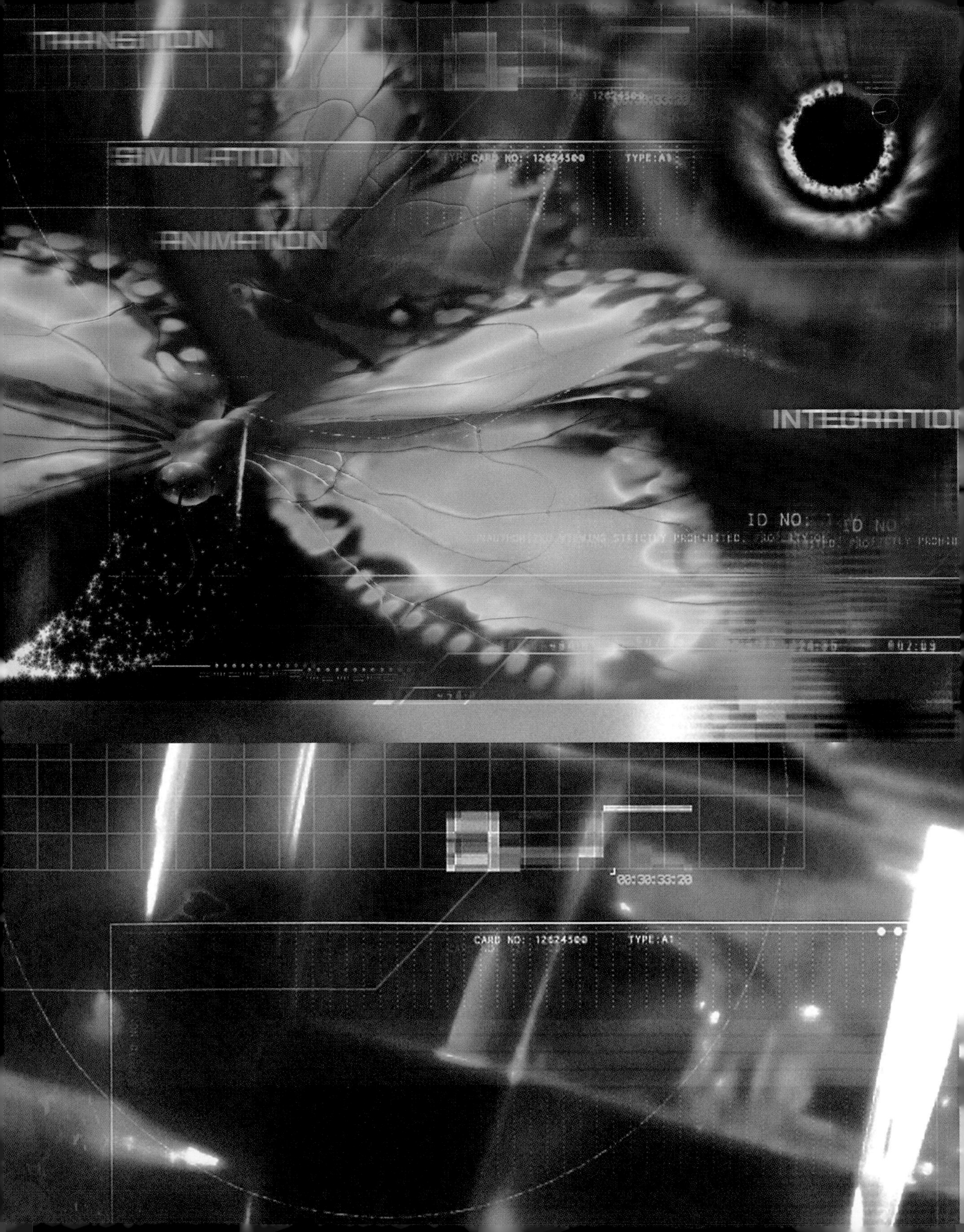

TRANSITION

SIMULATION

ANIMATION

INTEGRATION

CARD NO: 12624500   TYPE:A1

ID NO: ID NO

UNAUTHORIZED VIEWING STRICTLY PROHIBITED.

00:38:33:28

CARD NO: 12624500   TYPE:A1

Glossary

4:3 The standard display aspect ratio of a traditional television set. See *aspect ratio.*

#

8-bit For video, a bit depth at which color is sampled. Eight-bit color is common with DV and other standard-definition digital formats. Some high-definition acquisition formats can also record in 8-bit, but they usually record in 10-bit. Refers to 8 bits per color channel, making a total of 24 bits in an RGB image and 32 bits in an RGB image with an alpha channel.

16:9 The standard display aspect ratio of a high-definition television set. See *aspect ratio.*

Action Safe The area inside a border that is 5 percent smaller than the overall size of the video frame. Some or all of the Canvas image beyond this border will be cropped by the video display monitor or television. How much is cropped varies among different TV manufacturers. See *Title Safe.*

A

AIFF (Audio Interchange File Format) Apple's native uncompressed audio file format created for the Macintosh computer, commonly used for the storage and transmission of digitally sampled sound.

alpha channel An image channel in addition to the R, G, and B color channels that is used to store transparency information for compositing. In Motion, black represents 100 percent transparent, and white represents 100 percent opaque.

anamorphic An image shot in a wide-screen format and then squeezed into 4:3 frame size.

anchor point In the Properties tab of the Inspector, the point that is used to center changes to a clip when using motion effects. A clip's anchor point does not have to be at its center.

animation The process of changing any number of variables, such as color, audio levels, or other effects, over time using keyframes or behaviors. See *keyframe.*

aspect ratio The ratio of the width of an image to its height on any viewing screen. Standard TV has an aspect ratio of 4:3; HDTV's is 16:9. See *high definition.*

audio mixing The process of adjusting the volume levels of all audio clips in an edited sequence, including the production audio, music, sound effects, voice-overs, and additional background ambience, to turn all of these sounds into a harmonious whole.

audio sample rate The rate or frequency at which a sound is sampled to digitize it. The standard sampling rate for digital audio is 48 kHz; CD audio is sampled at 44.1 kHz.

audio waveform A graphical representation of the amplitude (loudness) of a sound over a period of time.

AVI A PC-compatible standard for digital video no longer officially supported by Microsoft but still frequently used. AVI supports fewer codecs than Quick-Time. Some AVI codecs will not play back in QuickTime and will thus be inaccessible in Motion without prior format conversion.

B

batch export The ability to export multiple clips and/or sequences with a single command by stacking them up in a queue. In Motion, the "Export using Compressor" option can be used to generate a batch export.

Bezier handles The "control handles" attached to a Bezier curve that allow you to change the shape of the curve.

black level The measurement of the black portion of the video signal. This level is represented by 7.5 IRE in the United States; Japan (NTSC) and PAL measurements are represented by 0 IRE. See *NTSC; PAL.*

blanking The black border around the edges of a raw video image. This is the image created by the video camera CCDs—the photosensitive receptors that translate the lens image into digital information. The very edge of the picture is usually worthless. These black pixels should be cropped out of your image if you plan to composite it over the top of other footage.

blend modes The methods used to combine overlapping elements. Blend modes use different mathematical formulas to combine the pixels, creating different effects between the elements.

bluescreen A solid blue background placed behind a subject and photographed so that later the subject can be extracted and composited onto another image. See *greenscreen.*

Broadcast Safe A color-correction filter that provides a fast method of dealing with clips whose luminance and chrominance levels exceed the broadcast limits for video. Only recommended as a final fail-safe.

cache An area of the computer's memory (RAM) dedicated to storing still images and digital movies in preparation for real-time playback.

C

calibrate The process of adjusting a feature for accuracy.

Canvas The window in Motion in which you can view your edited sequence.

center point Defines a clip's location in the X/Y coordinate space in the Canvas.

chroma The color information contained in a video signal consisting of hue (the color itself) and saturation (intensity). See *hue; saturation.*

clip A media file that may consist of video, audio, graphics, or any similar content that can be imported into Motion.

clipping Distortion that occurs during the playback or recording of digital audio due to an overly high level.

close-up Framing a subject so that it fills the frame. Usually used for dramatic storytelling.

codec   Short for *compression/decompression*. A program used to compress and decompress data such as audio and video files.

color correction   A process in which the color of objects is evened out so that all shots in a given scene match.

color depth   The possible range of colors that can be used in a movie or image. Higher color depths provide a wider range of colors but also require more disk space for a given image size. Broadcast video is generally 24-bit, with 8 bits of color information per channel. Motion works natively with 8 bits per channel of red, green, and blue.

component video   A type of analog video signal where the luminance and chrominance signals are recorded separately, thereby providing better video quality. The signal can be recorded in an analog form (Y, R-Y, B-Y) as in a Beta SP, or in a digital form (Y, Cr, Cb), as in a Digital Betacam.

composite   The result of combining many different elements—some moving, some still. As a verb it refers to the process of combining these elements, or *layers;* as a noun it refers to the final resulting image. It's also sometimes referred to as a *comp.* In visual-effects work, the idea of a composite is to create a single image, which presents the illusion that all the elements were captured by a single camera filming the scene. In motion graphics, the concern isn't so much to convince the audience that everything was shot "in camera" as it is to present a stylistic and coherent blend of elements. See *layers.*

composite video   A type of analog video signal that combines all chroma and luma information into a single waveform running through a single pair of wires. This can result in analog "artifacts" affecting the quality of the video signal. See *chroma; luma.*

compositing   The act of creating a composite.

compression   The process by which video, graphics, and audio files are reduced in size. The reduction in the size of a video file through the removal of perceptually redundant image data is referred to as a *lossy* compression scheme. A *lossless* compression scheme uses a mathematical process and reduces the file size by consolidating redundant information without discarding it. Compression is irrelevant with clips imported into the Motion Canvas, since all clips are decoded into fully uncompressed frames before caching to system RAM. Compression is, however, a consideration in the final export of a composition to disk. See *codec*.

contextual menu A menu that "pops up" on the screen and whose content changes depending on where you click. Usually accessed via a Ctrl- or right-click mouse action.

contrast The difference between the lightest and darkest values in an image. High-contrast images have a large range of values from the darkest shadow to the lightest highlight. Low-contrast images have a narrower range of values, resulting in a "flatter" look.

cut The simplest type of edit, where one clip ends and the next begins without any transition.

cutaway A shot that is related to the current subject and occurs in the same time frame—for instance, an interviewer's reaction to what is being said in an interview or a shot to cover a technically bad moment.

data rate The speed at which data can be transferred, often described in megabytes per second (MBps). The higher a video file's data rate, the higher quality it will be, but it will require more system resources (processor speed, hard-disk space, and performance). Some codecs allow you to specify a maximum data rate for a movie during render.

D

decibel (dB) A unit of measure for the loudness of audio.

decompression The process of creating a viewable image for playback from a compressed video, graphics, or audio file. Compare with *compression*.

desaturate To remove color from a clip. Desaturation of 100 percent results in a grayscale image.

digital Describes data that is stored or transmitted as a sequence of 1s and 0s.

digital video Video that has been captured, manipulated, and stored using a digital format, which can be easily imported into your computer. Digital video can come in many different formats, such as Digital-8, DVCPRO, DVCAM, or DV.

dissolve A transition between two video clips in which the second one fades up over the top of the first one, eventually obscuring it.

Dock The strip on the Macintosh Desktop where you can store alias icons of the programs you use most frequently.

drop-frame timecode NTSC timecode that skips ahead in time by two frame numbers each minute, except for minutes ending in *0*, so that the end timecode total agrees with the actual elapsed clock time. Although timecode numbers are skipped, actual video frames are not skipped. See *timecode*.

drop shadow An effect that creates an artificial shadow behind an image or text.

dub To make a copy of an analog tape to the same type of format.

duration The length of a clip or a sequence from its In point to its Out point, or the length of time it takes that piece of video to play.

DV (digital video) A digital standard created by a consortium of camcorder vendors, which uses Motion JPEG video at a 720x480 resolution at 29.97 frames per second, stored at a bit rate of 5 MB per second at a compression of 4:1:1. This format does not provide timecode capabilities or an audio track for the cue channel.

DVCAM A standard-definition digital videotape recorder format that records an 8-bit, 5:1 compressed component video signal with 4:1:1 color sampling. Recorded using ¼-inch tape. Supports two tracks of audio with 16-bit, 48 kHz audio sampling, or four tracks of audio with 12-bit, 48 kHz audio sampling.

DVCPRO Panasonic's native DV (digital video) component format that records an 8-bit, 5:1 compressed component video signal using 4:1:1 color sampling (PAL uses 4:2:0). This format supports two tracks of audio with 16-bit, 48 kHz audio sampling, or four tracks of audio with 12-bit, 48 kHz audio sampling. DVCPRO adds a longitudinal analog audio cue track and a control track to improve editing performance and user-friendliness in linear editing operations.

DVD A disc that is the size of a CD but uses higher-density storage methods to significantly increase its capacity. Usually used for video distribution, DVD-ROM discs can also be used to store computer data.

dynamic range The difference, in decibels, between the loudest and softest parts of a recording.

effects A general term used to describe filters and behaviors added to an object in Motion.

E

envelope The visual curve of an audio waveform's pan or level. Essentially the same as a keyframe curve (the term *envelope* coming from the audio engineering world; the term *curve* coming from the digital animation world). See *pan*.

export The method by which a final composite is rendered out to the hard drive as a single QuickTime movie, image sequence, or still frame.

fade The process of transitioning an object from fully transparent to fully opaque, or vice versa.

F

favorite A custom effect that is used frequently. You can create favorites from any element or group of elements in your Layers tab.

field Half of an *interlaced video* frame consisting of the odd or the even scan lines.

FireWire Apple's trademark name for its implementation of the IEEE 1394 protocol used to connect external hard drives, cameras, and other digital devices to computers. It provides a fast interface to move large video and audio files to the computer's hard drive. FireWire exists as two standards: FireWire 400 and FireWire 800. FireWire 800 has twice the bandwidth of the traditional FireWire 400 and uses a different hardware connector.

frame A single still image from either video or film. For video, each frame is made up of two interlaced fields. See *interlaced video*.

frame blending A process of inserting blended frames in place of frames that have been duplicated in clips with slow motion, to make them play back more smoothly. Frame blending is available in the Scrub filter, part of the registration incentive pack of plug-ins.

frame rate   The speed at which the individual images making up a moving sequence play back. It's stated in terms of frames per second (fps). Film in 16mm or 35mm is usually shot at 24 fps; NTSC video is 29.97 fps; PAL video is 25 fps. HD can have several different frame rates.

framing   Composing a shot for the best presentation of the subject, taking into consideration the size of the subject in the frame and how it is positioned.

frequency   The number of times a sound or signal vibrates each second, measured in cycles per second, or *hertz*. Audio recordings are made up of a vast collection of waveforms, using many different frequencies of sound. Each frequency in a recording is associated with an audio pitch. The frequencies of an audio recording can be changed to disguise a voice or to clean up an unwanted noise.

G

gain   In video, the level of white in a video picture; in audio, the loudness of an audio signal.

gamma   A curve that describes how the middle tones of an image appear. Gamma is a nonlinear function often confused with *brightness* or *contrast*. Changing the value of the gamma affects midtones while mostly leaving the whites and blacks of the image unaltered. Gamma adjustment is often used to compensate for differences between footage acquisition formats.

generators   Clips that are synthesized (or generated) by Motion. Generators can be used as different kinds of backgrounds and elements for visual design.

GPU (graphics processing unit)   The central processor inside a modern computer graphics card.

gradient   A generated image that changes smoothly from one color to another across the image.

grading   The process of color-correcting footage to achieve a desired look.

greenscreen   A solid green background placed behind a subject and photographed so that later the subject can be extracted and composited into another image. See also *bluescreen*.

H

Hi8 A high-end consumer analog videotape format that has a quality between that of VHS and DV.

high definition (HD) High definition was created to increase the amount of pixels onscreen (a higher definition) as well as to solve many of the frame rate and cadence problems between film and video. There are two main types of HD footage. The highest is 1080, with a native resolution of 1920x1080. The other is 720, which has a native resolution of 1280x720. Both formats can have different frame rates and can be either progressive or interlaced.

high-key images Images that are made up of mostly light values.

histogram A window that displays the relative strength of all luminance values in a video frame, from black to super white. It is useful for comparing two clips in order to match their brightness values more closely. Available in the Levels filter.

hue A specific color or pigment, such as red.

I

icon An onscreen symbol that represents a program or file.

importing The process of bringing files of various types into a project in Motion's Canvas. Imported files can be created in another application, captured from another device, or included when you import another Motion project.

In point The first frame of an object to be displayed in the Canvas.

Insert edit To insert a clip into an existing sequence into the Timeline, which automatically moves the other clips (or remaining frames of a clip) to the right to make room for it. An Insert edit does not replace existing material.

interlaced video A video scanning method that first scans the odd picture lines (field 1) and then scans the even picture lines (field 2), which merges them into one single frame of video. Used in standard-definition video.

J

jiggle To move a parameter away from its current value, then move it back to that original value. Used to force Motion to create a keyframe in Record Animation mode.

jog To move forward or backward through your video one frame at a time.

JPEG (Joint Photographic Experts Group) A popular image file format that lets you create highly compressed graphics files. The amount of compression used can be varied. Less compression results in a higher-quality image.

jump cut A cut in which an abrupt change occurs between two shots, with no continuity from one to the other.

K

keyframe A point on the Timeline where a specific parameter value has been set. Motion interpolates between keyframes to create in-between frames.

keying The process of creating a mask (key) to eliminate a specific background area in order to composite foreground elements against a different background.

L

layers Containers that group several objects in a Motion project. Layers can be nested inside other layers. Filters and behaviors applied to a layer will affect all the elements contained within it. Known in other applications as *precompositions*.

letterbox Describes when video is displayed to fit within a standard 4:3 monitor, resulting in a black bar at the top and the bottom of the picture.

linear editing A video-editing style in which a program is edited together by copying shots from the original source tapes to a master tape, one by one. Because the assembly is linear, any changes made to an earlier point on the tape result in the rest of the edited tape having to be reassembled from that point forward. See *nonlinear editing*.

looping Repeated playing of the playback range. On by default.

low-key images Images that are made up of mostly dark values.

luma Short for *luminance*. A value describing the brightness information of the video signal without color (chroma). Equivalent to a color television broadcast viewed on a black-and-white television set.

Luma Key A filter used to key out a luminance value, creating a matte based on the brightest or darkest area of an image. Keying out a luminance value works best when your clip has a large discrepancy in exposure between the areas you want to key out and the foreground images you want to preserve. See *keying* and *matte.*

luminance See *luma.*

M

markers Indicators that can be placed on a clip or globally in a project to help you find a specific location while you edit. Can be used to sync action between two clips, identify beats of music, mark a reference word from a narrator, and so on.

marquee The black-and-white animated dashed lines that highlight a selection.

mask An image, clip, or shape used to define areas of transparency in another clip. Acts like an external *alpha channel.* A mask is an application of a matte.

master shot A single, long shot of dramatic action from which shorter cuts, such as close-ups, and medium shots are taken in order to fill out the story.

matte An effect that uses information in one layer of video to affect another layer. Mattes are useful when you want to use one clip to selectively hide or reveal part of another—for example, to reveal parts of a video layer with a round spotlight shape. Matte filters can be used by themselves to mask out areas of a clip, or to create alpha channel information for a clip in order to make a transparent border around the clip that can be composited against other layers. See *alpha channel.*

media file A generic term for elements such as movies, sounds, and pictures.

midtones The middle brightness range of an image. Not the very brightest part, not the very darkest part.

MiniDV cassette A small cassette used for the DV digital videotape format.

mini-Timeline The small timeline at the base of the Canvas that solos the timing events for the selected object, filter, mask, or behavior.

mono audio A type of sound in which audio channels are taken from a tape and mixed together into a single track, using equal amounts of audio channels 1 and 2.

motion blur An effect that blurs any clip with keyframed motion applied to it, similar to blurred motion recorded by a camera.

motion path A path that appears in the Canvas showing the path a clip will travel based on *keyframe* points that are applied to the clip.

MPEG (Moving Picture Experts Group) A group of compression standards for video and audio, which includes MPEG-1, MPEG-2, and MPEG-4.

MPEG-4 A global multimedia standard based on the QuickTime file format, delivering scalable, high-quality audio and video streams over a wide range of bandwidths, ranging from cell phone to broadband, that also supports 3D objects, sprites, text, and other media types.

N

nest To place a layer into another layer so that it effectively acts as a single object in the new layer.

non–drop frame timecode NTSC timecode in which frames are numbered sequentially and run at 30 fps. NTSC's frame rate, however, is actually 29.97 fps; therefore, non–drop frame timecode is off by 3 seconds and 18 frames per hour in comparison to actual elapsed time.

noninterlaced video The standard representation of images on a computer, also referred to as *progressive scan*. The monitor displays the image by drawing each line, continuously one after the other, from top to bottom.

nonlinear editing A video-editing process that uses computer hard disks to random-access the media. It allows the editor to reorganize clips very quickly or make changes to sections without having to re-create the entire program.

nonlinear editor (NLE) An editing platform (usually on a computer) used to perform nonlinear editing.

nonsquare pixel A pixel whose height is different from its width. An NTSC pixel is taller than it is wide, and a PAL pixel is wider than it is tall.

NTSC (National Television Systems Committee) The standard of color TV broadcasting used mainly in North America, Mexico, and Japan, consisting of 525 lines per frame, 29.97 frames per second, and 720x486 pixels per frame (720x480 for DV). See *PAL*.

NTSC legal The range of color that can be broadcast free of distortion according to the NTSC standards, with maximum allowable video at 100 IRE units and black at 7.5 IRE units.

on the fly The process of marking an In or Out point or creating markers as the Canvas or Audio Editor is playing back.

O

opacity The degree to which an image is transparent, allowing images behind to show through. An opacity of 0 percent means an object is invisible; an opacity of 100 percent means the object is completely opaque.

Out point The last frame of an object to be displayed in the Canvas.

overscan The part of the video frame that cannot be seen on a TV or video monitor. Broadcast video is an overscan medium, meaning that the recorded frame size is larger than the viewable area on a video monitor. The overscan part of the picture is usually hidden behind the plastic bezel on the edge of a television set.

Overwrite edit An edit where the clip being edited into a sequence replaces an existing clip. The duration of the sequence remains unchanged.

PAL (Phase Alternating Line) This system is the European color TV broadcasting standard, consisting of 625 lines per frame, running at 25 frames per second and 720x576 pixels per frame. See *NTSC*.

P

pan To move a camera left or right without changing its position. The term has been adapted in computer graphics to refer to the movement of individual video elements.

PICT The native still-image file format for Macintosh developed by Apple Computer. PICT files can contain both vector images and bitmap images, as well as text and an alpha channel.

pixel Short for *picture element*. One dot in a video or still image.

pixel aspect ratio The width-to-height ratio for the pixels that compose an image. Pixels on computer screens and in high-definition video signals are square (1:1 ratio). Pixels in standard-definition video signals are nonsquare.

playhead A navigational element on the scrubber bar that shows you the frame you are on in the Timeline, Canvas, Keyframe Editor, or Audio Editor. You can drag the playhead to navigate through a sequence.

postproduction The phase of film, video, and audio editing that begins after all the footage is shot.

preset A portion of a Motion project saved into the Favorites section of the Library.

Q

QuickTime Apple's cross-platform multimedia technology. Widely used for editing, compositing, CD-ROM, Web video, and more.

QuickTime streaming Apple's streaming-media addition to the QuickTime architecture. Used for viewing QuickTime content in real time on the Web.

R

ramping Employing variable speed effects to vary a clip's speed throughout playback. Achieved in Motion using the Scrub filter, part of the registration incentive pack. Also called *time remapping*.

real time Refers to the ability to play back video content during preview at exactly the same frame rate as the final intended output. Can also refer to the ability to update parameters and instantly see the result of the change.

real-time design Motion's revolutionary system of compositing together video elements in real time.

redo To reverse an undo, which restores the last change made to a project.

render The process by which the computer calculates final frames for a project. In Motion, the rendering takes place in the GPU of the graphics card.

RGB An abbreviation for *red*, *green*, and *blue*, which are the three primary colors that make up a color video image.

rotation To rotate a clip around its anchor point without changing its shape.

S

safe zones The two sets of lines representing Action Safe and Title Safe areas in the Canvas. See *Action Safe*; *Title Safe*.

sampling The process during which analog audio is converted into digital information. The sampling rate of an audio stream specifies how many samples are captured. Higher sample rates are able to reproduce higher-pitched sounds. Examples: 44.1 Kbytes, 48 Kbytes. Greater bit depths during sampling increase the dynamic range (changes in volume) of the audio.

saturation The purity of color. As saturation is decreased, the color moves toward gray.

scale An adjustable value that changes the overall size of a clip. The proportion of the image may or may not be maintained.

scrub To move through a clip or sequence with the aid of the playhead. Scrubbing is used to find a particular point or frame or to hear the audio.

SECAM (Sequential Couleur Avec Memoir) The French television standard for playback. As with PAL, the playback rate is 25 fps and the frame size is 720x546. Primarily a broadcast medium; editing for SECAM broadcasts is still performed in PAL.

Select/Transform tool The default arrow-shaped pointer, which allows you to select items in the interface. For example, you use it to select a clip or edit point.

sequence An edited assembly of video, audio, or graphics clips.

shot composition See *framing*.

SMPTE (Society of Motion Picture and Television Engineers) The organization responsible for establishing various broadcast video standards, like the SMPTE standard timecode for video playback.

snapping The process by which the playhead or an object in the Canvas "snaps," or moves directly, to guides, markers, or edit points when it is moved close to them.

solo The process of temporarily disabling all objects other than the selected objects in order to improve real-time performance.

sound byte A short excerpt taken from an interview clip.

square pixel A pixel that has the same height as width. Computer monitors have square pixels, but NTSC and PAL video do not.

standard definition The term used to differentiate traditional television broadcast signals from those of new high-definition formats. Standard-definition broadcast signals are usually 720x486 (for NTSC) or 720x576 (for PAL). See *high definition.*

stereo audio Sound that is separated into two channels, one carrying the sounds for the right ear and one for the left ear. Stereo pairs are linked and are always edited together. Audio-level changes are automatically made to both channels at the same time.

straight cut An edit in which both the video and audio tracks are cut together to the Timeline.

streaming The delivery of media over an intranet or over the Internet.

super black Black that is darker than the levels allowed by the CCIR 601 engineering standard for video. The CCIR 601 standard for black is 7.5 IRE in the United States and 0 IRE for PAL and NTSC in Japan.

super white A value or degree of white that is brighter than the accepted normal value of 100 IRE allowed by the CCIR 601 standard.

T

talent An actor in a clip.

thumbnails Small square icons displaying a frame of the represented clip.

TIFF (Tagged Image File Format) A widely used bitmapped graphics file format that handles monochrome, grayscale, and 8- and 24-bit color. There are two types of TIFF images: one with an alpha channel and one without.

tilt To pivot the camera up and down, which causes the image to move up or down in the frame.

time remapping The process of changing the speed of playback of a clip over time. The equivalent of varying the crank of a film camera. Available in Motion via the Scrub filter, part of the registration incentive plug-in pack.

timecode A unique numbering system of electronic signals laid onto each frame of videotape that is used to identify specific frames of video. Each frame of video is labeled with hours, minutes, seconds, and frames (01:00:00:00). Timecode can be drop frame, non–drop frame, time of day (TOD), or EBU (European Broadcast Union—for PAL projects).

timecode gap An area of tape with no timecode at all. Timecode gaps usually signify the end of all recorded material on a tape, but they may occur due the starting and stopping of the camera and tape deck during recording.

Timeline A window in Motion for displaying and editing the timing events for all objects, filters, and behaviors.

Title Safe Part of the video image that is guaranteed to be visible on all televisions. The Title Safe area is the inner 80 percent of the screen. To prevent text in your video from being hidden by the edge of a TV set, you should restrict any titles or text to the Title Safe area.

tracks Layers in the Timeline that contain the audio or video clips in a project.

transfer modes Another term for *blend modes*.

trimming To precisely add or subtract frames from the In or Out point of a clip. Trimming is used to fine-tune an edited sequence by carefully adjusting many edits in small ways.

underscan To display video on a computer or video monitor with a black border around the edge, so that no part of the frame is hidden from the viewer (for example, the Action Safe area is not cropped out, as it would be on a normal television set). Computers display underscan video.

U

undo A feature that allows you to cancel out the last change made.

variable speed See *time remapping*.

V

Vectorscope A window in Final Cut Pro that graphically displays the color components of a video signal, precisely showing the range of colors in the signal and measuring their intensity and hue. It can be used to calibrate the color in video signals being captured from videotape, as well as to compare two clips for purposes of color correction. Motion projects can be referenced in Final Cut Pro to take advantage of its Vectorscope.

video-in-text effect   When a video image is matted inside the shape of text.

VTR / VCR   (videotape recorder/videocassette recorder)   A tape machine used for recording pictures and sound on videotape.

VU meter   (Volume Unit meter)   An analog meter for monitoring audio levels.

W

white balance   To make adjustments to a video signal being recorded in order to reproduce white as true white. For example, if the white in a shot is too green due to fluorescent lighting, white balancing adds enough magenta to make the white appear neutral.

white level   An analog video signal's amplitude for the lightest white in a picture, represented by IRE units.

wide-screen   A format for shooting and projecting a movie in theaters in which the original footage doesn't get cut off because of the 4:3 aspect ratio. With the advent of high-definition video, wide-screen 16:9 video is coming into more popular use. See *16:9*.

wide-screen mask filter   Adds black bars across the top and bottom of a 4:3 image that crop it to a 16:9 format.

X

x-axis   Refers to the *x* coordinate in Cartesian geometry. The *x* coordinate describes horizontal placement in motion effects.

Y

y-axis   Refers to the *y* coordinate in Cartesian geometry. The *y* coordinate describes vertical placement in motion effects.

YUV   The three-channel PAL video signal with one luminance (Y) and two chrominance color difference signals (UV). It is often misapplied to refer to NTSC video, which is YIQ.

Z

z-axis Refers to the *z* coordinate in Cartesian geometry. The *z* coordinate describes perpendicular placement in motion effects.

zoom To change the magnification of your Canvas or Timeline.

Index

THINKSTOCK
footage

fresh. fast. royalty-free.

Your royalty-free resource. Thousands of useful clips. Pay once... use the clip forever. Broadcast quality.

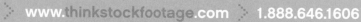
www.thinkstockfootage.com   1.888.646.1606

SPEED OR QUALITY.

Chroma key solutions for those that demand both

www.reflecmedia.com

Available through Resellers in 45 countries Worldwide

CREATIVE CODE DESIGN

BROADCAST DESIGN

3D ANIMATION

COMPOSITING

MOTION GRAPHICS

WWW.CREATIVECODEDESIGN.COM.AU

18 SECOND AVE EPPING   SYDNEY   AUSTRALIA   PH: +612 9869 0746   EMAIL: STUDIO37@OPTUSNET.COM.AU

Become a Certified Apple Pro!
Through the Apple Pro Training Series

The Apple Pro Training Series is the official training curriculum for Apple Pro applications.

Upon completing the course material in this book, you can become a certified Apple Pro by taking the certification exam at an Apple Authorized Training Center. Certification is offered in Final Cut Pro, DVD Studio Pro, Shake, and Logic. Successful certification as an Apple Pro gives you official recognition of your knowledge of Apple's professional applications while allowing you to market yourself to employers and clients as a skilled, pro-level user of Apple products.

To find an Authorized Training Center near you, visit:
www.apple.com/software/pro/training

Final Cut Pro HD
Diana Weynand
0-321-25613-1 • $44.99

Advanced Editing and Finishing Techniques in Final Cut Pro HD
DigitalFilm Tree and Michael Wohl
0-321-25608-5 • $54.99

Final Cut Pro for Avid Editors
Diana Weynand
0-321-24577-6 • $44.99

Final Cut Express 2
Diana Weynand
0-321-25615-8 • $44.99

Optimizing Your Final Cut Pro System
Peachpit Press
0-321-26871-7 • $54.99

Logic 6
Martin Sitter and Robert Brock
0-321-20040-3 • $44.99

Shake 3
Marco Paolini
0-321-19725-9 • $44.99

DVD Studio Pro 3
Adrian Ramseier and Martin Sitter
0-321-25610-7 • $44.99

Color Management in Mac OS X
Joshua Weisberg
0-321-24576-8 • $44.99

Soundtrack
Mary Plummer
0-321-24690-X • $39.99

Motion
Damian Allen
0-321-27826-7 • $44.99

To order books or find out more about the Apple Pro Training Series, visit:
www.peachpit.com/applepro